FLORIDA STATE
UNIVERSITY LIBRARIES

JUN 1 1 2001

TALLAHASSEE, FLORIDA

BRITISH POLICY TOWARDS FRANCE, 1945–51

British Policy towards France, 1945–51

Roger Woodhouse
*Lecturer in the Department of Political Science
and International Studies
University of Birmingham*

in association with
KING'S COLLEGE, LONDON

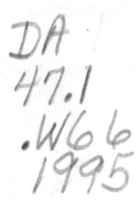

 First published in Great Britain 1995 by
MACMILLAN PRESS LTD
Houndmills, Basingstoke, Hampshire RG21 6XS
and London
Companies and representatives
throughout the world

> This book is published in Macmillan's *Studies in Military and Strategic History* series
> General Editor: Michael Dockrill

A catalogue record for this book is available
from the British Library.

ISBN 0-333-63737-2

 First published in the United States of America 1995 by
ST. MARTIN'S PRESS, INC.,
Scholarly and Reference Division,
175 Fifth Avenue,
New York, N.Y. 10010

ISBN 0-312-12489-9 (cloth)

Library of Congress Cataloging-in-Publication Data
Woodhouse, Roger.
British policy towards France, 1945-51 / Roger Woodhouse.
p. cm.
Based on the author's thesis (doctoral, University of Birmingham)
Includes bibliographical references (p.   ) and index.
ISBN 0-312-12489-9 (cloth)
1. Great Britain—Foreign relations—France. 2. France—Foreign
relations—Great Britain. 3. Great Britain—Foreign
relations—1945- 4. France—Foreign relations—1945-1958. 5. Great
Britain—Foreign policy. I. Title.
DA47.1.W66 1995
327.41044—dc20   95-1365
                                                                    CIP

© Roger Woodhouse 1995

All rights reserved. No reproduction, copy or transmission of
this publication may be made without written permission.

No paragraph of this publication may be reproduced, copied or
transmitted save with written permission or in accordance with
the provisions of the Copyright, Designs and Patents Act 1988,
or under the terms of any licence permitting limited copying
issued by the Copyright Licensing Agency, 90 Tottenham Court
Road, London W1P 9HE.

Any person who does any unauthorised act in relation to this
publication may be liable to criminal prosecution and civil
claims for damages.

10 9 8 7 6 5 4 3 2 1
04 03 02 01 00 99 98 97 96 95

Printed and bound in Great Britain by
Antony Rowe Ltd, Chippenham, Wiltshire

To Kate

Contents

Preface		ix
Introduction		xi
1	**The Road from Ruin**	**1**
	Economic Co-operation	1
	The Monnet Plan	8
	Integrated Planning	16
2	**Steel**	**21**
	The German Industry	21
	Supply and Demand	26
	The British Industry and Europe	30
3	**Coal**	**34**
	Coal and the Monnet Plan	34
	The European Coal Organisation	37
	German Coal	44
4	**The Saar**	**51**
	British Policy	51
	Quadripartite Deadlock	55
	Tripartite Agreement	62
5	**The Ruhr**	**67**
	The Bizone	67
	Dismantling and American Aid	74
	Reprieve and Rehabilitation	79
6	**The Marshall Plan**	**89**
	Bizonal Participation	89
	European Steel Co-ordination	94
	British Coal	100
7	**The Schuman Plan**	**105**
	The British Reaction	105
	The Plan in Context	108
	The Background to the Negotiations	112

8	**The Parting of the Ways**	**125**
	The Limits of Integration	125
	The German Question	132
	The New Europe	136
	Notes	140
	Bibliography	173
	Index	178

Preface

This book is based on a doctoral thesis written between 1989 and 1993 in the Department of Political Science and International Studies at the University of Birmingham, under the supervision of Dr Martin Kolinsky. The final year of research was supported by the University by the award of the Kirkcaldy Scholarship.

R.W.

Introduction

As German armies were sweeping across Europe in June 1940 the British Prime Minister, Winston Churchill, made an unprecedented offer: faced with a common enemy, Great Britain and France would cease to be two sovereign states but would merge to form an Anglo-French Union with a common citizenship. The prime mover in this plan was the Frenchman co-ordinating the mobilisation of the material and productive resources of the two countries: Jean Monnet. The offer came too late, however, for any response. A plane took Monnet and other leading figures in an eleventh-hour dash to Bordeaux, to where the remnants of the French government had fled in disarray, but no authority could be salvaged to bestow upon the Union any degree of legitimacy.[1] For the next four years France remained under German domination while a bloody and destructive war raged around the world. In February 1945, with France finally liberated and Germany facing total defeat, the proposal resurfaced. However, questioned in the House of Commons, the Foreign Secretary, Sir Anthony Eden, replied that no renewed offer of an Anglo-French Union had been made.[2] In April, Churchill himself, when asked whether such a move was still government policy, answered that it was not.[3]

To some extent this reflected the attitude of the Prime Minister to General Charles de Gaulle, wartime leader of the Free French and now head of the French provisional government. Churchill thought it preferable to await overtures from France, as any display of eagerness '...would give de Gaulle every opportunity for misbehaviour'.[4] In the event, however, the task of steering Anglo-French relations through the conflicting interests in the aftermath of war did not fall to Churchill and Eden. Following the outright victory of the Labour Party in the General Election of 26 July 1945 it was the new Prime Minister, Clement Attlee, and his Foreign Secretary, Ernest Bevin, who took their seats at the Potsdam Conference already in progress with the Soviet Union and the United States. Among other things, that conference agreed the principle that, although divided into separate zones of occupation, Germany would be treated as a single economic unit. Details on this and all outstanding matters were to be finalised by a Council of Foreign Ministers which would meet as required. France, not represented at the conference, had been granted a zone of occupation and was now invited to participate in future decisions through the medium of this quadripartite machinery.[5]

Britain and France were therefore to be partners in the process of remodelling Europe for the post-war era. It was fitting that they should be. Though France had been rapidly overrun, leaving Britain to stand alone, the fight against Hitler's Germany was a struggle upon which the two countries had embarked together. Mightier powers had later become embroiled in the conflict but the war had its beginnings in Anglo-French opposition to German territorial ambitions. Britain's commitment to this common cause had been symbolised by the offer to marry her destiny to that of a France already succumbing to the German onslaught. Five years later, with the enemy subdued under four occupying armies, the Allies were engaged in fixing the post-war international order with Germany helpless at their feet. Yet, by the Summer of 1950, Britain was reduced to the role of bystander as France and a rehabilitated and vigorous German Federal Republic buried their differences to become the nucleus of a new Europe.

Jean Monnet, who had made a flight to Bordeaux even as France fell, in the hope of cementing an Anglo-French Union, was now building a union of a different kind and with a partner few would have guessed in the days after Allied forces had evicted the armies of the Third Reich from French soil. The announcement on 9 May 1950, that France and West Germany were to place their coal and steel production under a common supreme authority, was a landmark in European integration but was also a watershed in Anglo-French relations. Britain was, of course, welcome to join the Franco-German scheme. Something had been lost, however. After five years of war the idea that the unity of Britain and France was paramount still survived. After another five years of peace that vision had been eclipsed by the reality of a new Europe in the making.

With hindsight, there is a compelling sense of the inevitable in the development of the modern European Community from its genesis in the Schuman Plan, via the Treaty of Rome, Single European Act and Maastricht. From this perspective the moment of creation is scarcely separated from the decision of the United Kingdom not immediately to join France and Germany in the venture. The impression is one of an idea whose time had come, a snap decision by a short-sighted British government, and an opportunity missed.

In fact, the shape of post-war Europe, the future of its coal and steel industries in general and those of Germany in particular, were questions with which Britain and France had long grappled. Production and demand, control and military occupation were woven together in a thread which ran through Anglo-French relations as the two allies sought order in the chaos left by the war against Hitler. The resources of Germany's industrial heartlands in the Ruhr and the Saar, their role in the recovery of Europe and their ultimate place in the post-war European economy were subjects to which Britain and France had returned time and again. In such matters the Schuman Plan was on well-trodden ground. True, the Franco-German initiative, although concerned with coal and steel, was ennobled by a vision of the future in which it was the first step to a new community of nations. The choice of the sectors in which economic integration would start was not without its particular history, however. Neither was the conduct of Anglo-French relations in the years before the Schuman Plan without its own guiding vision of a Europe to come. Against this background, caught between hope and necessity, Britain and France arrived at the crossroads.

1 The Road from Ruin

ECONOMIC CO-OPERATION

As the new Labour government took office in July 1945 the future shape of intra-European relations remained uncertain. In France, the newspaper *Le Monde* called for the creation of an Anglo-French partnership of real substance as the kernel around which a wider association of nations could form. This was a subject close to the heart of the francophile British Ambassador in Paris, Duff Cooper, who wasted no time in sending a cutting back to the Foreign Office.[1] The Ambassador also addressed a letter to the new Secretary of State for Foreign Affairs, Ernest Bevin, who replied that the question of relations with France was one which he proposed to review at an early date.[2]

Bevin asked for a full meeting to be arranged with the Western Department of the Foreign Office, in preparation for which he intended to seek the advice of the Chancellor of the Exchequer and the President of the Board of Trade.[3] These he arranged to see on 10 August 1945. On that occasion the feeling of Bevin's colleagues was that, although British trade policy should offer general support for France, it was too early to consider entering into binding long-term commitments.[4] It was to the future that Bevin was looking, however. On 13 August 1945 he assembled his people in the Western Department and explained that his ultimate objective was a system of political, military and economic co-operation in Europe with a close Anglo-French relationship as its cornerstone.[5] This was welcome news to Duff Cooper, who felt that Bevin's policy and sentiments towards France could not be better.[6] In the Department, however, the opinion was expressed that: 'The "grand design" clearly ought to be kept a secret inside the four walls of this Office.'[7] It would be overstating the case to suggest that the Foreign Office was actively hostile towards the idea of a policy in Europe founded on an Anglo-French entente. The documentary record does nevertheless display evidence of a certain lack of enthusiasm among Bevin's officials. On the other hand, Duff Cooper and his colleagues at the British Embassy in Paris seem to have been better disposed towards Bevin's vision and were consequently susceptible to French approaches on this subject, which were then dutifully relayed to London. In July 1946 the head of Economic Affairs at the French Foreign Ministry had an informal conversation with the British Embassy on the general subject of trade agreements. He then went on to say that relations between the two countries ought to be considered on a higher plane and that it should be possible to find a means of linking their economies on a much more satisfactory basis.[8] This kind of canvassing did nothing to earn the sympathy of Foreign Office stalwarts such as Sir Oliver Harvey, who took the view that such grandiose ideas should be carefully curbed.[9]

Despite Sir Oliver's reservations, however, these overtures were fully compatible with Bevin's policy as expressed in August of the previous year. Furthermore, it was becoming apparent that economic questions were going to be deciding factors in post-war Europe. In August another official noted that the imbalance in trade between Britain and France was proving an impediment to the treatment and eventual solution of a number of problems.[10] In the exchange of memoranda which followed, it emerged that the main concern was the poor state of health of the French economy and its effect upon the United Kingdom. The conclusion was that the French economic difficulties offered an opportunity to press home an advantage in a number of minor matters in dispute, such as the sale of UK surplus supplies in North Africa and the settlement of certain pre-occupation debts. Any generosity towards the French should, however, be on the basis of a *quid pro quo*, even if this were in the form of promises rather than hard cash.[11] This attitude, although understandable, nevertheless failed to capture the spirit of Bevin's avowed policy towards France. The pressure from the Paris Embassy to embark upon discussions with the French was acknowledged, however, and arrangements were made for a visit to France by a party from the Foreign Office. In preparation, an interdepartmental meeting was arranged to gauge official opinion elsewhere in Whitehall and as an opportunity for representatives to clear their minds.[12]

As for the Foreign Secretary, his mind was already clear. In May 1946 Bevin assured his French counterpart, Georges Bidault, of his love for France and remarked that if the two Empires were co-ordinated they would represent the greatest mass of manpower in the world.

> M. Bidault said that he wished he could revive the proposal for common citizenship made by Mr. Churchill to M. Reynaud in 1940, but he feared that it was too late to carry the proposal, or, at least too soon to revive it.[13]

There remained possibilities for action on a less ambitious scale, however. In August 1946 Bevin again convened a meeting with the Western Department and, almost a year after the first exposition of his 'grand design', he returned to the same theme. Rather than attempting a dramatic gesture, Bevin had decided to concentrate on putting economic relations between Britain and France on a closer footing. To this end he wished to examine the possibility of establishing something in the nature of a customs union, which might later be extended to Belgium, Holland and Luxembourg.[14] He was informed that the matter had already been explored tentatively with other Departments, but without a firm directive it could be taken no further. Bevin gave instructions that a paper should be prepared for him to present in Cabinet in due course. His officials were at pains to point out, however, that trade with France was hampered by the fact that the French were not producing those goods which Britain most desired to purchase. In particular the United Kingdom was anxious to obtain supplies of steel. The difficulty was that France could not raise production without more coke, suitable qualities of which could most conveniently be produced from the coal mined in the Ruhr, in the British zone of occupation. Thus from an early date it was clear that any meaningful consideration of mutual economic support would inevitably encounter the question of Germany's position in the post-war economic order.

Here was a clash of interests and a difference in outlook. The main concern of the French was to extract the maximum amount of fuel possible from Germany. The British, on the other hand, were inclined to retain enough to ensure a certain level of economic activity in their zone. Britain's position was spelled out in June 1946 in a Cabinet Paper presented by the Chancellor of the Exchequer.[15] At the heart of the matter was a continuing failure to implement the principle agreed at Potsdam that Germany should be treated as a single economic unit. On this basis the mainly industrial British zone should receive surpluses of foodstuffs from the Soviet and other zones. Without these deliveries, the Treasury calculated that for 1946 it would be necessary to spend £91 million on imports (including £59 million on food) plus £10 million on civil administration. Against this, on an optimistic estimate, £49 million might be received in revenue from exports. If Britain was to maintain her zone of occupation, the choice was between either achieving a balance of payments or calling upon the British taxpayer 'to carry the Germans on his back'.[16]

A plan favoured by France was to detach the Ruhr politically from Germany and place the area under international control. This was a suggestion which received strong support from Duff Cooper, who made his views known in a long despatch on the subject which was printed for distribution to the Cabinet.[17] These arguments were refuted, however, in a paper which was circulated over Bevin's initials.[18] Besides rejecting the proposal as being economically unsound, this reply raised doubts as to the durability of such an arrangement, which would in effect deny the population normal political rights under a repressive régime. It was pointed out that such methods were no longer generally employed: 'Even when dealing with primitive peoples'[19] Furthermore, France had performed a similar experiment in 1923 which had stifled the Weimar Republic and paved the way for the rise of the Nazi Party. On balance it was felt that a repetition would be inadvisable.

Despite their differences on these wider issues, Bevin felt that Britain and France could find scope for economic co-operation, even on such a humble level as the home market for vegetables being increasingly supplied from French sources. This was an example he mentioned to his Principal Private Secretary, who shared the insight with the Western Department.

> I quote these suggestions by way of illustration of a determination on the Secretary of State's part to put our commercial relations with France on a fruitful basis as the first step in the building up of a closer relationship with France and thereafter with Western Europe.[20]

These sentiments were echoed by Duff Cooper in a letter to Bevin on 21 August in which he stressed his belief in the desirability of eventual economic integration between Britain and France.[21] In the same letter Cooper referred to a proposed meeting between Bevin and the French Foreign Minister, Georges Bidault, and was therefore clearly aware that only the previous day this latter had written, over Bevin's head, to the Prime Minister suggesting that talks be held on economic matters in Paris, where a British delegation was already installed for the Peace Conference then in progress.[22] In his letter Bidault decried the import controls, which he blamed for France's adverse trading balance with Britain, and expressed his astonishment that the recovery plans of the two countries should be worked out and put into effect without mutual consultation, even at the risk of creating economic rivalries for the future.[23]

Bevin was in Paris in person and, despite the snub, seized the opportunity presented by Bidault's direct appeal to Attlee. On 5 September 1946 he met with Bidault at the Quai d'Orsay in the presence of Alphand and Chauvel on the French side and Duff Cooper, Hall-Patch and Hoyer-Millar for the British. Bidault opened by reiterating the points in his letter. Bevin warmly welcomed the French approach and agreed that much could be done to rationalise the British and French economies with a view to eliminating pointless rivalry.[24] He went on to say that in the current circumstances, when both sides had to keep their policies under constant review, it was difficult to lay down a rigid plan of concerted action which would remain valid over time.

It would be better to review the immediate day to day problems as they came and to settle them in a spirit of mutual co-operation in the belief that out of this would grow an increasingly closer permanent association in all economic matters.[25]

It was agreed that machinery should be established for regular consultation and that this should take the form of an Anglo-French committee of experts. Bidault then returned to the theme of harmonising the plans for the reconstruction of the respective economies. Bevin affirmed that he regarded this as desirable and that it should be a matter for the proposed committee.

The setting up of this committee could, therefore, hardly fail to entail a serious assessment of the more or less vague ideas regarding Anglo-French co-operation which had been floated on occasions over the previous year. Even when these had emanated from the Foreign Secretary himself they had been greeted with varying degrees of scepticism by his own officials, but with the new committee approved by the Cabinet, the way was open to engage the entire Whitehall machinery.[26] In October the Board of Trade wrote to the Treasury suggesting that an effort ought to be made to decide what Anglo-French 'economic co-ordination' could, or should, mean.[27] The letter went on to mention possible reactions in the United States to any agreements which might be entered into with the French, as the financial agreement by which Britain was granted American credits was hedged with non-discrimination obligations.[28] In the circumstances it would be difficult to give the French any undertakings to purchase goods which could not be sold on the British market under conditions of fair competition. The letter's author also devotes three paragraphs to the subject of steel, to which he attaches some importance, but concludes gloomily that: 'To raise steel with the French at this stage would seem to involve risk of the Committee becoming a new arena for bickering over the future of the Ruhr.'[29] As had been indicated to Bevin by members of his own Department on 8 August, this was bound to be a major stumbling block in any genuine co-ordination of economic and industrial effort with the French, and one which it would be extremely difficult to avoid.

The new Anglo-French committee was the subject of a Board of Trade paper.[30] The committee was to review the balance of trade and payments and also to consider problems and suggest solutions on an *ad hoc* basis. Of most concern, however, was the third of the terms of reference:

(C) to consider how to prevent conflicts between the reconstruction and modernisation plans of the two countries in accordance with the declared objectives of the two Governments as regards world trade ...

The paper noted that the above represented a change, suggested by the Board's President, to an original draft running:

> ... to consider how the reconstruction and modernisation plans of the two countries can be *helpfully related to each other* etc.[31]

The difference in wording represented a considerable dilution of the spirit of the original, from an active involvement in a common effort, to a more passive interpretation which would limit the degree of co-operation to avoiding a clash of interests. To some extent this was understandable. As President of the Board of Trade, Stafford Cripps was bound to take a cautious view of any proposals which would unduly restrict his Department's room for manoeuvre in its dealings with any particular country. Nevertheless, under the new terms of reference he had felt able to give the new committee his full support in Cabinet.[32]

On the other hand, the general tone of the discussion document produced by the Board of Trade was certainly not overwhelming in its endorsement of Anglo-French economic collaboration and took the view that the French were angling for advantages to assist their own reconstruction but for which they had little to offer in return to a world-class trading nation such as Britain, which could have no use for the kind of cartels and price-fixing rings which, it was assumed, the French had in mind. In any case the Board felt that it had already taken an enlightened attitude to the United Nations proposal for an Economic Commission for Europe (to the extent that it had not opposed its establishment in principle) and was consequently not anxious to support many more initiatives as it lacked:'the manpower to engage in a multiplicity of economic "talking shops" set up without any well defined and clearly useful objectives'.[33]

The proposed course of action was therefore to participate in the machinery of Anglo-French consultation but with reservations. With regard to the possibility of contacts between British and French private enterprise, the Board thought that this should be permitted, if the question arose, on the understanding that any projects emerging from such talks should be self-supporting, or at least require no subsidies from the government.

On 21 October 1946 an interdepartmental meeting was convened to discuss the line to be taken when the new committee began its work. Represented were: the Board of Trade, the Ministry of Supply, the Dominions Office, the Ministry of Food, the Treasury, the Cabinet Office and the Lord President's Office. A member of the Foreign Office staff arrived half an hour after the start of the meeting in response to a telephone call, and quickly gained the impression that there seemed little determination to make anything concrete out of item (C) of the terms of reference of the committee.

> In particular the Ministry of Supply were unwilling to commit themselves on the question of coordination of steel production in the long term and they feel that any arrangements for steel in the next two years would entail discussions on coal and thus on the future of the Ruhr which I imagine we wish to avoid.[34]

In this and other aspects of the question the meeting generally endorsed the tentative approach outlined in the Board of Trade paper. The Treasury made the point that it was engaged in a product-by-product analysis of dollar imports with a view to seeking alternative supplies from outside the dollar area, and that in this respect France could not be considered in isolation from other European countries. The fear that Britain might attempt to economise on foreign currency and increase exports by expanding home production in competition with traditional French exports was seen as the prime motive for the French interest in co-operation. On the whole the meeting addressed the subject in terms of a straightforward calculation of advantage.

> ... we should need to be careful of encouraging the expansion of production which might ultimately compete with our own exports ... we need not go out of our way to warn the French that our demands on them might not out-last a few years.[35]

Given that the purpose of the meeting was to discuss possible means of economic co-ordination, these remarks did not augur well for the likelihood of establishing confidence between the two partners in the venture.

The ramifications of closer collaboration were not in fact lost on the Board of Trade, which hosted a meeting on 8 November to discuss the unavoidable exchange of information which would be implicit in such a relationship. Present were representatives of the Lord President's Office, the Central Statistical Office, the Treasury and the Economic Section of the Cabinet Office. In the event a reasonably balanced discussion ensued. A degree of reluctance to give away too much was evident but it was thought that it should be possible to open a dialogue on the general economic problems with which Britain and France were faced.[36] The tone of the meeting was not one of ill will towards the French, but rather a lack of belief in 'ambitious and nebulous' projects and a feeling that ideas such as combined planning and division of labour between the two countries were unrealistic.[37] In fact it was a little too early to judge in what measure the reconstruction plans of Britain and France could be related to each other as neither country had, at that stage, published its programme for the anticipated period of post-war recovery. To this extent British officials were working in the dark on rather unfamiliar territory without the benefit of any concrete example of how economic collaboration might function in practice. In these circumstances it was perhaps natural that a cautious and conservative attitude should prevail pending a full exposition of the French intentions in the matter of their own economic recovery.

THE MONNET PLAN

Jean Monnet and his team began work on the *Plan de Modernisation et d'Équipement* in April 1946 and the finished result of their labours was accepted as policy in January 1947. Well before the preliminary study was completed the mere fact that the work was in hand had an effect on the way in which Anglo-French relations were considered, as any discussion of economic 'collaboration' or 'co-operation' was obliged to anticipate the Plan's eventual implementation. Even after their amendment in line with the suggestion of Sir Stafford Cripps, the terms of reference of the Anglo-French Economic Committee meant that the Monnet Plan would necessarily be at the heart of any further debate on the subject of economic relations between the two countries. The Plan could therefore serve to give substance to what might otherwise remain nothing more than a vague notion that something should be done to set matters on a more satisfactory footing. Here was a point to which all discussion had to return and which would be difficult to gloss over. This high profile recalled Monnet's strategy to ensure acceptance of his ideas at home in France, where his aim was to mobilise the French working population across the whole political spectrum to create an apparatus more durable than the government itself.

> Ministerial instability was an evil for France, but hardly more than an inconvenience for the Plan. In the twenty years which followed, three Planning Commissioners saw twenty-eight governments come and go.[38]

At the end of 1946, without the benefit of this historical perspective, it was difficult to assess the forthcoming Plan's likely impact but, as public awareness grew in France, interest spilled across the Channel. In December 1946 the *Conseil du Plan* published an outline of the proposed methods, which Duff Cooper forwarded to the Foreign Office with the observation: 'these methods of execution call for a considerable effort of organisation. Moreover, the French are to be asked to pay their taxes, which will be extremely repugnant to them.'[39] Cooper's colleagues back in London were less concerned about the French taxpayer than they were about the implications for Anglo-French relations. Joint discussion of the Monnet Plan seemed unavoidable but the Foreign Office sought to delay this until the return from America of their economic expert, Edmund Hall-Patch. In the meantime Robert Marjolin, Monnet's deputy, visited London and left copies of the completed Plan with the Economic Section of the Cabinet Office and the Board of Trade. It was clear that the French would expect some response in the same spirit that had given rise to the Anglo-French Economic Co-operation Committee. The Foreign Office therefore tended to the view that it would be as well to include the Plan on the agenda for the next meeting.

> All I have in mind is that we listen to the exposé of the plan and invite their concrete suggestions for any future action. We might lay down the basis for future exchange of statistical information and discuss in general how our minds are working on this problem. The Board of Trade representative should be able to cope with such simple developments.[40]

This slight was unjustified. In fact the official concerned was Harry Lintott, an able and open-minded civil servant who was later to become Deputy Secretary-General of the OEEC. Lintott felt that high-level contacts between Britain and France would be inappropriate before Ministers were in possession of the forthcoming Economic White Paper, but approved of exploratory talks at the official level. In this he enjoyed the support of his President, Stafford Cripps.[41] Their cautious approach was in contrast to the position taken by Hector McNeil, Minister of State at the Foreign Office, who, they understood, was in favour of immediate discussions at the highest level. It was agreed that if this suggestion were brought before the Cabinet it should be opposed by Cripps.[42]

That same day it transpired that the French Prime Minister, Léon Blum, had sent a special emissary with a personal message for Clement Attlee, the main object of which was to ask for British help in the matter of coal supplies, but which also touched on the subject of hastening the integration of the two countries' plans. Lintott, who was informed of this development, realised that Bevin would raise the matter in Cabinet that afternoon and again made the point that there was no objection to preliminary talks in the context of the Anglo-French Economic Co-operation Committee as long as these did not exceed the scope of a general discussion of the Monnet Plan and did not stray into areas where any undertaking by the British side would be premature.[43] In this sense the Board's reluctance to rush headlong towards economic integration was prudent and Lintott was making a valid point: there could be no correlation, on whatever scale, between the two reconstruction plans while no British equivalent of the Monnet Plan existed. Duff Cooper had always believed that the Board of Trade was fundamentally opposed to collaboration between Britain and France,[44] but it was unreasonable to expect the Board to lead a messianic crusade towards a union the benefits of which would be mainly political. However much he personally desired such a relationship, and whichever way the balance of opinion lay among the officials at the Foreign Office, the fact remained that such developments fell within the Board's ambit and, in the absence of overriding considerations imposed at Cabinet level, were bound to be examined on their merits. In this instance there was a case for avoiding precipitate action on the grounds that the British Government was not yet in a position to commit itself in the full knowledge of what its own long-term requirements were likely to be.

At the Cabinet meeting Cripps made it clear that he would prefer to avoid early discussions with members of the French government. Bevin was nevertheless unwilling to send a wholly discouraging reply to Blum's overtures and it was agreed that it should be possible to hold talks at the official level without being drawn into detailed consideration of the Monnet Plan and integration of the British and French economies.[45] In the letter, drafted by Bevin, which Attlee sent to Blum following the Cabinet meeting, the opportunity was welcomed to study the means of making the economies of the two countries as far as possible complementary.

> This is an idea which we are certainly willing to explore ... we feel that as a first step preparatory to wider conversations it would be very useful if our officials could ... learn more details about the Monnet Plan which is clearly of great interest to this country.[46]

If this conveys an eagerness to examine the repercussions of the Monnet Plan for Anglo-French relations which did not in fact prevail in the Cabinet, the letter does at least confine itself to the use of the term 'complementary' rather than 'integrated'.

This was in keeping with the Treasury attitude as expressed to the Foreign Office a few days earlier:

> I believe it is really important to get away from the idea of integration and to get fixed in everybody's minds that what we should aim at is complementary economies ... we encourage them to do what they do best and vice versa ...[47]

It was this kind of minimalist attitude which would prove to be incompatible with Anglo-French co-operation in the age of the Monnet Plan. The Plan did not aim to stimulate those activities which the French 'do best'. It was not a plan for perfume and ladies' fashions nor even primarily for cheese and wine. Its overriding concern was with coal, steel, electricity and all the requirements of modern industry. The increase of the working week to 48 hours, the difficult decision to defer the rebuilding programme for private housing and the other austerity measures were not aimed at satisfying the UK luxury market. The French were determined to cast and to smelt, to forge and to press, to weld and to rivet efficiently and economically; that is to say that they wanted to do the *same* things as the British. The very existence of the Monnet Plan precluded any 'compatibility' of the two economies if the term were taken to mean a division of labour favouring British manufacturing industry to the detriment of the French. If any such misapprehension existed, it should certainly have been dispelled by the publication of the full details of the Monnet Plan, a digest of which appeared in *The Economist*, giving the proposed increases in steel output, car production and textile manufacture, and corresponding rises in power-generating capacity and coal consumption.[48]

For British delegates to the Anglo-French Economic Co-operation Committee, the situation was further clarified at the discussions arranged in Paris at the end of January 1947. The meetings took place in a relaxed and friendly atmosphere and brought a positive response from the British side. In contrast to the preparatory interdepartmental meetings, when the idea of sharing information with France had been viewed with distaste, the British members of the Committee were won over by the frankness of their French colleagues and all agreed that economic collaboration would mean nothing unless Britain were equally open in return.[49] All in all, the British representatives were fascinated and impressed by what they learned of the Monnet Plan. Some of the problems which could be foreseen obviously had political implications beyond the purview of the officials involved but these were not presented as excuses for doing nothing, but rather as points which emerged from a reasoned analysis of the opportunities for further action. It was, however, apparent that the usefulness of the various options open was in direct proportion to the magnitude of the political problems they were likely to raise.

Harry Lintott thought that the best approach would be to compare the long-term investment programmes of suitable industries in the light of the international supply-and-demand situation. This would have lent itself to one sector in particular: the steel industry. Britain had no comprehensive plan to compare with the Monnet Plan but a development plan for steel had existed since May 1946.[50] Lintott could see, however, that any move along these lines would lead inevitably to the question of Germany.

> But I am afraid that if we get going with the French on steel before the level of the German steel industry is finally decided they will be dragging it in as a King Charles's head at every turn.[51]

One of Lintott's colleagues also conceded that the principle of Britain and France exchanging information had a certain appeal, but wondered what would happen if this revealed a duplication of effort. The problem as he saw it revolved around the amount of control governments had over the investment programmes of private enterprise. In the case of nationalised means of production there would, of course, be no difficulty regarding control of investment, but such flagship industries might be expected to contribute to export revenue.

> Assuming that the steel industry were nationalised would H.M.G. want to have its hands tied by any sort of inter-governmental agreement as to the limits of its export target for steel?[52]

For his part, Lintott acknowledged that a number of daunting problems existed but was of a mind to overcome them by means of a genuine constructive effort. Looking to the future:

> if the two countries are, in respect of a particular industry, aiming at targets which, when added together, are going to be palpably too large in relation to any foreseeable condition of world supply and demand, it seems to me in the spirit of economic planning that some effort should be made to adjust the total target to the right level in advance rather than wait for the adjustment to be made by an appropriate number of bankruptcies.[53]

James Meade, head of the Economic Section of the Cabinet Office, gained the impression that in this regard what the French mostly had in mind was a mutual adjustment of the two countries' plans for capital development of various industries in order to avoid an eventual combined over-capacity. As all recognised, the obvious sector to start with was steel, but, although the French made their interest apparent, this was a subject from which the British side shrank because every time it was raised 'the level of German industry promptly landed in the middle of the conversations'.[54] This was a thorny problem which could perhaps be skirted around for a short while but, as the Board of Trade recognised, it would be preferable to give an indication at the outset of how far the government would be prepared to go.[55]

It was in this spirit that the Economic Section of the Cabinet Office had begun its first appraisal of the Monnet Plan in December 1946. This was ready in time for the Anglo-French discussions in January 1947 and British delegates thus had about six days in which to marshal their thoughts before the Paris talks.[56] The paper prepared for them pointed out that Britain and France had different priorities as far as economic planning was concerned and also different means at their disposal. The Monnet Plan started from the premise that basic industries had to be modernised at all costs and everything else could wait. French recovery was thus based on bold and partial long-term plans, whereas the British effort tended to concentrate on those immediate problems which seemed most amenable to current control. Nevertheless the paper foresaw a possible future convergence of approaches and put forward some preliminary views on six possible degrees of 'closeness' of integration:

1. Periodic, informal exchanges of ideas.
2. Noncommittal exchange of information on targets.
3. Formal mutual declarations of policy on tariffs, etc.
4. Integration of investment programmes of nationalised industries; and agreed policies towards the control of private investment.
5. Barter agreements, combined purchase agreements and long-term contracts.
6. A customs union.

The paper's author acknowledged that political factors would necessarily predominate in any decision, but observed that Britain and France had an interest in each other's economic development which friendly collaboration would acknowledge.[57] James Meade had attended the Paris talks and had gained the impression that, although the French ideas were not precise, they envisaged integration up to and including the fourth degree of closeness on the Section's provisional scale.[58] In common with the Board of Trade however, Meade foresaw repercussions beyond the narrow view of any bilateral arrangements.

> ... it is a question how far such discussions could usefully go without bringing in other countries. The French are themselves preparing a Steel Plan for the whole of Europe – involving, it is understood, a very low level of German steel output.[59]

There was thus, among those concerned, a consensus regarding what the French were hoping for by way of a British reaction to the Monnet Plan and what obstacles stood in the way of a favourable response. Further progress now required a decision at the highest level and it was therefore thought that in the first instance Meade's paper should be considered by the Steering Committee on Economic Development, which was chaired by the Permanent Secretary of the Treasury and was the main official body reporting to Ministers on economic policy.[60]

In the meantime Meade's section drafted a special paper on the theory of integration of investment.[61] This took the view that, as a general principle, such an approach would have the advantage of removing much of the guesswork from planning production for export; the benefits being in proportion to the extent that the two countries were influenced by their planners. Problems were foreseen, however, in the practical execution of joint planning of investment programmes. Difficulties could, it was thought, arise if technical innovations later undermined the rationale for concentrating some particular industry in one country. A further area of uncertainty concerned the means of implementing planning decisions as pressure on raw materials and productive capacity eased and government controls on industry were relaxed. If all that remained were Town Planning and Factory Act controls, there would be little leverage over private industry.[62] The scope for integration would then depend upon the extent to which the Labour government held the commanding heights of the economy through its control of the nationalised industries, assuming that the French government could also find the means to exercise similar control over its key industries. These problems notwithstanding, the author drew the tentative conclusion that: 'Not to "integrate" investment programmes may be equivalent to "disintegrating" the two economies by an equally arbitrary (but much less helpful) intervention in the market.'[63] This paper was not circulated outside the Economic Section but a synopsis of the points arising in discussion of it within the Section was made available to the Board of Trade.[64]

In order to prepare the ground as far as possible before the Steering Committee's discussion, the Board of Trade held a number of internal meetings followed by an interdepartmental meeting on 14 February 1947. The mood here was generally positive. The representative of the Ministry of Fuel and Power saw no obstacle to divulging technical plans for the mining industry but thought that little help could be given in forecasting the future trend of coal exports. The Treasury took the view that the government should seek to establish a framework of planning within which French and British industrialists could negotiate with each other directly, though Meade saw a danger of price rings and market sharing organisations springing up under such an arrangement.[65] The opinion was also expressed that steel was a special case which would require separate attention.[66]

Although the record of the meeting conveys the impression that the representatives were in all good faith attempting to clarify in what ways their various Departments would be likely to be involved in the overall obligations of Anglo-French co-operation, it is clear that the limits of useful discussion had by this time been reached unless a clear directive could be obtained to draw all the strands together into a single policy. The natural route to ministerial level was through the Steering Committee. This committee had not met for a while because of pressure of work on its members engaged in the preparation of the Economic White Paper. With the pressure eased, it was anticipated that the committee would resume its business. On 15 February 1947 its Chairman, Sir Edward Bridges, wrote to the Secretary suggesting that the paper on the Monnet Plan could be included on the agenda for the next meeting.[67] The committee met on 26 February and dealt with this item as follows:

> Sir Edward Bridges said that the White Paper adopted the same general approach as the Monnet Plan, viz that a plan of this kind could only be carried out by the combined effort of the whole nation and demanded co-operation between government and the people.[68]

To all intents and purposes that was the end of the matter. Despite all the preparatory work which had been undertaken with regard to the implications for Anglo-French relations, the committee touched only upon the aspect of the Monnet Plan which had parallels in domestic policy.

On 1 March 1947 a Board of Trade official observed that since the interdepartmental meeting on 14 February no progress seemed to have been made at any level.[69] In July, the same official chose to raise the matter at a briefing for delegates to the conference on the Marshall Plan in Paris.

Mr Sanders said that the delegation would be glad to have a summary of the Monnet Plan and our views of it ... Mr Makins said that he thought a paper had already been prepared in the Foreign Office.[70]

Two days prior to the meeting of the Steering Committee in that February, the *Observer* newspaper had called for a common Anglo-French economic plan under the headline: 'A Path For The Bold'.[71] Less than six months later interest in the subject had dwindled to the point where the senior official in charge of economic matters at the Foreign Office was barely conversant with the body of documentation available to him.[72] In the intervening period no further meetings had been held or papers produced in any Department, at any level.

INTEGRATED PLANNING

The Monnet Plan provided a focus for previously vague ideas on Anglo-French economic co-operation. After January 1947 this subject could not be tackled constructively without reference to the Plan's targets and how British economic development might relate to them within the overall pattern of supply and demand for the key sectors involved. The French ambition was not merely to recover from the effects of the war but to overcome the legacy of stagnation from the inter-war years.[73] The twin objectives of modernisation and higher productivity enshrined in the Plan had been adopted as policy by the French government and also enjoyed the backing of the trade union movement.[74] Under its terms of reference the Anglo-French Economic Co-operation Committee was charged with considering how to prevent conflicts between the reconstruction and modernisation plans of the two countries. The French had produced such a plan, had explained it to the British and were pressing ahead with its implementation. It remained for His Majesty's Government to define the British position. The principle of seeking to avoid clashes of interest presented a range of options which were identified, discussed and reported upon, but which never became embodied in government policy. After a brief and intense flurry of activity consideration of the issues was abandoned. James Meade, who remained as head of the Economic Section until September 1947, recalls that interest in co-operation based on the Monnet Plan seemed merely to fizzle out, while at the same time other more pressing matters came to the forefront of attention.[75] This recollection of events is consistent with the shortage of documents on the subject after February

1947 and suggests that the failure to pursue the matter was not the result of a major policy overhaul.

Of course, one of the impediments to economic co-operation with the French was the lack of any equivalent to the Monnet Plan in Britain, where there was general uncertainty as to what economic planning might entail.[76] There was nevertheless a fascination with Monnet's technique of associating both management and workers with the formulation of policy. Monnet himself tended to the view that a similar approach should be adopted in the United Kingdom.[77] This was an aspect of economic planning which had a certain appeal for Sir Stafford Cripps and the one which he made clear he would prefer Monnet to emphasise when he visited Britain for proposed informal conversations with industrialists. Monnet had hoped that the intention was that from these initial contacts there would emerge a representative group to exchange views with his planners in Paris. He was disappointed, however, as

> the President's idea was rather that M. Monnet should spread the gospel of consultation between government and industry in the preparation and execution of economic plans than that this should be a step in Anglo-French 'joint planning' or 'integration'.[78]

As a general rule Cripps attached considerable importance to the role of economic relations in international affairs, as he made clear in a speech to an intake of Foreign Office new entrants in 1945.[79] On the subject of the Monnet Plan, however, he inclined to the opinion that substantial discussions with the French were best postponed until after the Economic White Paper had been debated in Parliament.

It was in preparation for this debate, scheduled for 10 and 11 March, that the Steering Committee took Meade's paper on the Monnet Plan on 26 February 1947, with a view to gleaning suitable material for Ministers' speeches. The absence of any discussion of the paper's references to Anglo-French economic integration would therefore seem to reflect the relative urgency accorded to matters bearing on the impending debate rather than any lack of sympathy for the concept of co-ordinated planning. In particular it would be wrong to impute any obstructive intention to Bridges, whose cursory treatment of the paper echoed almost word for word the advice from the Prime Minister's office that the relevance lay in Monnet's technique for promoting co-operation between government, industry and people.[80] A rudimentary machinery of consultation for this purpose was eventually established under the Central Economic Planning Staff (CEPS).

The CEPS was set up with Sir Edwin Plowden at its head in March 1947 and was the nearest that the Attlee government came to the French system, though by the time it was operational the momentum of the initial interest in joint planning had been lost. The delay was understandable, however. Even after the long-awaited Economic White Paper and its subsequent debate in Parliament the organisational means were lacking. In the circumstances it seemed reasonable, therefore, to

> defer discussion of long-term economic collaboration with the French until after Sir Edwin Plowden has got into the saddle and inter alia has had the opportunity to consider the implications of Anglo-French collaboration in relation to his own task.[81]

Plowden's appointment was made public on 27 March 1947 but because of a bout of influenza which turned to jaundice he did not start work until the beginning of May.[82] On 20 May 1947 a meeting endorsed Plowden's proposal to create a Planning Board consisting of two representatives from each side of industry, the Permanent Secretaries of the Board of Trade, Ministry of Labour and Ministry of Supply, and himself as Chairman.[83] This never developed into a nucleus of Anglo-French collaboration or played any major role in British planning but became something of a 'fifth wheel' in the CEPS apparatus as the system evolved.[84] In any case, by the time Plowden was installed and his staff engaged their immediate concern was the chronic shortage of fuel and raw materials and the rapid depletion of Britain's foreign exchange resources. When alleviation of these problems came, through the Marshall Plan, it was natural that the British planning effort should be directed towards the operation of the European Recovery Programme.

In fact the only attempt by the Attlee government to produce a general economic plan for more than one year at a time was in the form of the long-term programme submitted to the OEEC, and it was in this context that the French returned to the possibility of integrated plans in November 1948.[85] In his memoirs, Plowden covers this later episode in a chapter entitled: 'A First Attempt at Anglo-French Co-operation'.[86] This would seem to suggest that the still unresolved question of collaborative planning did not figure on the list of outstanding matters requiring his urgent attention when he took up his duties in May 1947. Indeed, Lord Plowden confirms that, to his recollection, the matter was never raised with him.[87] When the French Ambassador, René Massigli, called at the Foreign Office in December 1946, he urged for integration on the basis of the Monnet Plan and expressed his fear that otherwise British interests might become bound up with the German economy to the detriment of relations with France.[88] Bevin agreed that this was a reason to press ahead while the opportunity existed.[89] The Foreign Secretary could be guilty of procrastination, however, and had already deferred Cabinet discussion of the paper which he had instructed his officials to prepare on the desirability of an Anglo-French customs union, or similar arrangement.[90] The reason for this postponement was the hope that elections might hasten the establishment of a stable régime in France.[91]

In the meantime the fact that his premiership was certain to be short-lived did not prevent Bevin from agreeing to conclude an Anglo-French alliance with Léon Blum at the head of a caretaker government in January 1947. Article IV of the Treaty of Dunkirk states that:

> the High Contracting Parties will by constant consultation on matters affecting their economic relations with each other take all possible steps to promote the prosperity and economic security of both countries ...[92]

This was open to a certain amount of interpretation, but *The Times* noted that: 'The significance will be great indeed if the official wording is taken to imply, as it has been suggested informally that it should, a plan to integrate plans.'[93] This was not beyond the bounds of possibility if the terms of reference of the Anglo-French Economic Co-operation Committee were given a suitable interpretation. The practical difficulties were obvious and not all of Whitehall would have welcomed such a move with unbridled enthusiasm but, in the event, the matter was not taken to a conclusion. The subject provoked no clashes in Cabinet, and no flights of oratory either condemned or defended the notion that integration was desirable or possible. There were, of course, other calls on Ministers' time. In addition, the Cabinet was depleted during the period in question by the attendance of Ernest Bevin at the Council of Foreign Ministers in Moscow and the illness of Herbert Morrison. As Lord President of the Council it was this latter who had overall responsibility for economic policy.[94] In his absence it was the cautious Sir Stafford Cripps who was handling economic matters in addition to his duties as President of the Board of Trade. There may well have been elements in the Civil Service and the government who would have fought Anglo-French integration tooth and nail, but the battle-lines were never drawn and the minimalist view of economic co-operation prevailed by default.

Despite the lack of a conclusive outcome, however, the episode had served to bring to the forefront of attention issues which might otherwise have escaped detailed examination. In the process, previously ill-defined ideas regarding Anglo-French economic relations were measured against the stringencies of the Monnet Plan in an appraisal which extended beyond the confines of the Foreign Office. Above all, at a time when much remained to be decided in Europe, it provided the opportunity for the French to explain their objectives for the reconstruction period in the context of their relations with Britain. This raised questions in regard to the wider pattern of international production and trade for which British policy lacked immediate answers. The exercise had nevertheless revealed the pitfalls involved in moving from a position of general willingness to co-operate with France in economic matters to one of practical association with French ambitions.

2 Steel

THE GERMAN INDUSTRY

During the course of the Anglo-French talks on the Monnet Plan in January 1947 it became clear that the French regarded the prospects for the fulfilment of their recovery programme as being to a large extent dependent upon the place reserved for German industry within the overall pattern of post-war reconstruction in Europe. The corollary of this basic conviction was that Anglo-French economic co-operation must necessarily encompass an agreement on a common position with respect to the curtailment of Germany's considerable industrial potential. This view was forcefully put by Hervé Alphand, Director General of Economic Affairs at the Quai d'Orsay, in a memorandum handed to Sir Mark Turner of the Control Office for Germany and Austria one week after the close of the Paris talks.[1] It was emphasised that a prime concern of the French was the German steel industry, and Alphand pursued this point the following week in conversation with British officials: 'On steel, Alphand said that there were two parts to the subject, firstly the level of the German steel industry and, secondly, the allocation of steel capacity among the countries of Europe.'[2] The French were convinced that productive capacity in Western Europe as a whole exceeded the maximum peacetime requirement and that the German industry should be reduced below its pre-war level to compensate. Alphand developed this theme when he called on Hall-Patch ten days later and put the case that Germany should not be allowed to manufacture for the export market. According to French calculations, German internal consumption would require a quantity of between 7.5 and 8 million tons of steel a year, of which 6.5 to 7 million tons could come from home production, the balance being imported principally from the Saar.[3] As the level of German industry was still a matter for quadripartite decision, Alphand hoped that a common Anglo-French line could be agreed before the next Council of Foreign Ministers, which was due to start in Moscow in March. It was agreed that British experts would study the matter and submit the results to Ministers for consideration. Thereafter, British representatives would be prepared to travel to Paris for discussions before the departure of the delegations for Moscow.[4]

In fact British experts had given this question a good deal of consideration since the end of hostilities without arriving at a figure as low as that recommended by any of the other three occupying powers. The government had no interest in seeing the German steel industry restored to preeminence in Europe but was nevertheless anxious to promote a level of output commensurate with a viable economy in order to defray the continuing cost of occupation.[5] The largest part of the total German steelmaking capacity was located in the British zone but was subject to the quadripartite Level of Industry Agreement, which circumscribed the economic benefit which could be drawn from the considerable manufacturing potential in the area and left no real possibility of recovering the costs of occupation.[6] From the outset Britain had been thinking in terms of a reduction by half of the German pre-war productive capacity of 23 million tons a year to 11.5 million tons.[7] As a gesture towards the other occupying powers this was reduced by 1 million tons but nevertheless remained the highest figure put forward to the Allied Control Authority in December 1945.[8] As that year drew to a close Britain was ready to countenance a reduction down to 9 million tons but even this figure did not form a basis for agreement and discussion was deferred.[9] By the time the Level of Industry Plan was agreed in March 1946, the total capacity to be retained in Germany had been further beaten down in discussion to a figure of 7.5 million tons with the additional proviso that actual output should be restricted to a lower level of 5.8 million tons.[10]

From the British point of view this was hard to accept and the possibility was raised of denouncing four-power control at the Paris Council of Foreign Ministers in May 1946 and abandoning the Level of Industry Plan completely.[11] Nothing so drastic in fact occurred, but in October Bevin publicly came out in favour of a figure of 11 million tons.[12] By December he was determined to pursue British interests regardless of any four-power agreement. 'He thought that we should go straight ahead with our policy and if this involved breaches of the Level of Industry Plan we should commit the breaches and argue about them afterwards.'[13] Despite growing British dissatisfaction, however, the Allied agreed level remained at 7.5 million tons capacity and 5.8 million tons actual production and this was how matters stood when Alphand presented the French case at the end of January 1947.

During the Anglo-French talks on the Monnet Plan the previous week the British delegation, in the absence of clear guidance from the Cabinet, had shied away from discussion of the steel industry for fear that they would 'stub their toes against the German problem'.[14] As Alphand recognised, however, a definite British position would have to be agreed before the impending Council of Foreign Ministers in Moscow and the moment was therefore opportune to put forward the French point of view in the hope of influencing policy in this respect. In fact Attlee had already decided on the appropriate means of addressing this question and had taken the step of reconstituting the Overseas Reconstruction Committee to include the Minister of Supply.[15] This development prompted the expert on steel at the Ministry of Supply, Frank Lee, to go on record in favour of 11 million tons for the level of the German industry: a figure which he felt both the Russians and the Americans were now disposed to accept.[16]

As Chairman of the Overseas Reconstruction Committee it fell to Bevin to take charge of the policy review. On 5 February 1947 Lee was given the task of arranging for urgent interdepartmental consideration of the question. Bevin asked for account to be taken of the points recently put forward by the French and for representatives of the British steel industry to be involved.[17] Lee accordingly convened a working party gathered from the appropriate Departments supplemented by Sir John Duncanson of the British Iron and Steel Federation, Mr Wheeler of Guest, Keen and Baldwins, and Dr Colclough, adviser to the Iron and Steel Board. Meeting in February 1947, this group was in session at the time when interdepartmental activity following the Monnet Plan talks was at its peak; an overlap which sometimes deprived the work on Anglo-French economic co-ordination of expert advice.[18] For the French, few questions had more bearing on their plans for the future than the relative strength of the German steel industry. More than any general theory of economic integration they would have welcomed a pledge of British support for their point of view. This now hinged on the findings of Lee's working party.

Bevin, despite his expressed preference for an increase in the permitted level of German steel capacity, specifically requested that the proposals in Alphand's note on the subject be taken into account. He also asked that representatives of British steel interests be consulted. Whether nationalised or private it was unlikely that the industry would welcome an inflated German export potential. The review therefore promised to give French concerns the most sympathetic hearing which could be expected in the circumstances and, whatever the outcome, the exercise would at least serve to bring before the Cabinet a problem of European reconstruction to which France attached considerable importance.

The French view was set out in the document handed to Sir Mark Turner by Alphand on 28 January 1947.[19] While in no way denying that curtailment of Germany's potential for waging war was one of their main aims, the French were nevertheless at great pains to establish a sound economic basis for their recommendations. These revolved around a further reduction of the existing limit of 7.5 million tons capacity on the grounds that the Level of Industry Plan included the Saar as part of Germany. Alphand's proposal involved detaching the Saar and placing its resources under French control; the area's share of the total permitted capacity being deducted to leave 6.3 million tons. Saar steel totalling 1.2 million tons could then be exported back across the new border, restoring the availability of 7.5 million tons and thereby raising *per capita* consumption in the now truncated Germany. The cost of these imports would be offset partly by the revenue from manufactures but mainly by virtue of the extra coal made available for export as a result of the reduction in the German steelmaking capacity.

In this way, the French memorandum argued, Germany might achieve economic viability without affecting the steel export sales of other Western European producers. This was a matter of great concern to the French, who were of the strong opinion that there was already a looming problem of over-capacity due to the loss of former overseas markets in countries which were now developing their own steel industries. Even allowing for the requirements of post-war reconstruction, this was seen as imposing a ceiling on the quantity of steel from European producers which could be readily disposed of. Given that Britain and France were planning to expand and modernise their production facilities, the French took the view that German competition would be to the detriment of both, and should therefore be nipped in the bud. This, in essence, was the French position which Lee's working party was required to take into account.

After a series of meetings the working party fixed on 10 million tons per year as a suitable revised level of steel production in Germany (excluding the Saar).[20] This was the minimum which they considered compatible with a viable economy. The figure did not provide for any exportable surplus but allowed for the use of steel in the manufacture of other goods for export. The report estimated that this level of output would correspond to a *per capita* consumption below that of many industrialised countries in the mid-1930s. Although above *French* pre-war consumption it would be less than the target figure in the Monnet Plan and was regarded as barely adequate in the circumstances. 'In view of Germany's reconstruction needs, reduction of consumption to the level obtaining during the depression would indefinitely retard her recovery.'[21] From this it followed that an appropriate source of supply had to be secured for German requirements. The report estimated that imports on the necessary scale, even financed as much as possible by coal exports, would involve a balance of payments deficit of £40 million a year. The working party was, in any case, highly sceptical that the overall European surplus anticipated by the French would materialise in the foreseeable future. Germany would therefore have to rely on her own resources, which would need to be adequate for the task.

On the subject of possible future competition from Germany the report considered that the greater danger would be to hold down German capacity to a level which might later come under pressure for an upward revision requiring a new large-scale construction programme.[22] This conformed to the view of Sir Mark Turner.

> To give the Germans an opportunity to build a major steel works, after the completion of the French and our own modernizing plans...would be to present the Germans with an opportunity of undercutting us in all our export markets.[23]

The fact that the situation in Germany could not be regarded as permanent was not lost on the Overseas Reconstruction Committee when it met to consider the report. Following a suggestion that the production of certain special steels should be prohibited, the Committee decided that, as controls were bound to be relaxed over time, it was preferable to avoid any measures which would then be difficult to administer.[24] With regard to the overall size of the industry it was agreed that at the forthcoming Council of Foreign Ministers an attempt should be made to reach agreement for an annual production of 10 million tons.[25] This course of action was approved by the full Cabinet the following day.[26]

Anglo-French talks aimed at defining a common position in advance of the next session of the Council of Foreign Ministers were held in Paris on 28 February 1947 in a frank and cordial atmosphere.[27] Nevertheless, after dissecting the copious statistical material presented, neither side felt able to concede the main points at issue.

> The discussions ended with an agreement to differ. The French representatives did not accept, but did not dissent strongly from the British view that German domestic needs should be put at 10 million ingot tons. But they maintained their contention that German steel capacity should be limited to the production of say 6.5 million ingot tons, any balance needed above that figure being met by imports from the Saar and elsewhere.[28]

This met with the British criticism that imports on the necessary scale would have an adverse effect on the balance of payments, which the French delegation countered by reciting 'an ingenious catalogue of savings and alternative exports' that would fill the gap.[29]

The British delegation were unconvinced, but their overriding concern was the question of whether there would in fact be a sufficient quantity of steel available on the open market to meet the needs of German ancillary industries in the absence of an adequate indigenous source of supply. The Chancellor of the Exchequer had already expressed reluctance to call upon the taxpayer to 'carry the Germans on his back' beyond the end of that financial year.[30] The possibility that the British public might again be expected to shoulder that burden at some future date because of a lack of steel which could perfectly well have been produced on German territory was not an attractive prospect. For their part, the French would not be shaken in their belief that, rather than a *shortage* of steel, the danger was of an impending glut.[31] The British remained sceptical and, to illustrate their point, mentioned that the United Kingdom was not certain of achieving its own steel programme on schedule. On this subject they wondered whether the French might have had any second thoughts regarding the feasibility of the Monnet Plan target. 'They had, however, abounding self confidence in their own capabilities and without being offensive there was nothing to do but accept their statement.'[32]

The possibility of the failure of the Monnet Plan had been taken into account by Lee's working party, who had only included the Plan's figures in their calculations with the caveat that full achievement was doubtful.[33] This view was shared by the Economic Intelligence Department, which warned of dire consequences if German steel capacity were not kept at a high enough level to make good the shortfall with imports from the Ruhr should the need arise.[34] There was also already some doubt as to whether France could be prevailed upon to maintain deliveries of steel to Germany from the Saar if French industrialists were clamouring for supplies.[35] These misgivings coloured the British attitude at the discussions in Paris. Nevertheless the exercise served to air differences on a subject which would continue to preoccupy the French throughout the years of post-war recovery.

SUPPLY AND DEMAND

Fundamental to Anglo-French differences regarding the German steel industry were two widely separated outlooks. The British view was that steel would continue to be in short supply for a number of years to come, whereas the French prognosis was that, failing remedial action, supply would rapidly outstrip demand. These contrasting views were held in a period of grave shortage which was strangling the output of those British industries upon which a sound post-war economy might be founded. In October 1946 John Wilmot reported to the Lord President's Committee:

I am sorry to have to present such a gloomy picture to my colleagues. But I fear that in considering all our plans in the immediate future we must face the fact of a continuing shortage of steel in relation to a demand which has reached abnormal levels.[36]

In January 1947 the possibility was even raised of discouraging the flow of manpower into metalworking industries because of lack of steel.[37] For a nation founded on a solid industrial base and a Labour government committed to full employment this was a matter for serious concern and boded ill for Britain's prospects.

Indeed, unless supplies can be considerably increased at once and maintained at a much higher level than at present, lack of this raw material more than any other will cripple production in a wide range of industries.[38]

In 1947 steel was still subject to government allocation and, by the middle of the year, engineering industries not engaged in the manufacture of priority items were receiving approximately 45 per cent of their requirements.[39] In the first quarter of that year, when the British delegation was discussing the level of German steel capacity in Paris, home production actually fell to the equivalent of an annual output of 11.25 million tons.[40] In the light of this level of performance it is possible to justify the view expressed to the French during the Paris talks that there was an element of doubt regarding the early attainment of the ultimate target of 16.25 million tons. On the other hand, the French were understandably willing to accept the same target in a spirit of optimism as they wished their British counterparts likewise to take the Monnet Plan figure at face value, thereby arriving at a projected overall European supply sufficient to obviate the need for any increase in German production.

Given the importance of the question it was understandable that the British should prefer the safer course of action based on a more conservative estimate. Their caution, however, proved to be ill-founded. One year later not only was France able to begin exporting small quantities of steel to Britain, but the British were able to use the threat of competition from other European suppliers to force an early start to French deliveries originally scheduled for later in the year. This ploy proved successful and prompted the comment that the French 'may well have begun to think seriously about the duration of the present seller's market'.[41] In fact, since the early days of the Monnet Plan, the French had made no secret of their very real anxiety in this regard. It was the British, rather, who clung to the view that the steel shortage was a durable phenomenon and who persisted in planning on the basis of the most pessimistic scenario despite the existence of conflicting opinions.

Although making no attempt to emulate the Monnet Plan, the Attlee government published each year an Economic Survey of developments and policy in the principal areas of activity. In February 1948 the Survey forecast that the major limiting factor for industry would be the shortage of steel. It was predicted that this would pose acute problems of control and allocation but it was equally recognised that 'no system of control can make eight tons do the work of ten'.[42] This outlook reflected the views of Austin Robinson, a Cambridge economist serving as a member of the Central Economic Planning Staff. Alec Cairncross, then an economist at the Board of Trade, disagreed strongly with the assumption that the situation was immune to treatment.

> I have never believed this, and what has been happening lately suggests that we have been too cautious in our target for the industry, precisely because we did not take sufficiently into account the methods that might be used to squeeze more from existing capacity...I am not by any means sure that it will be putting it too high to suggest that we can get 16 million ingot tons by 1951 from the capacity already in existence, apart altogether from what is in course of construction.[43]

In fact it proved possible to remove general-purpose steel from government control in June of the following year.[44] Furthermore, by December 1949, the Board of Trade was forecasting home production for 1950 at a level of 15.79 million tons.[45] This represented a considerable improvement on the view offered at the Anglo-French talks in February 1947 that the United Kingdom would not achieve production in excess of 16 million tons per year for *at least ten years*. Less than three years later, however, that target was already appearing feasible and French optimism in accepting the figure was within a few thousand tons of being vindicated.

The general supply situation in Europe had also improved. In its report of February 1947 Frank Lee's working party on steel had concluded that, although the future was uncertain, there was: 'no reason to suppose that, at any rate within the next ten years, European producers need think of looking for a market in Germany'.[46] By January 1949, however, the Ministry of Supply was expecting an available surplus for export of 1.5 million tons among the member countries of the OEEC.[47] This had been foreseen by those most closely involved as early as May 1948 when an official at the British Embassy in Paris spoke with Sir John Duncanson of the Iron and Steel Federation, who had served on the original working party.

> Duncanson told me a day or two ago that in his opinion there would be an overproduction of steel in the U.K. before long, and we should have to start looking for a home for it. Oddly enough, René Fould, a big ship builder, said just the same thing last evening about France.[48]

The Board of Trade agreed that the worst of the steel shortage might possibly be over by the end of 1949 but noted that:

> the Central Economic Planning Staff however do not think there is a prospect of any change for some time to come. Perhaps the truth of the matter is that Sir John Duncanson is much too optimistic, the C.E.P. too pessimistic.[49]

The idea of actually treading a middle path between these two possibilities does not seem to have been raised, however, and government policy remained predicated on conditions of continuing shortage.

In March 1950 the Economic Commission for Europe reported that the steel shortage had, on the whole, been overcome and that productive capacity in Europe would in future exceed the demand for its products.[50] This conclusion had already been drawn by the French in January 1947; the same month that the Economic Section of the Cabinet Office put forward the possibility that considerable surplus capacity might appear after the immediate period of reconstruction.[51] Admittedly this report had been in preparation for several months and was therefore somewhat out of date for the purposes of the Anglo-French exchanges of view then taking place.[52] Compiled before the publication of the Monnet Plan, it had taken the highest output ever achieved in France: 11 million tons rather than the Monnet Plan target of 15 million tons. Working on the basis of the *lower figure*, the Economic Section calculations nevertheless proved to be nearer the mark than the new survey on which the British based their position at the Anglo-French discussions at the beginning of March 1947.

In fairness, the course of European reconstruction was at that moment still largely uncertain. Soon, however, the pace of events took on a new rhythm as the influence of American policy made itself felt. Following the failure of the Moscow Council of Foreign Ministers to reach an agreement on the level of the German industry, the United States pressed for a figure of 12.5 million tons a year for internal consumption *plus* a further 1 million tons destined for export as the figure for the combined British and American zones of occupation. Inviting his Cabinet colleagues to reject the American scheme Bevin added that: 'acceptance of the American figure would be likely to revive French suspicions of our intentions in Germany and might cause a setback in our relations with the French Government'.[53] This was only to be expected. At the Paris talks, Britain and France had come close to agreement on a level for Germany's domestic requirements but had remained divided on the question of sources of supply. Regarding the future of the steel industry in Europe as a whole, the two sides had agreed to differ over the interpretation of the figures but neither had proposed that Germany should produce any steel for export. Only three months later the level of output envisaged for the Bizone undermined at a stroke the statistical basis of the forecasts and presaged the re-establishment of Germany among the first rank of European steel producers.

THE BRITISH INDUSTRY AND EUROPE

The question of the future of German industry intruded into the subject of Anglo-French economic co-operation with an undeniable logic. Following the Monnet Plan discussions in January 1947 a Board of Trade official wrote:

> I am rather forced to the conclusion, which I gather coincides with what was said in the Paris talks, that what the French are really driving at is Anglo-French/German economic integration. Here I think we have to be very cautious.[54]

Elsewhere this reasoning was pursued yet further. Frank Lee, the Ministry of Supply steel expert, gave his opinion as:

> I feel in my bones that, leaving security and technical considerations on one side, a purely Anglo-French tie-up in steel would be wrong: there would be much more to be said for working out a scheme of concerted development for Western Europe (Germany, Belgium, Luxemburg, France and ourselves) as a whole. But of course that would raise pretty formidable political, economic and technical questions.[55]

There were, of course, the interests of the United Kingdom to consider. Details of the British steel development programme had been published the previous year based on the plans produced by the Iron and Steel Federation for modernisation and expansion of a privately-owned steel industry.[56] The Labour government was committed to a policy of nationalisation for the industry which entailed the adoption of the same proposals regarding degree of specialisation, location of the various production processes, output targets etc. In respect of this sector of the economy at least, Britain was therefore already in a position to compare her long-term objectives with those of France when the Monnet Plan was published at the end of 1946. On the possibility of the two national steel plans being integrated, *The Times* pronounced that this would be a futile exercise unless, for example, Belgian intentions were known.[57] In fact Anglo-French integration was never pursued to the stage where lack of a European dimension became the limiting factor.

Despite his penchant for economic co-operation, Ernest Bevin shared with his Cabinet colleagues a commitment to expansion of the British steel industry which precluded any forfeiture of control. His personal argument in favour of nationalisation was that a steel industry in private hands would lack the incentive to sustain, through good times and bad, a level of output in keeping with the national interest.[58] He was also wary of relying on imported steel: a practice which he saw as 'making the usual mistake of gambling on other people supplying us'.[59]

As Europe emerged from conditions of shortage, however, there was scope for reciprocal arrangements based on local strengths and weaknesses. One such was the Anglo-French Steel Agreement of March 1948. This provided for the supply of semi-finished steel and rolled steel joists to Britain on a sliding scale as French production increased; the arrangement to be on a commercial basis with the added incentive to France of regular deliveries of coiled steel strip produced in Britain.[60] Though advantageous to both sides, a particular element of expediency was evident on the part of Britain. At the Anglo-French Economic Co-operation Committee in September 1948 the British delegation pressed for increased deliveries to take into account steel produced for France in the Saar.[61] On the other hand, the London Committee concluded in February 1949 that no contract for French steel should be entered into for 1951/52 unless the French could guarantee increased supplies in the intervening period.[62] Within a year of this decision the supply situation had eased to the extent that the Steel Agreement was judged to have outlived its usefulness from the British point of view, leading to the Escape Clause being invoked.[63] Rather than a long-term rationalisation of production, the British objective was thus clearly the relief of the existing shortage.

As plans for nationalisation of the British steel industry neared fruition a Cabinet Paper was produced reviewing the lines of argument which members of the government might use in support of the Iron and Steel Bill once its provisions had been made public. Paragraph 7 was devoted to the international implications:

> If closer economic integration of Western Europe is ever to mean anything the iron and steel industry must be at the heart of it. This means that, if the iron and steel industry of Western Europe is to be effectively integrated on economic and strategic grounds, the necessary regulation must be carried out under Government auspices rather than left to the free play of private enterprise.[64]

Far from commending this as an argument in support of the Bill, the Foreign Office felt that it should be placed under a heading: 'Points to Avoid', rather than court the risk of government policy being misrepresented as wholesale nationalisation of the steel industries of the Marshall Plan countries in the interests of European integration.[65] Bevin could himself see that if the argument were ever advanced in support of the Bill it could be demolished by drawing on examples of countries where the industry was still in private hands. For this reason he preferred to change the paragraph in question to a reference to the importance of an efficient British steel industry to Europe generally.[66] His wishes were reflected in the reissued version, which laid emphasis on the benefits to European reconstruction of a higher level of British production than could be expected from a steel industry in private hands. It was thus at Bevin's request that the allusion to European steel integration was expunged from the array of arguments which Ministers were authorised to deploy in favour of the forthcoming nationalisation.

The Iron and Steel Bill received the Royal Assent in November 1949. Six months later the announcement of the Schuman Plan heralded the advent of European steel integration round a Franco-German nucleus. The declaration, on 9 May 1950, that the two countries intended to place their total production of coal and steel under a High Authority, was made without prior consultation with Britain. Bevin enquired of the French Ambassador, René Massigli, whether the offer extended to Britain and was informed that it was open to all European countries, which naturally included the United Kingdom. The Ambassador nevertheless gained the impression that the Foreign Secretary was only controlling himself with an effort.[67] Bevin's wrath stemmed from the feeling that the British had been deliberately kept in the dark and that, in spite of protestations to the contrary, the Plan was contrived to exclude the United Kingdom.[68] Even if true, this was hardly cause for complaint as the French had long sought a common outlook on the post-war European steel industry but had met with little more than evasion and procrastination from Britain. This was despite the fact that cross-Channel division of labour in steel production had been quoted by Bevin as an example of developments which might emerge from the work of the Anglo-French Economic Co-operation Committee: 'The French might, for example, produce some kinds of steel or textiles and Great Britain other kinds.'[69] This was perhaps, however, merely an off-the-cuff example to illustrate the general mutual benefits which Bevin genuinely hoped would accrue from closer economic ties between the two countries. As far as any meaningful co-operation in this field was concerned, progress was impossible without taking into account the wider implications; in particular the extent to which German steel would affect the overall pattern of production and supply as the normal flow of commerce was resumed. This was a hurdle which Anglo-French co-operation failed to clear and a problem which eventually found a solution of a different kind.

3 Coal

COAL AND THE MONNET PLAN

Invasion and long occupation took a considerable toll on France and, unavoidably, the effects on political and economic life persisted after the Liberation. In addition to physical damage to industrial plant and transport infrastructure the country lingered for a period in political limbo as first one, then another Constituent Assembly strove to arrive at a constitution. As 1946 drew to a close, however, the road ahead became clearer with the acceptance of the constitution of the Fourth Republic in October, followed by the publication of the Monnet Plan in November. When, in December, Léon Blum took office at the head of a Socialist caretaker government pending the election of a President, the moment was ripe for the British Labour government to take stock of the situation. Returning from six weeks in New York at the Council of Foreign Ministers and the United Nations, Ernest Bevin summoned the French Ambassador and said that, to his mind, the rehabilitation of France was the fundamental problem in Europe. Accordingly he had always sought closer ties between Britain and France, perhaps not through grand gestures but rather by a pragmatic, methodical approach to everyday matters affecting both countries.[1] The Ambassador said that in this regard there were three main issues: French recovery, the German level of industry, and Anglo-French relations. He argued that these were in fact one question and that the deciding factor was coal.[2]

The importance of this particular commodity had been emphasised to Herbert Morrison by Jean Monnet at a luncheon in Washington as early as May 1946.

> At the moment French economy had arrived at a point at which ... only lack of coal could arrest progress. But if the coal was not forthcoming, the whole process would be slowed up with all the possibilities of political extremism, financial collapse and social chaos.[3]

This point was forcefully reiterated in a letter handed to Attlee by Jules Moch, acting as Blum's special envoy, on 3 January 1947.

> One or two million tons of coal or thereabouts per month will decide between our economic reconstruction and our political destruction. I do

not in any way exaggerate when I say that the fate of democracy and socialism in France and consequently in Europe is at stake for this amount.[4]

Bevin was well-disposed towards giving all possible assistance to Blum's government in these circumstances, and faithfully echoed the substance of his argument in Cabinet.[5] The problem was that, in the middle of a severe winter, the coal supply in Britain was rapidly proving insufficient even to meet basic requirements at home, far less providing an exportable surplus adequate to France's needs.[6] This shortage was an obstacle to providing material help but Bevin was nevertheless concerned to make some effort to support the French government. Blum's letter had also raised the possibility of economic discussions between the two countries and Bevin was therefore at pains to carry his Cabinet colleagues in an appropriately encouraging response to at least this request. As a result, the letter from Attlee which was despatched two days later paved the way for the Anglo-French discussions on the Monnet Plan later that month.[7]

It was no secret that the targets for industrial output envisaged in the Monnet Plan depended on increased supplies of coal, the most accessible source of which was to be found in the British zone of occupation in Germany. The total imports necessary were estimated at 18.5 million tons for 1947, rising to 22 million tons for 1950. Of this, between 10 and 15 million tons per year would be required from the Ruhr.[8] The war and the Allied victory had also taken their toll on Germany, however, with the result that lack of equipment and shortage of manpower restricted the amount of coal mined. In late summer 1946 the Ruhr coalfields were only exporting at a rate equivalent to approximately 12 million tons annually, of which France could expect to obtain something in the region of 3.5 million tons based on a projection of the existing distribution of exports.[9] In other words the success of the Monnet Plan required, in round figures, the entire annual export tonnage of the Ruhr at the 1946 level. The situation was open to improvement as time went by but, with increased output, the British authorities were faced with the dilemma of how much of the extra tonnage to plough back into the task of setting German industry back on its feet while the liberated countries were desperate for more exports. Early in 1947 Jean Monnet made his own position clear.

He said that he was glad there were signs of increased production from the Ruhr, but unless some arrangements were made very soon for France to benefit from this increased production he did not think there was much hope of the French plan for modernisation being carried through and still less hope of any successful co-operation between our two countries in the economic field. He had made this plain to Sir Edward Bridges.[10]

Later the same month Monnet took the opportunity to present an exposé of the latest position to the British delegation at the Anglo-French talks in Paris on the subject of the German steel industry.[11] Working on the import requirement of 18 million tons of coal for the current year, Monnet explained that 9 million tons should be obtainable from the United States and 1 million tons from Poland, leaving a balance of only 8 million tons from Germany. He had believed that, as production from German mines rose, this figure would be attainable but it was in fact proving to be the case that, as output increased, more coal was being retained for German internal consumption. In the light of the conversations then in progress this caused him some concern as any further rise in the level of German industry would jeopardise the whole Monnet Plan.[12]

Monnet's remarks went to the heart of the matter; French recovery could be best achieved and more easily sustained if it progressed in advance of the re-establishment of Germany's industrial base. This perspective on the realities of the post-war period was clearly inseparable from the Anglo-French relationship: 'That is the primary meaning of an alliance with Britain: an explicit recognition by the British that France must be favoured, deliberately and consistently before Germany.'[13] As the French Ambassador indicated to Bevin at the end of 1946, the deciding factor was coal. Given sufficient supplies France could take advantage of the period of quadripartite control over Germany to acquire at least a headstart in re-equipment and modernisation and to establish markets for the increased output of her industries. From the point of view of France the worst possible scenario was one in which a resurgent German industry enjoyed the full benefit of large indigenous fuel supplies while French blast-furnaces and factories marked time on a restricted régime.

In avoiding this ruinous state of affairs British support was crucial and could be brought to bear at a number of points. Not only was Britain the occupying power in the Ruhr but she was, in normal circumstances, an exporter in her own right. Britain was also a member of the European Coal Organisation (ECO), to which fell the task of overseeing fair distribution of this indispensable commodity. There was thus considerable scope for Britain to intervene in France's favour on a matter the importance of which had been made abundantly clear on many occasions. Nevertheless, at the end of March 1947, the French Ambassador was impelled to write to the British Prime Minister in terms which again held out the spectre of impending social and economic collapse in the event of France's vital needs remaining unsatisfied.[14] That such an appeal should have been necessary at that late date indicated the intractable nature of the problem. For two years the subject of coal had soured Anglo-French relations, during which time the French had unremittingly pressed their case without managing to secure imports adequate to their needs. Although sympathetic to France's predicament, Britain's response through the means at her disposal succeeded only in producing an atmosphere of acrimony and uncomprehending disappointment. With the best will in the world British policy was constrained by considerations beyond the desire to stimulate French recovery and it was these factors which proved decisive in the difficult conditions which prevailed in the immediate post-war years.

THE EUROPEAN COAL ORGANISATION

The problem of sharing a restricted coal supply pending a return to peacetime conditions had been addressed by the British coalition government before the end of hostilities. In October 1944 the Ministry of Supply produced a note for the Transitional Period Committee proposing the formation of a European Coal Organisation and recommending that other Allied governments be approached in this respect.[15] Talks eventually got under way on 1 March 1945 and continued for five weeks between representatives of the United Kingdom, France, the United States and the Soviet Union. Progress was hampered to such an extent by Soviet obstruction over small details that, at an informal meeting of the other countries on 7 April, the possibility was raised of arranging matters between just the three of them. In the event, when the Provisional European Coal Organisation came into being on 18 May 1945 the membership consisted of: Belgium, Denmark, France, Greece, Luxembourg, the Netherlands, Norway, Turkey, the United Kingdom, and the United States.[16] With effect from 4 January 1946, this was formally constituted as the European Coal Organisation, consisting of a Council and a full-time staff including a Chairman and a Secretary-General, with headquarters in London. Its stated purpose was 'to promote the supply and equitable distribution of coal and scarce items of coal-mining equipment'.[17]

The task of ensuring an equitable distribution of coal proved to be fraught with peril but certain basic principles were quickly established. In a situation of chronic shortage it was accepted that no importing country would be able to obtain its full requirements but each would have to be content with an agreed 'level of satisfaction' calculated against total availabilities for a three-month period on the basis of indigenous production, pre-war consumption, alternative sources of energy, and damage sustained during hostilities. On the basis of these guidelines a fair division was ultimately determined by the Allocations Proposals Committee subject to unanimous agreement.[18] Supplies were then drawn from a pool of total declared export availabilities after allowing for a small number of permitted bilateral deals. By the accepted criteria regarding 'level of satisfaction' Britain was, in any three-month period, ineligible for an allocation but contributed small amounts to the pool. As a general principle export tonnages from the largest suppliers, the United States and Germany, were declared for allocation in their entirety.

These arrangements, though the best that could be contrived in the circumstances, were not ideal and were always susceptible to pressure from individual members seeking concessions on various grounds. The French in particular displayed a penchant for robust lobbying which exasperated the British. Following an attempt by France to obtain greater freedom in the matter of bilateral agreements a British official opined that: 'I am afraid it is going to be very difficult to get the French to play fair. This is a typical performance.'[19] The French, however, were more concerned with economic survival than impressing their colleagues with a display of the virtues appropriate to the cricket pitch. Their determination increased when, in 1946, industrial action by American miners drastically reduced the amount of coal for allocation from the ECO pool. The British response, although sympathetic, was inevitably limited by the realities of the situation.

> Gouin has presented request for additional 500 000 tons of coal monthly due to American strikes. This is of course quite impossible. Foreign Secretary is however most anxious to make some concession and political gesture before French elections.[20]

The Minister of Fuel and Power immediately made available from British stocks an additional 100 000 tons for the ECO pool.[21] The Foreign Secretary also hoped to arrange an extra contribution from German sources over the months of June and July. He did not, however, envisage that this should go straight to France, but rather that it should be subject to the due process of the Allocations Proposals Committee of the ECO, where the French case would nevertheless be given all possible support by the British and American delegates.[22] For their part, the United States authorities in Germany were willing to release 60 000 tons from stocks in their zone, bypassing the usual allocation procedure in favour of a direct transfer of this quantity to France.[23] This did not, however, meet with the approval of the British, who were prepared to deplete stocks in their own zone by 100 000 tons, but felt that the total amount from both zones should be considered as a loan to the ECO, repayable from future deliveries when the situation improved.[24]

General Clay, the American Deputy Military Governor, took the view that if the loan went through the ECO, France would probably only receive a portion of the total and the whole object would be defeated.[25] The French, predictably, shared this opinion but it was the British view which prevailed and the head of Economic Affairs at the Quai d'Orsay was informed accordingly.

> M. Alphand reacted violently. He said that of the amounts advanced by the British and American Governments only part would reach France and the latter would be left with serious deficit…it was evident that His Majesty's Government's policy was to build up Germany at the expense of France.[26]

Receiving an assurance that the British delegate to the ECO would support the French case for a large share of the extra tonnage, Alphand then developed the theme that lack of coal was increasing the danger of economic collapse in France as a prelude to a slide into communism. This failed to impress his British listeners, who regarded the outburst as a typical example of the hysteria which the subject of coal tended to provoke in political quarters in France.[27]

Distribution of the 160 000 tons advance was considered by the ECO on 4 June 1946. A problem immediately arose when it was announced that the tonnage to be released from the British zone through normal channels might be subject to a shortfall amounting to some 75 000 tons. The Chairman proposed that, in order to maintain the anticipated pattern of allocations, the first call on the 160 000 tons loan should be for making good the deficit in the general pool. The response of the French representative was that France had prior claim to this tonnage and that he would leave the meeting if he did not obtain reasonable satisfaction.[28] The matter was only resolved when it was agreed that an appeal should be made to the Control Authorities to restore the original German availability. If the appeal proved successful France would receive 127 000 tons of the additional 160 000 and if the excess remained at only 85 000 tons France would get 63 000.[29] The British worried that if the French walked out it would herald the start of a free-for-all among coal importing countries.[30] Nevertheless, the French tactics were not viewed with approval.

> If the British public were to learn that so far from being grateful for our assistance the French Government had expressed disgust at its inadequacy their reaction would almost certainly be to think that it was a mistake to help them at all. The coal shortage is acute in this country and it is particularly unbecoming of the French to look gifts of coal from us in the mouth.[31]

That coal shortage was, within a few months, to give rise to a situation in which Britain was obliged to seek French support for her own manoeuvres within the forum of the ECO.

Meeting to discuss the deepening fuel crisis on 7 January 1947 Ministers considered the possibility of supplementing British supplies from overseas sources but decided that such a measure should be postponed for the time being.[32] The following month the situation had deteriorated to the point where it became necessary to suspend all exports of coal from the UK.[33] The same day the Minister of Fuel and Power announced that from the following Monday no electricity would be available to industrial consumers in London, the Southeast, the Midlands or the Northwest and that domestic supplies in those areas would be cut off every morning between 9 o'clock and noon, and every afternoon from 2 o'clock to 4 o'clock.[34]

The reaction from the United States was an offer of immediate assistance. At the soonest it would take fifteen days to ship coal across the Atlantic but there were already at sea, heading for Europe, a number of vessels which could perhaps be diverted to British ports. It was proposed that the American delegate to the ECO would support the reallocation of these shipments if such was the desire of His Majesty's Government.[35] The situation was analogous to that of the previous summer when General Clay had pressed for coal to be made available to the French directly but had relented following British objections that this would undermine the ECO. Britain now had the opportunity to pervert the normal functioning of that same organisation by laying claim to coal in transit to countries to which it had already been allocated. On this occasion, however, the British reputation for fair play remained intact and Attlee thanked Truman for his generous offer, which he declined on the grounds that the needs of Europe were no less pressing.[36] This response earned the approval of the ECO, which voted that a message of thanks and appreciation be conveyed to the British government.[37]

The coal shortage, however, continued to weigh heavily on British domestic politics. In the Debate on the Economic Situation in the House of Commons on 11 March 1947 a call was made for coal to be imported in order to establish sufficient stocks to guard against the possibility of similar hardships in the future.[38] This contribution to the debate served to focus the attention of the Cabinet on the subject once more and it was decided to invite the Minister of Fuel and Power to submit a paper to the Fuel Committee setting out the arguments for and against a policy of importing coal.[39] The Minister of State at the Foreign Office, Hector McNeil, insisted on submitting his own paper on the subject, in which he forcefully pointed out the overwhelming disadvantages for Britain's foreign relations.

> This would be particularly serious in the case of the French, so soon after the conclusion of the Treaty of Alliance and especially during the Meeting of the Council of Foreign Ministers in Moscow when we have every interest in acting in close concert with the French Government.[40]

McNeil also sent a telegram to Bevin in Moscow, apprising him of the mood of the Cabinet.[41] Bevin's reply was direct to Attlee and expressed the Foreign Secretary's complete opposition to the diversion of coal supplies from Europe to the UK. 'Effect on our foreign relations would be deplorable; we have had no coal mines affected by bombing, no railways seriously affected.'[42]

The last remark was a reference to the taking into account of war damage in the allocations procedure of the ECO. In fact, on none of the accepted criteria did Britain have any basis for making a claim against availabilities from the pool. In the meantime, however, the Chairman of the ECO had expressed to McNeil the personal opinion that, in the event of a British application, general agreement could be obtained for a 'special' allocation of up to 400 000 tons during July, August and September.[43] This assumed that the Americans could, by an exceptional effort, raise their contribution to the pool to a level of 3 million tons per month during the third quarter of the year. It also assumed that other member countries would be open to persuasion, perhaps by suggesting that Britain might otherwise extract her requirements direct from the coal mines of the Ruhr.[44]

This unsubtle approach would certainly have done very little to further the cause of Anglo-French relations. Informed of the direction in which ministerial opinion was drifting, Bevin was horrified.

> I see very grave objections to the possibility of a grant of special allocations to the United Kingdom being explored with the European Coal

Organisation. Such a move, which would be bound to become known, would make the position of the British delegation here intolerable.[45]

It would be especially embarrassing as the French were using the meeting of the Council of Foreign Ministers to press their case for more coal from German mines. When Bevin's telegram was considered in Cabinet the following day, Emanuel Shinwell, the Minister of Fuel and Power, was likewise of the opinion that it was not worth alienating France and the other European countries for such a small contribution to British needs.[46] Unusually, it was Attlee who opposed Bevin's view and proposed that, because of the critical position, an urgent approach should be made to the American Ambassador on the matter of additional supplies of coal. On this the Cabinet agreed.[47]

The response was that the United States would regard favourably any reasonable case which the UK might put to the ECO.[48] This course of action was finally decided at the meeting of the Fuel Committee on 16 April 1947, when the Minister of Fuel and Power was invited to make an immediate application to the ECO and to base the claim on 'special economic conditions' in the UK.[49] With this in mind the Foreign Office approached the American Ambassador with an enquiry which went straight to the crux of the matter: 'What will be the attitude of your government should the French oppose the UK application for an allocation of coal?'[50] The answer was unequivocal: 'Mr. Douglas immediately replied that if the French opposed our application the Americans would not favour it either.'[51] The Foreign Office envoys did not disguise from the Ambassador that they were sounding him out, as they imagined that, in return for co-operation in the ECO, France would require a *quid pro quo*; probably British support for the proposition that coal mined in the Saar should be considered as part of French production.[52]

At that time coal from the Saar was treated in the same way as the output of the Ruhr mines; that is, as a resource at the disposal of the Occupying Powers. In return for their support of the British application, the French expected Britain and the United States to issue a declaration to the effect that, as Ruhr production rose, coal from the Saar would be progressively withdrawn from ECO allocation and become the exclusive property of France.[53] Purely from the point of view of coal supplies, the British did not find this unreasonable.[54] Politically, however, such a declaration would in effect anticipate a general agreement on the question of the Saar which was still pending at the quadripartite level. In the few days between the French making their proposition and the meeting of the ECO there was no time to agree a common line with the United

States on this departure from four-power control and the best that could be contrived was to instruct the Paris Embassy to inform the French that there was no objection in principle to their plan, which would receive due consideration.[55] In the meantime the Americans had taken exception to the tactics of the French and were less inclined to support them in opposing Britain's application, as long as the British could press their case without damaging the ECO.[56]

In the event the British application received the full support of the United States at the meeting of the ECO on 21 May 1947.[57] The proposal put forward by the Chairman was that the UK should receive 200 000 tons per month during the third quarter provided that this did not reduce the availability of American coal below the level of 2.6 million tons per month achieved in the second quarter.[58] This plan met with a good deal of sympathy and would probably have gone through but for the French, who maintained an uncompromising hostility throughout the proceedings.[59] With discussions deadlocked at the close of the first day's session, the French Ambassador contacted Roger Makins asking for an assurance that, in the event of an agreement being reached the next day, the British would stand by their undertaking to give due consideration to the French proposals regarding the Saar. The British, however, could only promise that those proposals would be judged on their own merits.[60] The following day at the resumed meeting of the ECO the French finally agreed a scheme under which Britain would be eligible for 200 000 tons per month, conditional upon American availability reaching 3 million tons per month.[61]

By 1 August it was apparent that Britain would indeed receive the full 600 000 tons over the three-month period.[62] To put this figure in context it is instructive to consider the projected output of the British coal industry circulated to the Fuel Committee the previous week. This report presented the existing low performance as a temporary phenomenon and estimated that for the following year (1948) production would amount to 211 million tons, of which 7 million tons would be available for export to Europe.[63] Against this must be weighed the requirements of France, with a recovery programme based on *imports* of 18 million tons for 1947, rising to 22 million tons in 1950. From this viewpoint it would seem difficult to escape the conclusion that, in the conditions of shortage of 1947, France's was the greater need. Nevertheless it was deemed necessary to embark upon a bitter wrangle over an amount of coal which, in normal times, would be inconsequential alongside the huge output of British mines. For his part, Bevin remained implacably opposed to the idea of imports throughout the whole episode, but was overruled by Attlee who carried the Cabinet with him on an issue which was regarded as crucial.[64] Ronald Fraser, the

Economic Minister at the Paris Embassy and a privileged observer of these events, noted that:

> most interesting of all was the clear emergence of the fact that we are in presence of a battle between France and the U.K. for something that we both want and intend by all means to get, namely enough coal for our purposes.... There is here a real source of conflict between the two countries; but I suppose no Government at home would contemplate relaxing its efforts in this sort of deadly competition.[65]

A year earlier French attempts to circumvent the normal procedure of the ECO had been viewed with disapproval. In 1947, however, when Britain was herself faced with a fuel crisis it was the short-term national interest which ultimately assumed paramount importance over both the principle of equitable distribution and the Anglo-French relationship. Despite Bevin's attachment to both, the coal shortage had revealed the limits to which either could be taken in the stringent circumstances of the times.

GERMAN COAL

In order to relieve the British Military Government of the burden of the day-to-day running of the German coal industry, the North German Coal Control (NGCC) was established in July 1945 with responsibility for solid fuel production and distribution in the British zone of occupation. An existing cartel, the *Rheinische-Westfalen Kohlen Syndikat*, was replaced by a British distribution office. For each period of thirteen weeks the NGCC submitted advance estimates of production to the quadripartite Allied Coal Committee in Berlin, where the total tonnage to be made available for export from all the zones was then decided and advised to the European Coal Organisation for allocation among its members. The amount allotted to each destination from the British zone was then communicated to the NGCC, which arranged a breakdown of that figure into different qualities by arrangement with the Liaison Officer for the country concerned, and issued the necessary orders to the appropriate collieries, cokeries and briquette plants.[66]

The NGCC commenced its tasks bound by the terms of a directive proposed by the Americans at the Potsdam Conference stating that the export of coal from Germany should take precedence over the requirements of industrial production and civilian domestic consumption.[67] The British had certain reservations regarding the adoption of this principle but the Foreign Secretary at the time, Sir Anthony Eden, agreed with the view expressed by his officials that a prolonged argument on the subject would serve only to place Britain in the position of appearing to support the claims of the Germans against those of the Allies.[68] In the circumstances it was therefore thought that there was little choice but to align British policy with that of the United States and to apply the directive to the British zone, with the idea, nevertheless, that: 'the present wording of the United States draft would not prevent the Allied Control Council and the zone commanders having the last word in deciding how much coal could be exported'[69] It was later to prove that this would offer little opportunity to deviate from a régime dedicated principally to the supply of maximum quantities for export, regardless of the internal needs of the British zone. Once the principle had been established it would be very difficult to convince the French in particular that any relaxation was necessary or desirable. This task did not fall to Eden, however, but to his successor, Ernest Bevin.

In addition to the desperate needs of liberated Europe there were other urgent calls on German output, including the basic energy requirements of the producing country, without which it was difficult to ensure the normal operating conditions of the mines themselves or the efficient running of the railways. In the winter of 1945 when transport problems stifled exports to France, Bevin had every sympathy.[70] At the heart of the matter, however, lay the difficulty of extracting regular supplies from a devastated country. The difference between the British and French positions revolved around the extent to which Germany needed to recover in order to export coal at the desired rate. In an attempt to find common ground a conference was held at the Villa Hügel in Essen from 12 to 14 April 1946.

The French view emerged early in the proceedings:

> In effect, the object of the present conference would be to agree upon the minimum requirements of the British and French zones with a view ultimately to a quadripartite determination of a lower general level of internal consumption in order to maximise exports.[71]

The British reply was that essential requirements had already been cut below the minimum level. The two delegations developed their positions the following day; the British making the point that a certain amount of coal needed to be retained in Germany to supply those industries engaged in the repair and replacement of the equipment essential to the extraction and transport of that same commodity. In addition, the British zone was only existing by virtue of large quantities of imported necessities.

It is therefore essential not only to maximise the export of coal but to create exports of manufactured goods as the British would otherwise, in effect, be in the position of paying reparations to the Germans.[72]

The French accepted the point that consumption in Germany could not be reduced below a certain minimum figure without endangering the efficiency of the very facilities on which they were counting for supplies.[73] Nevertheless they took the view that the quotas currently allocated for German use were sufficient. They also emphasised the need for increased production in the French iron and steel industry, which was existing on a lower level of coal supplies than that in the Western zones of Germany.[74] The French delegation returned to this theme the next day and expressed the opinion that the allocations to the iron and steel industry in the British zone could be substantially reduced.[75] They also felt that, whatever the level of production achieved, a fixed amount of coal should be set aside for German requirements and the balance exported. The British thought that it was premature to fix a figure for internal consumption as even basic needs were not currently being met. At the end of the conference a press release announced that experts from both sides would 'examine in detail the many valuable suggestions put forward by the French Delegation'.[76] *The Economist*, noting that the talks had ended in good-will and understanding, expressed surprise in view of the previous clamour for more coal for France.[77] In fact, pressure continued unabated and, although the fundamental disagreement was glossed over in the final communiqué, the conference had done little to reconcile Anglo-French differences.

The following month the French appealed to the Allied Economic Directorate in Berlin against the tonnage allocated to export; especially France's share from the Ruhr, which amounted to a mere 3 per cent of output. The French steel industry, it was claimed, was only working at 35 per cent of its capacity and at less than 50 per cent of its 1938 level, as the quality of coal necessary could only come from the Ruhr. To this the Chairman replied that the matter was not within the competence of the Directorate but should be taken up with the ECO.[78] To some extent this was avoiding the issue. The European Coal Organisation could only apportion coal from tonnages placed at its disposal; the greater the contribution from the Ruhr, the greater the likelihood of France obtaining an allocation from this source commensurate with her requirements. The dilemma facing Attlee's Government was a choice between the viability of the British zone and compliance with French demands for ever more exports.

At a meeting held to discuss this problem the Control Office representative argued that more coal should be retained in the British zone to enable the production of manufactured goods. It was readily accepted that to reduce exports would be politically embarrassing and would pose severe economic problems for importing countries. On the other hand, to fuel German industry was the best way to reduce the balance of payments deficit in the zone.[79] The meeting concluded that the best course of action would be to concentrate on increasing production. In the meantime, however, it was becoming increasingly difficult to defer a decision. On 6 June 1946 the Minister of Fuel and Power gave the Cabinet an account of his visit to Germany and offered the opinion that, despite the obvious effect on relations with France, it would be necessary to declare a moratorium on coal exports.[80] The Foreign Secretary expressed opposition to this course of action on the grounds that it would amount to a unilateral decision regarding a resource nominally at the joint disposal of all four Occupying Powers. If the time ever came for the Potsdam Agreement to be cast aside, he would prefer the Soviet Union to take the initiative in doing so.[81]

At the meeting of the Overseas Reconstruction Committee on 21 June 1946, Attlee took the chair in Bevin's absence and Shinwell again came out in favour of a moratorium. The pitfalls were recognised but it was agreed that, political aspects aside, this would be the sound economic course.[82] A chance to ascertain what was politically possible was provided by the presence in Paris of delegations to the Council of Foreign Ministers. A series of informal talks between representatives of Britain, France and the United States served only to highlight the limits of tripartite discussion as, according to the Anglo-American view, increased production could only be stimulated by a corresponding rise in internal consumption, which would normally be a matter for quadripartite decision.[83] It was therefore left to the Council of Foreign Ministers to charge the Allied Control Council with the appointment of a committee of experts representing all four occupying powers. The committee was to report not later than 10 August 1946, first on measures to increase production, and secondly on principles of allocation.[84]

This earned the scorn of Emanuel Shinwell, the Minister of Fuel and Power, who had the opportunity to put his case for a moratorium to the French Ambassador personally. Shinwell was in complete agreement that France should receive more coal, but maintained that this would only be possible if exports were temporarily suspended in order to divert fuel to those German industries producing mining supplies. In his view, the latest move did nothing to help. 'He was not in favour of Committees when issues were already clear cut. He thought this one was particularly futile as anyone of common sense could see where the remedy lay.'[85] Shinwell was obliged to curb his impatience, however, as the report of the committee was delayed by a difference between the Soviet experts on one hand and the representatives of Britain, France and the United States on the other regarding division of output between internal use and export.[86]

An attempt to reconcile this difference failed to arrive at a common text and the final report acknowledged the divergence of opinion.[87] This document eventually went before the Co-ordinating Committee of the Allied Control Authority, composed of the four Deputy Military Governors. General Kurochkin upheld the view of his Soviet compatriots on the committee that, if Germany was to be treated as an economic whole, the corollary of quadripartite allocation of coal had to be quadripartite control of production. Failing agreement on this point the Soviet zone would in future declare to the Coal Committee only those tonnages judged surplus to its own requirements.[88] To this, General Robertson replied that if the Soviet Union no longer wished to participate in the established procedure, he would feel free to arrange the disposal of the output of the British zone between himself and his French and American colleagues.[89] Following this exchange, it was agreed to refer the minutes of the meeting, together with the report under discussion, to the Council of Foreign Ministers.

The British were not anxious to pursue the matter further. The break with the principle of quadripartite allocation provoked by the Soviet Union would facilitate the implementation of the cuts in coal exports which they had long sought. Approached for their support for a curtailment of 350 000 tons per month, the Americans had already agreed in principle to a figure of 150 000 tons for October and November, increasing to 350 000 tons for the following three months.[90] The prospect of a cut for October had been conveyed to the French.[91] Alphand had accepted this with reluctance and expressed his fears that the damage to public opinion in France would detract from the excellent effect of the recent establishment of the Anglo-French Economic Co-operation Committee.[92]

When the split with the Soviet Union regarding the report of the committee of experts became known, it was put to Alphand that a common position might be agreed amicably between Britain, France and the United States as disunity would produce no more coal for France and would give the Soviet Union every chance to fish in troubled waters.[93] Alphand, however, was strongly of the opinion that the report should be brought before the full Council of Foreign Ministers (CFM). Bevin made it clear to Georges Bidault, the French Foreign Minister, that he would resent any attempt to air grievances over coal in that forum. Bidault concurred but insisted that France needed an agreement on German coal as a matter of urgency. He did not want to seek discussion in the CFM and would prefer to settle the question between the British and the French.[94] Bevin thought that this would be difficult but agreed to further discussions on the understanding that these should be of an informal nature only. Nothing could be achieved on this basis, however, and the following month Bevin informed his French counterpart that: 'my own view would be that no very useful purpose would be served by further discussions between our officials, who have already gone over this ground exhaustively in recent months'.[95]

One impediment to an agreement was that, even had the political will existed to bleed Germany dry for the benefit of France, this would not be possible without the assent of the United States, especially in view of the anticipated fusion of the British and American zones of occupation.[96] With this move in prospect it was in Anglo-American interests to promote the economic viability of the area which was to form the Bizone. In October 1946 American support was obtained for the maintenance of the cuts in exports from the British zone into the following year.[97] Mindful of French domestic politics, Bevin hoped to delay any announcement until after the elections scheduled for 10 November 1946.[98] An advance warning of the impending cuts aroused French suspicions, however, prompting Alphand to ask whether the object was to increase steel production in the British zone.[99] It was explained that more steel was required to enable the zone to be run at all. Alphand replied that coal imports into France were already insufficient and that further cuts would have serious consequences for French recovery.

> M. Monnet had a long range plan for increasing the steel and iron industry in France, and limiting it in Germany...this plan could not be put into effect unless France could rely on German and British coal.[100]

Two months before the official publication of the Monnet Plan, this did not augur well for a joint Anglo-French approach to the problems of European economic reconstruction. On 24 September the left-wing newspaper *L'Humanité* had run a story that, with coal production rising in Germany, exports were being reduced as a result of the policies of those who would rebuild Germany before France.[101] This reflected a major anxiety of those in government circles, among them Alphand, who had little patience with the apparent benevolence of the Anglo-Saxon powers towards 'poor Germany' while France suffered for lack of coal.[102] Meanwhile the rebuilding of the German economy apparently continued at full speed.[103]

Although less dismayed by the prospect of a German recovery, the British were not, for all that, entirely insensitive to French fears. Under pressure from the French delegation assembled in Moscow for the Council of Foreign Ministers, an agreement was reached between France, Britain and the United States in March 1947. As the Soviet Union was no longer participating in the export allocation machinery the new system applied only to the three Western zones of occupation. The arrangement allowed for coal exports to increase according to a sliding scale as the mines attained progressively higher levels of output. When daily output of clean hard coal reached a total of 280 000 tons for the three zones, 21 per cent of this tonnage would be declared for export, rising by a series of increments to 25 per cent when daily output reached 370 000 tons.[104] This was arrived at despite misgivings being expressed by the Control Office, who felt that it was a matter for a decision by the Cabinet.[105] For the British delegation in Moscow, however, the overriding need was to reach an agreement behind the scenes on a tripartite basis before the subject of coal came before a plenary session of the Council, as it was clear that the French would otherwise cause difficulties during the discussion of this item.[106]

In the event, the French Minister for Foreign Affairs pronounced himself moderately content with the outcome. Although far from what he had hoped for, the agreement nevertheless demonstrated a new desire on the part of Britain and the United States to take account of the French point of view.[107] The Moscow sliding scale, applying only to the Western zones of occupation, also indicated a willingness on the part of Britain and the United States to pursue policies unhampered by the need to treat Germany as an economic whole. Moreover, when the Moscow Conference failed to reach an agreement on the German steel industry, the American reaction was to press for an inflated level of production at which even their British partners balked.[108] Of course, the sliding scale ensured that, whatever the pace of German recovery, the process would be subject to the same energy constraints as the Monnet Plan, as any effort to fuel German industry from increased coal production would automatically also benefit French industry *pro rata*. The fate of Germany was still largely obscure, however, and ideas were clearly evolving regarding the country's industrial potential and the degree of control that would in future be exercised over it. Faced with this looming uncertainty, the only concession which France could win for her own reconstruction programme was a level playing-field.

4 The Saar

BRITISH POLICY

Though by no means a panacea for France's economic problems, the tripartite agreement of April 1947 providing for a progressive increase in coal exports from Germany was welcomed as a step in the right direction. Reporting the generally favourable French reaction, Duff Cooper noted that comment in the press and opinion in government circles shared a common assumption.

> At luncheon the other day M. Blum and Monnet and others present were evidently pleased at the introduction of sliding scale and prospect which they too assume of getting all Saar coal for France.[1]

Such a development was certainly not foreseen in the sliding scale agreed in Moscow, which, on the contrary, linked export availabilities to the combined output of all three Western zones and thus implied the continued inclusion of Saar production in the total. Notwithstanding this detail, French optimism was not completely misplaced as the supposed entitlement to the Saar coalfields had a precedent in the fifteen years following the Great War, during which period ownership of the mines had been transferred to France; being subsequently returned to Germany in 1935. As the Second World War moved towards a conclusion the French let it be known that they hoped again to derive a positive benefit from the Saar by the terms of the peace settlement. The British, however, had regarded any commitment at that stage as premature, as was explained to Hervé Alphand in April 1945.[2]

At the Potsdam Conference in July 1945 the principles which would govern the occupation of Germany were established in the absence of the French, and consequently, when France took charge of the Saar as part of her zone of occupation, it was on the terms imposed by her allies, who retained joint control over the level of industrial activity and allocation of coal production.

As the prospect of a comprehensive peace settlement became ever more remote, French anxiety regarding the ultimate ownership and political control of Germany's material and industrial resources prompted a renewed appeal for British support. Although the future of the whole of Germany, and the Ruhr in particular, was a matter of concern, it was easier to raise the issue in respect of an area which was already in French hands and for which a reasonable case could be made. In February 1946 the French Ambassador left a note with the Foreign Office lamenting the continuing uncertainty and pointing out the difficulty of fixing the level of German industrial activity, and in particular the steelmaking capacity to be permitted, without first knowing whether or not the Saar was to go to France.[3] While accepting that the final political status of the Saar should be determined by the eventual peace settlement, the note proposed the immediate integration of the territory in France's economic and monetary system, including its incorporation in the French customs area and substitution of the franc for the mark. Communicating the same proposals to the Soviet and United States governments, the French expressed a request that they be most urgently considered by the four Foreign Ministers.[4]

Papers were already being prepared for the Cabinet on the future of Germany and, upon receipt of the Ambassador's note, Bevin arranged for its contents also to be taken into consideration.[5] The translation was accordingly annexed to a paper over Bevin's initials which took the view that an early decision on the matter was desirable

> as without such decision the plans for Germany's future economy may be drawn up on false premises. I would therefore ask my colleagues to agree that we should support the French request for an immediate discussion of this question by the four Powers...I also ask my colleagues to agree that the territory be transferred immediately to French administration.[6]

Bevin informed the Cabinet that he had been giving much thought to this and related matters and that he proposed to bring the issues before them in the near future.[7]

The papers prepared for the German Industry Committee of the Cabinet were considered at its one and only meeting on 15 March 1946. With regard to the Saar, the meeting agreed that Britain should endorse the French proposals provided that the assets transferred with the territory were regarded as forming part of France's entitlement to reparations.[8] On 17 April 1946 the full Cabinet agreed that this was an acceptable position pending a comprehensive solution to the question of Germany's future.[9] This view was echoed during the Foreign Affairs Debate in the House of Commons on 4 June 1946, when Bevin publicly expressed the Government's desire that the Saar should eventually go to France, preferably as part of a comprehensive solution to the German question.[10]

In supporting France's claim to the Saar the British government were in no way sailing in uncharted waters. Only eleven years after the end of the earlier French tenure of the territory the evidence of that period still provided a reasonable indication of the likely result. In 1934, the year before the referendum which returned the Saar to Germany, the Department of Overseas Trade, in its annual report on France, commented on the reduction in imports of coal from the United Kingdom, which was ascribed in part to: 'the acquisition of the Saar output, no longer statistically considered as an import, with its yearly extraction of 14 million tons, of which 28 per cent. is consumed in France'.[11] In other words the Saar was providing France with 3 920 000 tons of coal per year in normal operating conditions.

By comparison, in the third week of June 1946, 27 021 tons were delivered to France from the Saar as a result of normal ECO procedures.[12] At this rate France's share of Saar output for fifty-two similar weeks would be 1 405 092 tons. On the other hand, the figure for Saar pithead production for the same week extrapolates to an annual total of 7 710 040 tons,[13] of which France would receive 2 158 811 tons if supplied with the same proportion as in 1934 (28 per cent). Thus, a rule-of-thumb calculation would indicate that France could expect to benefit by about an extra 750 000 tons per year through direct control of the Saar, compared with receipts through ECO channels, even at the low level of output being achieved in June 1946. It was at the meeting of the Overseas Reconstruction Committee on 21 June 1946 that a moratorium on exports from Germany was considered.[14] Clearly, the transfer of the Saar to French control would soften the blow as far as France was concerned. The minutes of the meeting, however, record only that the principle that the Saar might be incorporated in the French economic area was agreed after a short discussion.[15]

Even if France could take immediate control of the Saar, coal was not the only factor in the equation. In 1943 the Foreign Office had prepared its *French Basic Handbook*, which contained a review of French iron and steel production over the inter-war years, both with and without the Saar, which indicated that possession of the Saar would increase France's total output of crude steel by something over 2 million tons per year. On the other hand, within her normal borders France could only produce 63 per cent of the metallurgical coke required for her own industry, and taking France and the Saar together only improved this figure to 70 per cent for the combined area.[16] Once in possession of the Saar, therefore, France would be faced with the choice of either running the steel industry at a level in keeping with the limited quantity of coke produced locally or aiming for maximum steel production by importing coke for the purpose, if any could be obtained.

In February 1946 an indication of French intentions emerged in a disagreement in the Allied Control Authority regarding the distribution, between the four zones, of the overall capacity of the German steel industry. Of the 7 500 000 tons per year to be retained, the American, British and Soviet representatives agreed that the portion in the French zone should be 1 000 000 tons, whereas the French themselves wished to keep in operation plant corresponding to an output of 2 075 000 tons.[17] A compromise was eventually agreed with the fixing of the retained capacity for the French zone at 1 210 000 tons, which left six plants, with a combined capacity of 1 875 000 tons, to be declared as available for removal as reparations, of which all but 300 000 tons was in the Saar.[18] Although temporarily redundant, if these plants were to remain *in situ* until such time as the Saar became part of the French economic system, France would be taking over a total productive capacity of 2 785 000 tons; about three quarters of a million tons in excess of the figure suggested in the Foreign Office handbook.[19]

In July 1946 a more up-to-date appraisal made the connection between the steel-production capacity of the Saar, as calculated by the Allied Control Authority, and the latest news emerging from the work on the preparation of the Monnet Plan, which appeared to envisage an ultimate steel capacity of 15 million tons, to be achieved in stages.

> The acquisition of the Saar, with approximately 3 million tons steel capacity would at once raise French total capacity to some 13 million tons....Thus the acquisition of the Saar steel-works offers a simple solution for the realisation of the 1950 steel target.[20]

This solution would have an advantage over new plant erected on French soil in that the increase in capacity would come complete with the necessary skilled workforce. The key factor, however, was coal supplies. Unless the French intended to neglect the metallurgical industries, running the Saar iron and steel plants at full capacity would reduce the amount of coal available to France for other purposes. The situation was complicated by the fact that quantity was not the only consideration. Saar coals were generally excellent for domestic consumption but would only produce usable coke if mixed with a certain amount of coal from other sources; suitable qualities being obtainable from the Ruhr and Aachen basins. So although an important contribution to the French economy, the absorption of the Saar would nevertheless not provide a complete solution to France's coal shortage.

Even with the acquisition of the Saar mines, France would still need to import at least 4–5 million tons of coking coal (or the equivalent in coke) per annum, as well as further quantities of ordinary coal, according to the actual level of industry and rate of domestic production.[21]

The Foreign Office survey also questioned the long-term ability of French industry to absorb the additional steel production. In the existing conditions of shortage France could obviously take any quantity of steel produced, but long-term prospects would depend on capturing some part of the former German export markets.[22] This meant that any enduring benefit which France might hope to derive from economic union with the Saar would depend ultimately on how far German industry was to be excluded from international competition by the occupying powers. By May 1946, however, Britain was already losing patience with the low figure for steel output imposed by the Level of Industry Plan and was looking for an upward revision.[23] In these circumstances, the quicker that the transfer could be confirmed, the greater would be France's chances of capitalising on her acquisition.

QUADRIPARTITE DEADLOCK

By late Summer 1946, though Britain openly supported the French case in principle, no definite steps had been taken to hasten the final take-over of the Saar. In September of that year, Bevin was approached by his French counterpart, who informed him that he proposed to bring about a customs union between France and the Saar, possibly before the next session of the Council of Foreign Ministers.[24] The following day it emerged that the French were in fact intending to create a customs barrier between the Saar and Germany, though for the time being maintaining the barrier between the Saar and France. While not seeking a formal blessing for this move, the French goverment wished to ascertain whether Great Britain or the United States would actually object.[25] For his part, James Byrnes, the US Secretary of State, disapproved and was resolved to offer the French no encouragement.[26] Georges Bidault later acknowledged the difficulty of unilateral action but warned that the French would insist on a solution at the next meeting of the Council of Foreign Ministers. For his part, Bevin felt that if the CFM failed to reach an agreement, France would be justified in taking unilateral action. In the meantime he would make a statement during the forthcoming Foreign Affairs Debate.[27] On 22 October 1946

Bevin accordingly supported the French entitlement to the Saar in the House, expressing the hope that the matter would be settled quickly.[28]

This was easier said than done. Progress at the Council of Foreign Ministers tended to be slow and the next session, in New York, was largely taken up with the subject of Trieste. As time ran out the French delegation accepted that discussion of the Saar would have to be deferred but warned that before the next session circumstances might lead France to take certain measures of an administrative nature.[29] There was no objection to this statement and the question of 'boundaries' was placed on the agenda for the next session, scheduled to start in Moscow in March of the following year.[30]

On 18 December 1946 the French Military Government in Germany issued two decrees, effective from 22 December, controlling the movement of persons, goods and capital between the Saar and the rest of Germany.[31] From Paris, Duff Cooper reported the mood in the capital in the first days of the new year:

> French journalist Pertinax told me recently that he had heard that you and Mr. Byrnes had in private conversation with Couve De Murville in New York told him that so far as Saar was concerned France could 'go ahead'. Something of the sort is generally believed in Paris.[32]

This was unequivocally denied by Bevin, who recalled that he had heard through Couve's remarks on the matter without comment.[33] Nevertheless, the French were behaving as if permanent economic union with the Saar were already a *fait accompli*. The curfew was lifted, one hundred Saar students were given facilities to study at French universities and it was announced that between seven and ten thousand Saarlanders detained as prisoners of war in France were to be allowed home.[34] However, the territory's resource most coveted by the French, its coal, remained at the joint disposal of the Western Allies while the greater part of its steelmaking plant was ear-marked for removal as reparations. In this respect the decrees issued in December 1946 took the French no nearer to their ultimate goal and, although they had every reason to hope that matters would eventually be settled in their favour, there still remained some details to be arranged.

One of the issues outstanding was the question of reparations. All of the Allies were entitled to an agreed share, expressed in monetary value, of industrial and other equipment designated for removal from Germany. Valuation, overall supervision, and the resolution of conflicting claims were dealt with by the Inter-Allied Reparations Agency (IARA).[35]

Obviously, if France took over the Saar, she would acquire in the process a certain amount of plant from the list on offer. There was no reason why, having obtained at a stroke equipment which other claimants would have had to dismantle and re-erect on their home territory, France should retain the right to a full quota from the rest of Germany. Furthermore, all valuations were on the basis of transportable plant, whereas, in the Saar, France would also benefit from immovable sections such as buildings, chimneys and the foundations of the heavy machinery. The Cabinet view was that France's balance on reparation account should be adjusted accordingly in advance of the final take-over.[36]

Also, the French had thrown their customs barrier round an area somewhat larger than anticipated. Although warned that 'certain adjustments' might be necessary,[37] Britain understood the Saar as being that territory lost to France in the 1935 referendum and was prepared to support a return to the *status quo ante*, but was not inclined to allow France another slice of German territory.[38]

The Americans, while agreeing in principle, were not inclined to press their opinion on the French.[39] It was therefore thought best to take the opportunity afforded by a Parliamentary Question to reiterate the British position.[40] Thus, on 3 February 1947, it was confirmed in the House of Commons that the support of His Majesty's Government was conditional only on a settlement of the questions of reparations and boundaries.[41] There was, however, no suggestion that Britain should withdraw her support for French economic union with the territory covered by the 1935 referendum, and a paper prepared for the Overseas Reconstruction Committee recommended that this position be maintained at the next Council of Foreign Ministers in Moscow.[42] This view was incorporated in the brief prepared for the British delegation, which also endorsed the assurance given the previous October that if quadripartite agreement proved impossible to achieve at the next attempt Britain would not stand in the way of any unilateral action subsequently taken by France. Nevertheless:

> In the event of the failure of the C.F.M. to agree to the French draft proposal we should make it quite plain to the French Government that our acquiescence in future unilateral action by the French to include the Saar in the French Customs Union does not entail acceptance of the proposed enlarged boundaries of the area.[43]

This was the British position presented to the Council of Foreign Ministers by Bevin on 19 March 1947.[44] The French response came in a visit to Sir Oliver Harvey from Couve de Murville, who let it be known that the French position was not absolutely rigid and suggested that informal talks on a noncommittal basis might serve a useful purpose.[45] This proved to be the case and Harvey was able to explain to Bevin that, whilst there still appeared to be no justification for the French desire to extend the Saar boundaries to the west, there was more substance in their claim to territory to the north, which was a dormitory area for Saar workers and included a section of an important railway line. Bevin felt that as long as the extension was defensible on sound economic arguments of that sort he would be prepared to give it his backing.[46]

While British and French officials made amicable progress behind the scenes, the main business of the CFM continued at the same ponderous pace which had characterised previous sessions and it was not until 10 April 1947 that the French, supported by the British and US delegations, moved for a decision on the Saar.[47] The following day Bidault returned to his theme and asked for the Council's immediate agreement in principle and the establishment of a committee of experts to finalise the details regarding borders and reparations adjustment. Bevin and Marshall both accepted this proposition but Molotov refused to be drawn on the subject and the matter was left in abeyance.[48]

As it began to seem that a decision would again be deferred until the next round of meetings, the British delegation considered what might be salvaged from the current session; in particular, whether it might be possible to arrive at a tripartite agreement before the conference broke up.[49] The French made it known that they had no intention of proceeding with full economic union with the Saar without the concurrence of Britain and the United States but gave notice that, if no agreement was reached at Moscow, they would take the step of introducing a Saar mark as legal currency throughout the territory.[50] At the Foreign Office, though certain difficulties were foreseen, the balance of opinion was in favour of trying to seal a tripartite agreement.[51] In Moscow, however, informal overtures revealed an impediment to further progress as it became clear that the Americans were not yet prepared to commit themselves.[52] The United States, it appeared, while acknowledging the advantages of a tripartite deal, was reluctant to abandon the principle of quadripartite decision on such a serious issue, but nevertheless promised to give the matter consideration before the next Council of Foreign Ministers.[53]

This reluctance formally to cede economic control of the Saar to France without Soviet approval was in contrast to the American readiness to establish with France and Britain the tripartite Moscow sliding scale for the disposal of the coal resources of the Western zones of Germany. Faced with further delays to economic union with the Saar, it would obviously be

The Saar

an advantage to the French if their partners in that agreement could be prevailed upon to countenance a similar arrangement by virtue of which France might benefit preferentially from coal mined in the Saar pending a final settlement of the area's status. In May 1947 France let it be known that if Britain and the United States were to join in a tripartite statement to the European Coal Organisation to this effect, the French delegate would take a favourable view of a British application for an allocation from the pool.[54] This tactic, however, succeeded only in arousing the antagonism of the US Secretary of State, General Marshall, who took exception to the French bargaining with coal supplied to the ECO by the United States for fair distribution.[55] Rather than forcing the Americans' hand, therefore, the manoeuvre led to an increase in US sympathy for the British case, leaving the French to play a 'lone and inept role' in the Allocations Proposals Committee of the ECO.[56]

Regardless of the attempt at horse-trading, the British were nevertheless inclined to accept the French claim to the Saar on its merits. On 16 May 1947, in keeping with exchanges of views with the French, Bevin went as far as to refer to the possibility of minor frontier adjustments in his speech during the Foreign Affairs Debate in the House of Commons.[57] The latest French proposals in this respect were presented on 19 May 1947 by the Ambassador, René Massigli.[58] The Foreign Office view was that, in the spirit of the Anglo-French Alliance signed at Dunkirk, and because the proposed frontiers were not altogether unreasonable, Britain should support the French claim as revised and should inform the US government accordingly, though it was felt that American approval was by no means guaranteed.[59]

The dilemma for the French was that they were anxious to go ahead with the introduction of the Saar mark but did not want to issue the currency over an area from which they might subsequently have to withdraw.[60] Bevin, who was reluctant to give his blessing to the proposed action without first consulting the United States,[61] cabled the Embassy in Washington with his personal opinion that early tripartite action was desirable.

> We do not see why we should continue to submit to Russian obstruction and we feel that the willingness of the present French government to conclude an agreement provides an opportunity of which we should take early advantage.[62]

On 4 June 1947 Bevin was informed that the French anticipated introducing the new currency in the Saar by 15 June and that, in recognition of the reservations expressed by the British and American governments, they were willing to make a further reduction in the area being claimed.

Accordingly, it was intended to withdraw the customs posts to a new line during the night of Saturday 7 June, prior to an announcement the following day.[63] Bevin immediately cabled the Washington Embassy with instructions to impress upon the State Department the hope that it would be possible for the United States to join with Britain in approving the French action.[64] The State Department, however, would not be rushed into a decision and by 6 June it appeared that the French move would necessarily precede any official American comment.[65] For his part, Bevin viewed the new frontier proposals as a great improvement and was not inclined to withhold British approval any longer.[66] The State Department expressed regret that they could not offer any support at that time and gave notice that they would reserve their position until after such announcements as the British and French governments might choose to make on the subject.[67]

On 10 June Britain provisionally accepted the new boundaries of the Saar pending an eventual peace settlement and a satisfactory agreement on the adjustment of the French reparations claim.[68] Three days later the United States Chargé d'Affaires in London informed the Foreign Office that, whilst the US government were not disposed to associate themselves with the British position, neither did they intend to raise any objection nor to make any formal protest at the French action. They were anxious, however, to be kept informed of any Anglo-French conversations on the subject of Saar coal.[69]

As this was as far as the Americans were prepared to go, it was left to the British and French to examine together the practical details of the next stages in the process. On 16 June 1947 an interdepartmental meeting on the subject was informed that the French were to send over a team of experts to propound their latest version of a formula for the progressive withdrawal of Saar coal production from German availabilities.[70] On 3 July 1947 the Ministry of Fuel and Power reported that the French had presented a series of proposals, the latest of which appeared at least to offer a hopeful basis for discussion.[71] The drawback of the French scheme was that, although it envisaged a graduated transfer of Saar production in order to allow losses to the ECO pool to be offset by supplies from the Ruhr, the different stages were based on a projected time-scale for improvement in Ruhr output rather than being linked to actual tonnages achieved. This formula failed to win the support of the Foreign Office, where it was felt that the operation would have to be managed on some more definite basis.[72] It was also becoming increasingly apparent that, in the wider context of inter-allied relations, events were moving in such a way as to preclude the resolution of the Saar question in isolation from the future economic development of Western Europe in general and the unfolding of American policy for the area in particular.

An opportunity to examine this aspect came during tripartite talks on the Western zones in August when Alphand called again for a declaration to the ECO to the effect that Saar production would be considered as French in advance of a final political settlement.[73] The meeting was informed that the British had already indicated their willingness to discuss this question and the US Ambassador accordingly undertook to convey the request to his government. In fact the ground had been previously prepared in a note issued by the French Embassy, the contents of which, it was explained to Makins, were mainly aimed at the Americans.[74] In this document it was recalled that coal mined in the Western zones of Germany was, in the first instance, divided between internal use and export according to the tripartite Sliding Scale Agreement, followed by allocation of the export tonnage by the ECO. As there was no Soviet participation at either stage, it was argued, the proposed redistribution of resources in France's favour fell outside the province of quadripartite control and there was therefore no reason to delay a Franco-Anglo-American meeting to settle the matter. As the sliding scale would in any case soon require revision, it was agreed that the subject might be discussed on the understanding that:

> The question of the incorporation of the Saar into France was outside the terms of reference of these talks, but the adjustments to the sliding scale which would accord with such an hypothesis could be examined.[75]

Despite the anodyne phraseology of this diplomatic fig-leaf, within three days a way out of the impasse of endless four-power discussions was in sight. On 10 September 1947 a working party of experts produced a formula for the progressive acquisition of Saar coal by France in nine increments; transfer to be complete when daily production in the combined British and American zones reached 330 000 tons, which was forecast for the fourth quarter of 1949.[76] The French were anxious for the proposed scale to be implemented forthwith, but encountered American opposition to any action which would pre-empt a final solution.[77] It transpired, however, that the US government was prepared to impose a deadline on further quadripartite discussions in return for an agreement by the French to fuse their zone of occupation with the Bizonal area already formed by the British and American zones. The French indicated that they would adopt this course of action in the event that the next session of the Council of Foreign Ministers should fail to result in the economic unification of Germany by four-power agreement.[78] The State Department now declared its willingness to accept the economic integration of the Saar into France by tripartite decision if the November CFM failed to reach an agreement.[79]

Meanwhile the French policy of anticipating a favourable final settlement continued with an announcement that it was intended to replace the Saar mark with the French franc.[80] Notice was also given that ownership of the Saar mines would be assumed by the French State at the moment of the currency reform.[81] These measures came into force on 20 November 1947, five days before the opening of the Council of Foreign Ministers in London.[82]

Discussion of the Saar question at the London CFM followed a similar pattern to that of the Moscow session. At the third meeting of the Council the French delegate, Georges Bidault, suggested that the question of the Saar was one point on which agreement might be easily reached. In response, General Marshall proposed the establishment of one or more Boundary Commissions but failed to win the support of the Soviet Foreign Minister, Molotov, who rejected the move as premature.[83] The following day Marshall returned to the subject but again Molotov refused to commit the Soviet Union and discussion of the question was discontinued despite Bevin's expression of incomprehension that a decision could not be reached, given that the French had, to his mind, established a good case for the matter to be dealt with promptly.[84] This did not prove possible and the conference broke up without reaching agreement, thereby leaving the way open for the United States to participate in a tripartite solution.

TRIPARTITE AGREEMENT

Following the London CFM, the French further tightened their administrative grip on the Saar with the enactment of a series of measures which brought wages policy, tax regulations and foreign exchange control into line with France. A mixed Court of Appeal was set up at Sarrebruck and the post of Military Governor was replaced by one of High Commissioner.[85] There was still, however, no hope of France deriving any tangible economic benefit from the Saar without the agreement of her Anglo-American allies and, by Christmas 1947, it was still unclear what progress the American attitude would permit. In the Foreign Office it was felt that there was no urgency to make the often-requested tripartite statement to the European Coal Organisation in advance of an agreement on the outstanding issues as this would amount to throwing away one of Britain's best bargaining counters on the question of reparations. It was thought that, in the event of another approach by the French, the United States might consent to join in an interim declaration to the ECO, on the strict understanding that this was for information only.[86]

In fact the United States proved willing to go even further, and tripartite talks on the Saar which took place in Berlin in early 1948 marked a turning-point in the American attitude. Accustomed to the caution which had characterised American policy until that point, the British delegation was taken unawares by an eagerness to settle the matter. On 1 January the functions of the ECO were taken over by the United Nations under the auspices of the Coal Committee of the Economic Commission for Europe. On 17 January the Foreign Office cabled Berlin that the line to be taken in the Saar talks was that there could be no announcement on coal to this body until the economic transfer of the territory to France had been formally approved by the three governments. The British delegation was to point out that it was already too late for a withdrawal of Saar coal from German availabilities to begin in the first quarter of the year, and to stress that a start from the first of April would depend on all outstanding issues being settled by that date. The French were to be informed that there was no question of changes being applied retrospectively.[87] A reply the following day expressed acute embarrassment and called urgently for new instructions as the Americans now intended to tell the French:

> That the sliding scale on coal withdrawals can come into force forthwith except that no disturbance of the first quarter allocation to E.C.E. should take place. They are willing with this waiver that the second quarter's withdrawals should be on the higher level which would have applied if withdrawals had commenced physically on 1st January, 1948.[88]

It was the American view which prevailed and, on 26 January 1948, identical letters were sent to the Coal Committee of the Economic Commission for Europe announcing that the three governments would in future regard the coal production of the Saar and of France as constituting a common resource.[89] Of further value to France was the fact that the agreed formula governing the transitional period corresponded more closely to French interests than that which had been floated during the talks in September. Instead of a scale based on improved levels of production in the Bizone, the output of the Saar mines would be placed at French disposal simply by means of a phased transfer in fixed stages at pre-determined intervals of time. By this arrangement the Saar was scheduled to contribute 825 250 tons of coal to the total German availability during the second quarter of 1948, falling to zero in the second quarter of 1949.[90] On 20 February 1948 this scale of diminishing obligation formed part of a tripartite agreement which established the principles of the economic union of the Saar and France to the satisfaction of the Western Allies.[91] On the question of reparations the French accepted a valuation of 70 million reichmarks, with outstanding questions relating to accounting procedure being left to the Inter-Allied Reparations Agency.[92] In addition to the value of plant remaining in the Saar, this figure included: 'Industrial equipment additionally retained in Western Germany in order to maintain the German economy at the permitted level despite the loss of the Saar.'[93] In other words, the immediate benefit to the French economy in terms of functioning plant was to be matched by the retention of an equivalent amount in the Bizone. Rather than a redistribution of productive capacity in France's favour, therefore, the Saar Agreement envisaged the continuation of the existing industrial balance of power but at a higher level of activity on both the French and the German sides.

The agreement of 20 February 1948 finally allowed France the free hand in the Saar which she sought. The attainment of this goal had been long in coming, though for nearly two years the French had enjoyed British support subject only to minor reservations. Staunch though that support was, it had not secured a decision in the Council of Foreign Ministers; nor had it hastened American acceptance of a tripartite alternative. In this respect the Saar episode demonstrated the limited influence which Britain could bring to bear in the service of French interests.

Failing quadripartite agreement, it was American backing which was the *sine qua non* of economic union and, confounded by Soviet intransigence, the Saar question eventually moved from deadlock in the CFM to a solution under the aegis of the United States. The pace of this development was, however, in no way accelerated by French or British pressure but was dictated solely by the evolution of American policy. On this aspect of the fate of Germany's material and industrial resources an Anglo-French consensus clearly existed, but this was not enough to expedite a favourable outcome. Within their zone of occupation the French had tightened their administrative grip on the coveted territory while arriving at a compromise agreement with Britain on the *de facto* boundaries of the Franco-Saar customs area. With regard to the core issue of definitive control, however, both Britain and France were obliged to let the matter run its course, with the result that resolution of the question was unavoidably out of phase with the demands of Anglo-French relations.

The Saar

In April 1947 the distribution of scarce coal supplies was a major source of friction between Britain and France which could have been smoothed by tripartite action regarding the Saar. By contrast, when the Saar Agreement was signed in February 1948 the situation had so improved that Britain was in a position to offer 6000 tons of coal per week for export to France.[94] By the end of May the French were even debating the choice between taking up this tonnage, for payment in sterling, or obtaining coal from the United States under the Marshall Aid programme.[95] In these circumstances Saar coal remained a welcome addition to French resources but was not, even on the simple time-bound formula of the Saar Agreement, the godsend which it would have represented the previous winter; neither did it offer the same prospect of an improvement in Anglo-French relations. In April 1947, a bare three months after the discussions on the Monnet Plan and within weeks of the signing of the Treaty of Dunkirk, the successful promotion of a cause to which both partners were openly committed would have demonstrated the value of Anglo-French co-operation. Allowing the matter to drift for another year was, on the other hand, a measure of the impotence of the lesser powers in the postwar era and an indication of the insubstantial nature of an Anglo-French axis amid the practical realities of the new order.

In particular, the penetration of American influence into Europe was inescapable. At the end of 1946 the British had joined their zone of occupation with that of the United States on the understanding that the basic tenet of economic planning would be that the Bizonal area should be self-supporting by the end of 1949.[96] Not that the Anglo-American partnership precluded British support for French aspirations in the Saar or detracted from British attempts to rally the United States to the French cause. On the contrary, British support continued unabated and expressed itself in numerous efforts to encourage American participation in a viable solution. Here was a contradiction, however. Britain welcomed the Saar Agreement but was nevertheless party to the requirement that the consequent gain to French productive capacity be balanced by a proportionate level of industry in the Bizone. There was consequently a dichotomy between British support for the principle of Franco-Saar union and indifference to the underlying motives of French long-term economic strategy.

From early 1947 it had been known that France hoped to maintain the German steel industry at an artificially low level in order to direct in excess of a million tons per year of Saar production towards the German domestic market.[97] Heedless of French plans, however, a paper prepared for the Anglo-American Bipartite Board recommended that, in the event of the separation of the Saar from Germany, the level of steel capacity in the Bizone should be adjusted upwards by 1.2 million tons, effectively blocking the export opportunity identified by the French.[98] This course of action was accepted as Bizonal policy from the first week of March 1947 onwards,[99] with the result that Britain supported France's claim to the Saar in the knowledge that achievement of the French ambition would, in this regard, be coincident with the undermining of its purpose. This policy was not, of course, pursued with malicious intent, but stemmed from two diametrically opposed theses with regard to the future of the market for steel in Europe; the French anticipating an impending glut, while the British forecast a continuing shortage. It was failure to reconcile such differences on matters of vital importance which left a void at the very heart of Anglo-French relations and, in the case of the Saar, cast French policy adrift in an economic environment inimical to France's long-term interests.

5 The Ruhr

THE BIZONE

The importance of American involvement in Europe was publicly acknowledged by Ernest Bevin during the course of the Foreign Affairs Debate in the House of Commons in October 1946, when he declared that: 'It cannot be too often repeated that the continuance of American interest in Europe is vital to the peace of Europe and particularly to the future of Germany.'[1] At the time, that future remained undecided as the quadripartite Council of Foreign Ministers failed time and again to agree a coherent plan encompassing all four zones of occupation. To the British this was particularly galling as their zone, containing the major part of the German industrial potential, continued to languish under the uncertainty, while foodstuffs were imported at their expense. With food on ration at home, the feeding of the German population was a burden which the United Kingdom could not bear indefinitely. This position was made clear by Bevin in a statement to the Paris CFM in July 1946, when he announced that, if an agreement on treating Germany as an economic unit continued to be elusive, His Majesty's Government would regretfully be compelled to take measures to ensure the economic viability of the British zone, in isolation if necessary.[2] The following day James F. Byrnes, the US Secretary of State, responded with an offer to the effect that his government would be willing to join the American zone with that of any other interested country.[3] Bevin recommended that this offer should be accepted in principle immediately pending a study of the details: a view which was endorsed by the Cabinet.[4] The Soviet Union dismissed the American offer out of hand, while the French government, wary of upsetting a delicate domestic consensus, preferred to defer consideration of France's participation to an indefinite future.

The American offer of zonal fusion therefore gave rise only to bipartite discussions with Britain.[5] From the outset the need to underpin the occupation of Germany with the economic strength of the United States assumed an importance which overshadowed Britain's relations with France. In particular, the Anglo-American negotiations coloured the British attitude to French overtures on the subject of coal supplies from the Ruhr, making difficult purely bipartite discussion of the matter.[6] In the coal crisis of that winter Bevin remained ever mindful of the plight of the French and, after the reduction in Ruhr exports imposed at the end of

1946,[7] was anxious if possible to avoid any cuts for the month of January. There were nevertheless other considerations, as he made clear in December: 'I am not prepared, however, to quarrel with the Americans if they insist that a further cut in Ruhr coal exports is necessary in the interests of the fusion of the two zones.'[8]

The outcome of the talks was somewhat of a disappointment from the British point of view in that, despite hard bargaining, the negotiations failed to shake American insistence that the running costs of the Bizone should be shared on a fifty–fifty basis.[9] The British would have preferred their partners to contribute a larger proportion of the budget but, as the talks progressed, it became apparent that there was little choice but to accept the terms offered. The agreement for the fusion of the two zones was finally signed on 2 December 1946 and came into effect on the first day of January 1947.[10] Although falling short of the degree of American support for which the British had hoped, it nevertheless held out the prospect of a more rational use of resources leading to eventual economic viability for the combined zones. The reluctant acceptance of an equal responsibility for running costs also had a positive side in that it entitled the British government to an equal voice on policy matters. This authority was to be undermined later that year, however, when the United Kingdom had to press to be released from the agreement on the grounds of insufficient reserves to meet her obligations in terms of dollar expenditure after the current appropriation.[11] Following further hard bargaining the renegotiated agreement relieved the United Kingdom of much of her financial burden but, in recognition of an increased contribution, allowed the United States a preponderant voice in decision making in the Joint Export–Import Agency (JEIA) set up by the original agreement for the purpose of conducting the external trade of the Bizone.[12] The sole check on American domination was the provision that either of the Military Governors could request a suspension pending further consideration of any proposed action which might prejudice the interests or conflict with the policy of his government.[13] At American insistence, however, the approval of both Military Governors was required to *maintain* the suspension of any course of action voted by weighted majority.[14] This effectively left Britain at the mercy of her partner, subject only to the persuasive force of the arguments put forward during the delay for reconsideration of any proposal in contention.

Once again, the United Kingdom had little option but to accept the American terms; the only alternative being to withdraw from Germany and accept that her days as a Great Power were over. Among other things, it was thought that this would work to the detriment of Anglo-French relations.[15]

Certainly, eight months after signing the fifty-year Treaty of Dunkirk, specifically directed against a possible resurgence of German power, Britain would have found a withdrawal from her zone of occupation highly embarrassing. On the other hand, to remain in Germany at the cost of relinquishing effective control over the massive economic potential of the Ruhr industries was to court the danger of allowing American interests to override the concerns so often expressed by the French on this subject.

In practice, however, it was when British and American views coincided that French interests were most easily overlooked. A subject on which both were agreed was the need to extend German participation in the running of the Bizonal economy. To this end, the Military Governors and their advisers met with German representatives in January 1948 to discuss the possibility of transforming the existing rudimentary machinery on the German side into an Economic Administration with a real function in the Bizonal organisation.[16] These talks achieved a rapid success. The participants assembled in Frankfurt on 7 January 1948, the day *before* the endeavour received the approval of the British Cabinet,[17] and within three days had reached agreement on the form and nature of the new structures.

The French reaction was one of horror and outrage. Although General Robertson, the British Military Governor, had informed his French colleague, General Noiret, that talks were to take place, no formal notification had been communicated to Paris, nor had any attempt been made to consult the French government, who were completely overtaken by the speed of events.[18] The French sense of shock was heightened by the fact that they were at that time awaiting a promised full-scale conference of the three Western powers on the future of Germany.[19] From the French point of view, therefore, the Frankfurt discussions seemed nothing less than a thinly-veiled move to pre-empt the forthcoming conference by the establishment of a form of German proto-government. The French protests, couched in the language of betrayed trust and wounded pride, came swiftly.[20] For his part, Bevin appeared equally surprised by the rapidity of events.[21] To the US State Department it seemed clear in retrospect that the conference on Germany and the talks on the Bizonal Economic Administration had been dealt with in isolation and that no connection between them had been formed in the minds of those concerned.[22] In an attempt to retrieve the situation the US Military Governor, General Clay, was advised that his government was now prepared to move to a settlement of the Saar question and that he should suggest that the French might respond by extending their co-operation on the matter of the new Bizonal organisation.[23] Two days later Bevin reported to the Cabinet that the

French had accepted the outcome of the Frankfurt discussions; a statement of which his colleagues took note with approval.[24]

This was all very well and good but the fact remained that, on a matter of obvious interest to France, Anglo-French relations had been marginalised by a concentration of attention on the development of the Bizone. Whatever inducement France might be offered to accept this state of affairs, she had nevertheless been presented with a *fait accompli*. That such treatment was inconsistent with the spirit of the Treaty of Dunkirk was pointed out by Sir Oliver Harvey, the new British Ambassador to France.

> Either our Alliance with France means nothing at all or we must treat her as an Ally, take her fully into our confidence in matters which she legitimately regards as of vital importance to herself and give her an opportunity to consider and offer comments on our plans before they are finally decided upon and enforced.[25]

This comment could equally be applied to another instance of a Bizonal policy decision prejudging an issue of crucial concern to France, when the atmosphere was soured at a critical moment by the revelation that secret Anglo-American talks had produced an agreement to dispense with the quadripartite Level of Industry Plan.[26] From an early stage it had been apparent to the British and the Americans that the economic viability of the Bizone could not be founded on such a restricted manufacturing base.[27] To the French this seemed to imply that so long as there was a Bizonal balance-of-payments deficit, the level of industry would always be under pressure for an upward revision.[28] In fact this was contrary to the intentions of the British, who regarded the setting of a reasonable upper limit on German industrial activity as a once-and-for-all exercise to be rapidly followed by the dismantling and removal of all industrial equipment in excess of the permitted capacity. This was a policy first advocated by General Robertson in July 1946.[29] As the Moscow session of the Council of Foreign Ministers moved towards deadlock on the subject of German industry in April 1947, it seemed to the members of the British and United States delegations that the time had come to agree the general lines of a joint contingency plan.[30] Robertson's view was that a bilateral level of industry plan should be prepared and that arrangements should be made immediately to dismantle down to that level.[31]

The bench mark of the German level of industry was taken as the total annual steel production, as this would impose an automatic limiting factor across a broad range of manufacturing activities. The opening of detailed discussions, however, revealed that the Americans favoured a figure of 13.5 million tons; a level which Bevin could see would cause friction with France.[32] The British preference was for a total of 10 million tons, but as the talks continued into the month of June, the interdepartmental working party on the subject conceded that a maximum of 11 million tons might be accepted as a last resort.[33] By July enough urgency was attached to the matter for the Overseas Reconstruction Committee, under Bevin's chairmanship, to authorise British representatives to negotiate up to a figure of 11.2 million tons for the Bizonal area alone.[34]

By this time discussions had been proceeding for nearly three months without any indication being given to the French. Meanwhile, in the wider scheme of things, events were taking place which were to shape the economic future of Europe. While the British and Americans formulated their plans for Germany, Marshall's speech of 5 June 1947 had given rise to the conference on European reconstruction in Paris between Britain, France and the Soviet Union, which opened on 27 June 1947. That conference broke down on 3 July 1947 as the Soviet delegation withdrew, leaving the way clear to issue invitations to all European countries to attend a new conference under the joint auspices of Britain and France.[35] In the circumstances, the British delegation felt that: 'It would only be embarrassing to the French to tell them at this stage that the United Kingdom was intending to take prior action in respect of Germany in the next few weeks.'[36]

It was certainly an awkward moment to reveal that, weeks in advance of the genesis of the Marshall programme for Europe, secret Anglo-American discussions had started to lay the foundations of a purely German recovery. French sensibilities aside, however, the proposed new conference could not fail to touch upon the position of the Bizone in European reconstruction. There was little choice, therefore, but to warn the French that it was likely that a revised level of industry would be announced in the near future.[37] By 12 July 1947 the British and Americans had settled on an annual level of steel production of 11.5 million tons for the whole of Germany (excluding the Saar), of which 10.7 million tons would be produced in the Bizone.[38] Bevin requested that no announcement should be made for the time being and that, in any case, the agreement should be communicated to the French before being made public.[39] When asked about the progress of the Anglo-American discussions, during a conversation with Georges Bidault three days later, Bevin said that it was the Americans who were pressing for an inflated level of industry while he was doing his utmost to hold them back.[40] With less than perfect candour, Bevin gave Bidault to understand that a decision was on the point of being reached which might involve a level of German steel production in the region of 11 million tons. Bidault replied that, at the very moment when they were engaged in a common effort to organise Europe along the lines of the Marshall Plan, such a decision taken on German industry before he had chance even to 'raise his little finger' would put France in a position where all could again be called into question.[41] It was agreed that their officials would meet the following day.

Bevin could see that the time for prevarication was past and cabled the Washington Embassy with the information that he was instructing Edmund Hall-Patch, Deputy Under-Secretary of State at the Foreign Office, to explain the situation with complete frankness.[42] Meeting with their French counterparts, therefore, Hall-Patch and his colleagues presented the Anglo-American motives in the most favourable light which diplomatic language could contrive but made no attempt to disguise the intention to retain in the Bizone sufficient capacity to ensure an actual production of 10.7 million tons of steel per year.[43] The French response came the following day in the form of a letter from Bidault expressing his dismay that, at this turning point in France's foreign policy, his government should unexpectedly be faced with a situation which threatened its very survival. In particular, Bidault's own position was precarious because the propaganda of the French Communist Party had claimed from the outset that the first consequence of the Marshall Plan would be German revival: a charge which he was on record as denying.[44]

In all fairness, Bidault had a genuine grievance. In a period when the Communist Party was a force to be reckoned with in French domestic politics, the coalition government headed by Paul Ramadier had not only expelled its Communist ministers that May but had later stood firm alongside Britain to set in motion the European Recovery Programme in the face of Soviet hostility. Its reward was to be suddenly confronted by a scenario certain to bring it under attack from both Left and Right, Communists and Gaullists alike: an Anglo-American plot to revive Germany.

A message from Bidault in impassioned terms was also received by Marshall, the US Secretary of State, with the result that the situation came under immediate review.[45] Likewise, in Britain Bevin informed the Cabinet that if the French government fell as a result of the anticipated outcry, the Paris conference on Marshall Aid might suffer irreparable disruption.[46] In the circumstances, Bevin favoured deferring the implementation of the Bizonal plan; a view which was endorsed by his colleagues.[47] This decision was conveyed to the US Government with the proposal that no action should be taken until September and that, in the meantime, the French should be given the opportunity to present their case.[48] To this the Americans eventually agreed and an opportunity was arranged.[49]

The tripartite talks opened in London on 22 August 1947 with prepared statements from the French delegation.[50] Stripped of rhetoric, the upshot of these was that France might accept the revised plan provided that French security was not jeopardised and German recovery did not take priority over that of the rest of Europe. In respect of the latter proviso, the French attached great importance to increased exports of coal and especially coke from Germany. The next day the British Chairman, Sir Gilmour Jenkins, said that the arrangements governing coal exports were subject to periodic revision, on which occasions suggestions from the French were always welcome and would always be given careful consideration.[51] From the French side Hervé Alphand indicated that, subject to the general points put by his delegation, he was prepared to waive his objection to the level of 10.7 million tons of steel production per annum for the Bizone.[52] The talks closed with the understanding that the new level of industry did not prejudge the future status of the Ruhr and that the proportion of coke in the export allocations would be reviewed.[53]

After all the furore these were the only prizes which the French delegation could carry home. Despite the need to keep France within the fold at a crucial moment in the European Recovery Programme there was a steadfast American resolve which had been communicated to the French in no uncertain terms.[54] For the sake of good relations, some minor modification to the level of industry plan would have been acceptable to the British, who were also prepared to hint that they might go a long way towards meeting the French on the subject of fuel supplies. The Americans, however, refused on principle to concede anything to the French which might be construed as a commitment.[55] The British, though more amenable, were placed very much in the position of junior partners by their recent request for an easing of the financial terms of the Fusion Agreement.[56]

For the French the discussions served little purpose but to cloak in a semblance of consultation a decision which they were powerless to change. For the British the talks paved the way for publication of the new level of industry plan without further delay. There was, however, a price to pay in terms of prestige. 'From our side the talks were rather unpleasant in that they demonstrated the weakness of our diplomatic position vis à vis the Americans, more particularly in regard to Germany.'[57] In this respect the episode had brought about a realignment of interests. Britain, for long the leading advocate of increased German steel production, had been overtaken and was now in the same position as France in that both had been prevailed upon to accept a level which they regarded as the absolute maximum. For the first time this was the same figure.

DISMANTLING AND AMERICAN AID

The revised Level of Industry Plan was expressed simply as the quantity of crude steel to be produced annually in the whole of Germany, excluding the Saar. The plan therefore allowed for the eventual attachment of the Saar to France and, in principle, also left the way open for a comprehensive quadripartite plan for the rest of Germany. In practice, however, the fact that the bulk of the steel industry was in the Bizone meant that form could be observed simply by including the notional output of the other zones in the global figure, without fear that this would hinder the implementation of the plan. Thus, of the 11.5 million tons total permitted production, 400 000 tons each was marked down to the French and Soviet zones, leaving 10.7 million tons for the Bizone.[58] The decision as to which plants in the combined zone would be surplus to requirements and therefore available for removal as reparations was then taken by the Bipartite Economic Panel and a list sent to the Inter-Allied Reparations Agency on 14 October 1947.[59]

That was not, however, the end of the matter. In October 1946 René Massigli had predicted that if the Americans put money into Germany, they would insist upon an expanded steel programme for the Ruhr.[60] A year later his fears were confirmed but he had not foreseen that American involvement would go even further than underwriting the cost of the Bizone, nor the consequences. By May 1948 the view in the State Department was that:

> We must not forget that this Government's position with respect to Germany as formulated at the time of the amended Bizonal Agreement must now be understood in relation to the subsequent and over-riding policy of the President and Congress as expressed in the Economic Co-operation Act which covers the European economic problem as a whole.[61]

This referred to the section of the act which laid upon the Economic Co-operation Administration (ECA) the legal obligation to take measures to ensure that plant scheduled for removal from the three Western zones as reparations would be retained *in situ* if this would further the European Recovery Programme.[62] The implications of this were accepted by all countries benefiting from Marshall Aid in their bilateral agreements with the United States.[63] In anticipation of repercussions on the German steel industry a preliminary study was carried out during May and June 1948 by a group under the auspices of the US Military Government and the

Economic Co-operation Administration. This group, headed by George Wolf, the President of the United States Steel Export Corporation, produced its report in August 1948.[64] This report represented a refinement of the blanket restriction on output tonnage in that it addressed the question of the form in which the steel should be placed on the market. The ceiling of 10.7 million tons per year for the Bizone applied to steel in its most basic form of ingots. These massive lumps of crude metal are not usually a traded commodity but undergo a series of rolling operations at the steelworks, to be sold in some useful form, such as bars or plates. At each stage a proportion of the original tonnage is lost in the transformation; so that Wolf estimated 10.7 million ingot tons would ultimately yield only 8.3 million tons of merchantable steel in those products which he identified as most needed.[65]

Basing his judgement on commercial principles of supply and demand, regardless of the political principles involved, Wolf was critical of the British stewardship of the Ruhr steel industry and urged that Bizonal self-sufficiency should take second place to the opportunity to export those items for which there was a seller's market.[66] Sir William Strang, Permanent Under-Secretary of the German Section at the Foreign Office, denounced the idea of a semi-official body of this nature encroaching upon the domain of high policy.[67] In the event, the report gave rise to much discussion but was never acted upon. Nevertheless it raised a pertinent question. Wolf's approach, based on the current world market situation, was perhaps not entirely appropriate, but it served to highlight the fact that an artificial limit to crude steel production was meaningless without taking into account the type and quantity of finishing capacity required. Whether for simple profit or for the greater good of European recovery, an ingot of steel needed to be processed into a form for which there was an actual requirement. This basic truth had far-reaching ramifications due to the operating conditions of the normal production cycle. A large steelworks might begin with the preparation and smelting of iron ore. The resulting pig-iron would then form the load of a furnace producing an ingot of crude steel for transfer to the rolling mill; heat being conserved by a rapid transit between stages. In addition, the exhaust gases from the furnaces or the on-site cokeries might be used for the generation of electric power. The dilemma facing the Allied authorities was that a steelworks on this scale might include a limited facility for producing one particular item of prime importance to the European Recovery Programme. In such a case, the choice would be between retaining the whole plant, involving perhaps a capacity for producing a million or more tons of crude steel, or running a single section without the benefits of integration in a larger operation.

If any sense was to be made of the obligation to retain suitable plant in Germany to assist European recovery, decisions of this nature were unavoidable. Under pressure from the US Congress, Paul Hoffman, the Economic Co-operation Administrator, invited a new committee of industrialists under George Humphrey to produce a further report. It was realised that this move would not meet with the approval of Britain or France.[68] Britain in particular resisted pressure to halt her dismantling programme while the new study was in progress as Bevin was of the opinion that once stopped it would be an uphill battle to resume it at a later date.[69] General Robertson, weary of American pressure and disgusted by arguments which he regarded as specious, was of a mind to be done with the matter once and for all by simply dismantling 40 per cent of the remaining plants, selected on a rule-of-thumb basis.[70] American pressure continued, however, and on 18 November 1948 the Cabinet suspended dismantling of the plants under review by the Humphrey Committee.[71] This included various chemical and engineering factories but it was already apparent that central to the whole exercise was the steel industry.

> Mr. Humphrey has recognised both the importance and the peculiar nature of the steel problem by appointing as a member of his Committee, but in an independent capacity, Mr. George Wolf, who led the Steel Mission to Germany earlier this year.[72]

It had been estimated that continued operation of those plants manufacturing the product range recommended in the earlier Wolf report would, in effect, entail the retention of the capacity to produce up to 14 million tons of crude steel a year.[73] Moreover, Wolf's inclination to divert a certain tonnage to export was seen as a threat to the long-term prospects of the British iron and steel industry on the world market.[74] The adoption of a second report along similar lines would therefore call into question the assumptions underlying Britain's steel development programme. This was the same threat which had hung over the Monnet Plan since its inception. The French, who had until this moment looked in vain for British protection against the looming menace of a revived German steel industry, now found a new willingness to co-operate.

The first British overtures met with suspicion and disbelief.[75] Eventually, however, the outline of a joint plan of action took form. The British floated the idea of pre-empting the Humphrey Report by voluntarily submitting a short token list of carefully selected plants for retention. The French fear was that if this failed to defuse the situation, too much ground would have been conceded to no effect. Rather than attempting to appease the Americans with such a gesture they preferred that any list presented should be conceived as a purely tactical move with further negotiations in mind.[76] At the end of September 1948 it was agreed at Foreign Minister level that, in any case, joint action would be the best approach.[77] Over the next two months, views were exchanged and a common posture generally maintained in preliminary contacts with the United States but no definite steps were taken until early December, when the members of the Humphrey Committee gave a preview of their report to British and French representatives before returning home.[78] At this moment British officials sought the views of their French colleagues before making their recommendations.[79] Though the two positions did not coincide exactly, there was considerable overlap. With regard to the steel industry, Humphrey proposed to maintain in operation a total of thirty-eight plants or sections of plants previously scheduled for removal. Of these, the British identified twenty to which they could agree, whereas the French inclination was to accept only thirteen, of which nine were on the British list.[80] This left a hard core of fourteen whole and part plants the retention of which both countries opposed.

The British remained convinced that the best strategy was to give ground immediately where possible, in order to hold the line on the important issues. The French indicated privately that they envisaged making substantial concessions at a later stage but for the moment would present a separate set of counter-proposals. At governmental level, Bevin assured the French Foreign Minister, Robert Schuman, that he and indeed the great mass of British politicians of all parties were determined to keep in step with France on this issue and that together they 'should be able to guide the United States Government aright'.[81]

To Sir Oliver Harvey it seemed that the situation now offered a golden opportunity to present a united front if Britain and France could agree to negotiate from an identical position.[82] For his part, Bevin remained in two minds and inclined to the view that it might be more important to seek a rapid end to the matter. It was left to one of his officials to recall that, in view of Bevin's conversation with Schuman, the French might regard such a move as an abrupt sacrifice of their interests.[83] It was also pointed out that Britain might soon be looking to France for support in respect of the curtailment of the German shipbuilding industry, whereupon Bevin agreed that the French should be approached with a view to arriving at negotiating strategies which were at least consistent in their positions of last resort.

Shipbuilding was one of a group of 'prohibited and limited industries' which were subject to restriction in pursuance of the Potsdam Agreement on the grounds that their products could be considered as materials of war.

The Anglo-American Level of Industry Plan of August 1947 had superseded the existing quadripartite agreement as far as steel was concerned but had left the future of these industries in abeyance. As the prospect of a general German recovery drew closer, however, the feeling grew in Britain that the subject was ripe for review and it was thought that the discussions on the Humphrey Report might offer the chance of a *quid pro quo*. It was therefore suggested to the French that this should be considered in formulating a combined approach.[84] The French, who were less worried than Britain by the spectre of Germany re-emerging as a maritime power but had grave concerns regarding the German chemical industry, agreed.[85]

This strategy suffered a setback when the Americans protested that to deal with the Humphrey Report and the prohibited and limited industries on the same agenda would only prolong the negotiations unnecessarily.[86] Over the following weeks Bevin steadfastly resisted American pressure to deal with the Humphrey Report immediately and in isolation.[87] Finally the United States agreed to take the two issues together provided that the whole matter could be resolved swiftly.[88] In the meantime contact had been maintained between British and French officials in an attempt to agree an 'order of retreat' to a common 'last ditch' position.[89] Arrangements were still incomplete when the call came to the negotiating table, but were hurriedly set in order by the deletion from the British list of two non-ferrous metal installations and the inclusion of three steelworks to which the French attached a greater importance.[90]

This was presented to the Americans on 16 March 1949 as the list of plants which the British and French insisted should be dismantled, regardless of their supposed value to the European Recovery Programme.[91] Discussions continued for the next two weeks and, as agreed, extended beyond the Humphrey Report to include a range of subjects, such as the electronics industry and radio-active materials, which Britain and France felt came within the scope of their legitimate security interests.[92] As the negotiations progressed it became clear that the Americans were determined to stand firm for retention in Germany of the Deutsche Edelstahlwerke at Krefeld, a small plant specialising in the alloy steels used in the manufacture of armour plate and jet engines.[93] The British were prepared to concede this point subject to satisfaction on the subject of shipbuilding.

After much bargaining of this nature the discussions closed on 31 March 1949. In respect of the Humphrey recommendations on steel, the Anglo-French 'last ditch' held firm with the exception of the Krefeld plant; the United States accepting that the other six items on the list should be dismantled and removed.[94] Based on their condition at the time of the

Humphrey study these six plants were capable of producing a total of just under a million tons of crude steel per year. Restored to normal working order, however, the Foreign Office assessed that the same equipment would have had an annual output of over 3 million tons.[95] Bearing in mind that the negotiations had also served to define the position regarding the prohibited and limited industries, removal of this productive capacity from German soil represented a reasonable outcome to the talks.

The joint response to the Humphrey Report was the first instance of common ground being established between Britain and France on the question of German industry. The British, however, were defending a position which, in terms of steel production, was at the top end of the range of figures, from about 10 million tons upwards, which they had favoured at different moments over the previous few years. For the French, on the other hand, the episode was merely the latest of a series of rearguard actions in a step-by-step retreat from the level of 7 million tons which they had advocated in 1945. For the purposes of British policy German self-sufficiency in steel equated to an optimum level of manufacturing activity which would permit a balance of payments without involving a greater presence in world markets than was strictly necessary. From the point of view of French economic planning, however, a German demand for steel satisfied entirely from domestic sources would deprive producers in the Saar of their most promising outlet.

Where French and British interests converged was in a common reluctance to see German steel diverted to export. There was little scope for this so long as self-sufficiency remained the guiding principle. The danger in the Humphrey proposals was that steelworks restored to full running order during conditions of shortage might prove resistant to operating on a reduced régime once the ceiling corresponding to domestic demand had actually been attained. By pressing for the removal of surplus capacity France and Britain were united in their determination to avoid this scenario. Starting from different policy imperatives the two governments thus finally established a community of interests at a crucial moment for Germany.

REPRIEVE AND REHABILITATION

On the question of the German steel industry Britain and France were able to present a common front, not through any evolution in thinking but precisely because one of Britain's original objectives had been achieved. With the acceptance of a total annual production commensurate with a viable domestic economy, British concerns now revolved around the need to maintain the *status quo* in the face of any pressure for an upward revision. The over-capacity threatened by the Humphrey proposals elicited a joint Anglo-French response, which nevertheless failed to address the wider question of the conditions under which German industry would ultimately be owned and operated. The new understanding was therefore confined to defending the existing quantitative controls against an American policy which would leave them susceptible to erosion. On the other hand, the scope and pace of developments concerned with the political control of German industry had already been largely determined by Anglo-American considerations, irrespective of French interests.

To some extent this was symptomatic of a growing disillusionment with the principle of quadripartite control. In July 1946 the failure of the Council of Foreign Ministers to arrive at a system for treating Germany as a single economic unit provoked the American offer, taken up by Britain, which eventually led to the formation of the Bizone. When the Moscow session of the CFM ended in deadlock in April 1947 the response was the formulation of an Anglo-American Level of Industry Plan. As failure followed failure it became clear that the London CFM scheduled for December 1947 would be the last chance to arrive at an acceptable settlement, though there was little optimism among the Western powers, whose preparations for the conference revolved mainly around agreeing at which point it could be deemed to have broken down.[96] On 15 December 1947 Ernest Bevin informed the Cabinet that the current round of meetings was unlikely to lead to agreement, and that unless there was a change in the attitude of the Soviet Union he saw no purpose in continuing discussions through the medium of the Council of Foreign Ministers.[97] The Council disbanded the same day with no plans to reconvene.[98] Unlike previous occasions, however, the breakdown of the London CFM in December 1947 was seen to open the possibility of an agreement embracing all three Western zones of occupation, thereby dividing Germany in two. Although France could be expected to extract a price for her co-operation, as the latecomer she had little choice but to accept much of the existing Bizonal organisation as it stood. Nevertheless this still left scope for seeking a tripartite agreement on the Saar and pressing for a special régime of international control for the Ruhr.[99] On the first of these conditions the ground had already been prepared and agreement was rapidly reached in February 1948.[100] The vexed question of control of the Ruhr, however, was left to the full-scale conference on the future of what now seemed destined to emerge as some form of West German state.

That conference convened in London in 1948, in two sessions from 23 February to 6 March and from 20 April to 1 June.[101] In addition to the occupying powers of the three Western zones, invitations went to the governments of Belgium, the Netherlands and Luxembourg. With proceedings under way, the French tabled a proposal for a system of continuing control over the Ruhr to include responsibility for the appointment of managers in the mines and steelworks and the approval of production plans and investment programmes.[102] By the end of the first session the functions of the proposed control body had been reduced to the allocation of coal, coke and steel between internal consumption and export, and preventing any action by Germany which would distort the normal conditions of trade in these products.[103] When the conference resumed in April, however, it emerged that the United States did not intend that the international authority should actually determine allocations but that it would confine itself to giving advice so long as West Germany remained dependent upon American aid. When pressed by Sir William Strang, the head of the British delegation, as to whether this meant that the powers of the authority in this respect would effectively be withheld during the four years of the Marshall Plan, the US Ambassador confirmed that this was precisely the case.

> It seemed to him anomalous that, while the United States were supporting Germany, other countries should be in a position to increase American financial responsibilities by controlling Germany's exports. He reminded the meeting that this represented no change in the position of the United States delegation.[104]

The preference of the United States was for the new authority to pass on its advice to the same Joint Export–Import Agency (JEIA), whose voting procedures would ensure an effective American veto.[105] The British view was that it was unacceptable for a supposed international organisation to be subordinate to the JEIA merely because that body provided a means of American control. The situation was complicated by the recognition by the Americans that it was perhaps inappropriate to state their aims openly in an international agreement; neither were the British anxious to set their hand to any document which was obviously the result of American dictation. Eventually there emerged the outline of a compromise which would have the effect of giving the proposed Ruhr Authority the power to make allocations, which would then be transmitted to the Military Governors for 'implementation' in accordance with the terms of any other international agreements in force.[106] By these indirect means the allocation process would be subject to the bilateral agreements (not yet concluded) between Germany and the United States in connection with Marshall Aid and, in the last resort, to the system of weighted voting in the revised Bizone Agreement.

After discussion with Bevin, Sir William Strang had a private conversation with the other heads of delegation and expressed his frank opinion that under these conditions the Ruhr Authority would be little better than a façade.[107] For the United States, Douglas thought that this was a harsh judgement; the Authority would serve a useful purpose by taking a wide view of the issues involved, thereby promoting the integration of the West German economy with that of the rest of Western Europe. Expressing the French view, Massigli said that although the powers of the Authority would be slight during the occupation period, they would be of real value as West Germany emerged from dependence on American aid as a self-supporting industrial nation.

For Sir William, who had wondered if the proposal was worth proceeding with, this exchange of views presented a dilemma. As far as Britain was concerned the only reason for accepting the establishment of the Ruhr Authority in such an emasculated form was as a means of securing French agreement to the setting-up of a German government. To follow the French lead in negotiations would, however, seem likely to result in conditions of American predominance which would be unacceptable to Britain on grounds of self-respect and public opinion. Rather than 'open the door wider to U.S. hegemony in Germany', Strang was determined at least to resist any increase in American supremacy beyond that inherent in the revised Bizone Agreement.[108] The final text of a statement of principles on the International Authority for the Ruhr (IAR) adhered to the formula by which the Authority would, during the occupation period, send its decisions to the Military Governors for implementation 'to the extent consistent with any agreements relative to the provision of financial assistance to Germany'.[109] This provided the means by which American interests could be safeguarded, but left the IAR devoid of purpose in a field already bristling with advisory bodies and hedged about with agreements of all kinds.[110] To the French, however, this offered at least the chance of retaining a degree of residual control when the American veto expired and a mature German government assumed its full powers.

The French experience in the wake of the 1914–18 war had demonstrated the difficulty of enforcing restrictions on German coal and steel without effective control at the level of the individual firm.[111] Provisions along these lines had formed part of the original French draft for the functions of the Ruhr Authority but had been dropped at an early stage of the

London Conference. Likewise the question of the ownership of the mines and steelworks had been left in abeyance. These basic industries had been taken into British control in August 1946 with the intention of breaking up the large pre-war cartels which had been the bedrock of German capitalism. To this end, 'Operation Severance' had split a number of large concerns into smaller firms, each with a nominal starting capital and each conforming to a company structure which would lend itself equally well to a number of different types of ownership, public or private.[112]

As an interim measure, the situation was brought up to date on 11 November 1948 by the establishment of two Bizonal bodies: the UK/US Steel Control Group and the UK/US Coal Control Group.[113] This action was pursuant to Military Law No. 75, which had been published the previous day.[114] The text of this law, the French were dismayed to learn, began with a preamble stating that the final decision on ownership was to be left to a duly elected German government. Coming on the very eve of another conference on Germany, this brought the French Ambassador to the Foreign Office in a great state of agitation.

> What the French Government so bitterly resented was that the two Governments should have now taken action in the matter without waiting for this further examination. . . . He could only suppose that we had acted as we did because we had at last succeeded in getting the Americans to agree to our thesis and wished to clinch matters before they changed their minds.[115]

The French suspected that Law No. 75 was a ploy to undermine their position on international ownership by means of the preamble, acceptance of which, they concluded, had been the price extracted from the Americans for admittance to the British system of control covering the major part of the German steel industry.[116] To some extent, it proved possible to assuage French outrage by granting France immediate membership of the same Control Groups without waiting for formal fusion of the three zones.[117] While appreciating this gesture, the French nevertheless maintained the view that the preamble to Law No. 75 ran directly counter to the fundamental purpose of the International Authority for the Ruhr. Furthermore, from the security aspect, it was claimed that to leave the ownership question to a future German government was tantamount to granting a privilege which the Reich had never before enjoyed. This, in the opinion of the French Minister for Foreign affairs, ran the risk of laying the foundations of German centralism and militarism, or at least of providing every opportunity for such tendencies to develop.[118]

The London conference on the Ruhr which ended on 28 December 1948 went some way to allaying French fears by the establishment of a Military Security Board which would, as part of its brief, co-operate with the International Authority for the Ruhr.[119] Further negotiations over the next few months thrashed out the terms and conditions under which the three Western zones would become a West German state. During discussions in Washington on the subject of the Occupation Statute which would then apply, Bevin insisted that any provisions should not detract from the right of the Germans to decide on matters of ownership.[120] The French returned to the charge in December, however, during the process of harmonising the British and American versions of Law No. 75, with a view to its extension to cover the French zone.[121] For their part, the Americans were agreeable to the excision of the offending section of the preamble, but for the British Labour government there was an important principle involved in leaving the nationalisation option open to the elected representatives of the German people. This was explained to René Massigli.

> The Secretary of State had instructed me to reply that he was too deeply committed to the Cabinet and to his Party to agree to any further concessions. I went over the past history of the question and explained to the Ambassador why Mr. Bevin was obliged to stand firm. The Ambassador, rather to my surprise, did not react violently but merely observed rather sadly that we seemed to have come to a deadlock.[122]

To a large extent any other reaction would have been to persist on an issue which was already curiously out of phase with the situation. Following the promulgation of the Basic Law on 23 May 1949, the Federal Republic of Germany had come into existence on 20 September and within two months had won important concessions with regard to the steel industry.[123] In these circumstances, regardless of whether or not Law No. 75 expressly provided for a free choice on the question of ownership, to attempt to impose a system at this late stage would be at best incongruous.

Within weeks of taking office, the Federal Chancellor Konrad Adenauer had written to the Allied High Commission expressing his dismay at the continued policy of dismantling in the new Republic. The Commissioners decided to agree to a meeting to exchange views on the subject.[124] It was already apparent that it would become increasingly difficult to pursue the dismantling programme in the face of growing opposition from the German people supported by a press and pamphlet campaign.[125] Although a tripartite policy, the onus for its implementation fell largely upon the personnel of the British zone where the bulk of the industry was concentrated. Fearing a rapid deterioration in relations with the Federal government so recently established, Bevin invited his American and French counterparts to meet to decide what action could be taken to defuse the situation. The three statesmen assembled in Paris on 9 November 1949.[126]

Opening the talks, Bevin was of the view that the first priority was to normalise relations with Germany. Dean Acheson went further and put forward the opinion that merely to aim at normal relations would leave the Federal Republic susceptible to the influence of the Soviet Union. He thought that the correct course would be a positive move to draw Adenauer's Germany into the comity of Western nations.[127] The following day Schuman informed the meeting that, with great difficulty, he had secured the assent of his government that concessions might be made regarding dismantling on the understanding that the existing limitations on production would remain.[128] Bevin thought that dismantling was now only useful as a bargaining counter.

> In conclusion I reminded my colleagues that the time for the execution of the dismantling policy had been set at Potsdam for $2\frac{1}{2}$ years. The policy had been delayed by so many different considerations and discussions that our attempts to carry it out now might become a little ridiculous. If we could get satisfactory arrangements on security I would be willing to pay a price for it.[129]

On the subject of steel, however, Schuman still had reservations on the grounds that over-production would result in unemployment, the political consequences of which would be felt not only in France but all over Europe.[130] This argument did not convince Acheson, who felt that nothing would be achieved in the economic field by destroying German plants, many of which would in any case require considerable expenditure to restore them to full working order. He assured Schuman that no Marshall Aid funds would be available for this purpose.[131]

On one steelworks, the Reichswerke at Salzgitter, Schuman was immovable. Otherwise it proved possible to agree seven plants which were open to negotiation with the German authorities. This list was incorporated in the directive to the High Commissioners as a basis for their discussions with Adenauer.[132] With these instructions, the Commissioners met with Adenauer on 22 November 1949. In return for the cessation of dismantling at the proposed plants, the Federal Republic agreed to apply for full membership of the International Authority for the Ruhr (where it already had observer status) and furthermore declared its determination to co-operate with the High Commission in the work of the Military Security Board. This agreement was embodied in a document which became known as the Petersberg Protocol.[133] Of the steelworks to be reprieved, most were of modest size. In the British zone, Ruhrstahl AG Henrichhütte, Hattingen, had an annual capacity of 386 000 tons, and, in the French zone, Hüttenwerke Siergerland AG, Charlottenhütte, Niederschelden, was rated at 140 000 tons.[134] The Deutsche Edelstahlwerke, Krefeld, with a capacity of 180 000 tons, was an easy concession to make because it had already been removed from the dismantling programme as a result of the Humphrey Report.[135]

On the other hand, the remaining four plants were those which had formed the hard core of the Anglo-French 'last ditch' position during negotiations on that report. With a combined annual capacity of 3 278 000 tons, these were the very steelworks whose destruction Britain and France had fought for and won in the face of American opposition.[136] Of these the most important was the August Thyssen works at Hamborn, with an annual capacity of 2.25 million ingot tons. In respect of this works the Humphrey Report had made the special recommendation that it should be kept in operation as long as the world steel shortage continued, but not later than 1 June 1954. It would then be closed down.[137] As this would, given full production, involve the redundancy of some 12 000 workers, the British view was that the closure would involve not a little resentment. 'In short it is considered that the postponement of dismantling the plant could only result in its remaining permanently in production in Germany, a result which we could not contemplate.'[138] Hamborn mostly produced a type of steel which, it was foreseen, would be particularly in over-supply when the situation improved. For this reason it had been decided in February 1949 to resist the Humphrey proposals to the limit. In the changed circumstances of that November it was necessary to sacrifice this achievement to the overriding need to bring into the fold a West German state that British policy had been instrumental in forming.

This immediately nullified the effects of the Anglo-French stance taken earlier in the year. That realignment of interests had come about with the first British defence of the *status quo* against pressure for upward revision of the level of industry. This represented a turning-point for Britain, whose policy had previously pursued the twin objectives of raising the level of steel production and encouraging a greater German participation in the running of the economy. With the attainment of the former, the latter would not be conducive to restricting production while unused capacity remained in Germany. By the time of the Petersberg Protocol, there was every indication that the ceiling on production would be reached early the following year. In France the Prime Minister and former Foreign Minister, Georges Bidault, was convinced that if plant were left *in situ* it would be used regardless of any limitation.[139]

That moment had not yet come, but as the Federal Republic of Germany stood poised to rise from the ashes of the Third Reich, the idea of a steel industry pared down to the bare minimum was clearly out of date. On 22 January 1950 Adenauer informed the High Commissioners of his intention to introduce legislation placing the reorganisation of the German iron and steel industry in the hands of the Federal government.[140] On 7 June 1950 the Combined Steel Group learned that *Land* and Federal authorities were proposing to make available funds of DM 20 million for the reconstruction of the August Thyssen works at Hamborn.[141] In the meantime, with the announcement of the Schuman Plan on 9 May 1950, the German steel industry had moved towards reinstatement among the ranks of European producers.[142]

To some extent the new Germany now in a position to treat with France as an equal was an Anglo-American creation, but it was also a product of the times. The formation of the Bizone was part of a process of polarisation which grew out of the deadlock in the quadripartite system. From the British point of view the prime objective was to relieve the burden on the Exchequer of feeding an area in temporary distress which was nevertheless potentially the most economically powerful in Europe. With American support it was possible to override the four-power process and create the conditions for a German recovery. The question of to what extent that recovery could be controlled was largely overlooked.

This was, however, a matter of immediate concern to France; a fact of which Britain had been made aware. In retrospect, it is tempting to concentrate on those aspects of this situation which gave rise to the most rhetoric at the time. Certainly, the two countries remained at loggerheads on the question of the régime which was to be imposed, and for a long time disagreed on the maximum production that was to be permitted. Nevertheless, this is to overlook a principle on which there was total agreement: namely that there existed a point at which German recovery should be halted. There was, moreover, no dispute about the method to be employed: every piece of industrial equipment surplus to requirements was to be taken apart and removed from German soil once and for all. On this issue Britain and France fought and won.

That victory, however short-lived, highlighted the essential community of interests between the two countries. No more than France did Britain wish to see an inflated German steel industry. While perfectly willing to allow the Germans a greater scope in the ordering of their own affairs, the

British had always seen that freedom within the context of an industry on a restricted scale, albeit at a higher level than the first preference of the French. In aiming for a viable economy for the Ruhr basin, however, Britain was engaged in a process which would ultimately place Germany at the crux of the division between East and West; between America and the Soviet Union. In these circumstances, the Anglo-French partnership bowed to the inevitable.

6 The Marshall Plan

BIZONAL PARTICIPATION

European post-war reconstruction, the division of Germany and the polarisation of world politics reached a turning-point together in the summer of 1947. On 5 June the US Secretary of State made a speech which held out the prospect of American assistance for a programme of European recovery. In Britain, Ernest Bevin immediately set in motion the process which would give form and substance to what rapidly became known as the 'Marshall Plan'. Informed that Marshall desired a co-ordinated response on the European scale, Bevin approached his French counterpart, Georges Bidault, and together they contacted the Soviet Foreign Minister, Molotov.[1]

From the outset it was apparent that any meaningful European response to Marshall's offer would necessarily include an agreed programme of reconstruction for Germany. At the conference between Britain, France and the Soviet Union which opened in Paris on 27 June 1947 this fact was readily acknowledged by the French, who nevertheless pointed out that the implementation of such a programme would raise precisely the questions which had defied solution in the Council of Foreign Ministers.[2]

By 3 July it had emerged that the Soviet Union was not prepared to join on the terms proposed, and the discussions broke down.[3] A sixteen-nation conference was then convened without Soviet participation. Only then was it revealed that the machinery of the CFM had already been bypassed in one respect by an Anglo-American agreement on the German steel industry.[4] Having accepted German participation in the European Reconstruction Programme in principle, the French were now confronted by the prospect of Marshall Aid underpinning a bilateral agreement to which they had not been privy.

The sixteen-nation conference closed on 15 July 1947[5] and the Committee of European Economic Co-operation (CEEC) was launched the following day by Ernest Bevin, who then relinquished the chair to Sir Oliver Franks. The Committee immediately began the first stage of its work, which was the production of a report to be submitted to the United States government on European resources and requirements over the next four years. To this end, questionnaires were sent to participating governments requesting information on a number of key economic indicators for the period to be covered, including the amount of steel which would be produced in each year. The French had already lodged a protest against the proposed increase in the Bizone, and in an attempt to prevent the disagreement from spilling over into the CEEC before the matter could be resolved, Sir Oliver Franks agreed with Hervé Alphand that the completed questionnaires from the Western zones of Germany would indicate any instances where the projected output exceeded the original 1946 Level of Industry figure.[6] Arriving at this compromise both delegates were under the impression that any discrepancy would be negligible and that both figures would be given purely as a matter of form.

The 1946 Level of Industry Plan allowed total German production to run at 5.8 million tons of crude steel per year from plant capable of producing 7.5 million tons, the majority of which was under Anglo-American control.[7] Franks had information that the figure returned by the Bizone in respect of 1951 would be in the region of 5.25 million tons, which, given reasonable estimates from the French and Soviet zones, would yield a total for the whole of Germany not unduly in excess of the old limit.[8] This illusion was dispelled on 1 August by a telegram from the British Military Governor stating that a reassessment of the situation had shown that, with favourable conditions and some reallocation of fuel resources, an output of 10 million tons in 1951 might be attainable.[9] The following day it was reported to London that, although certain members of the British element in Berlin had expressed doubts, the Americans were adamant that this figure should stand as the reply to the questionnaire.[10] This presented the Foreign Office with a dilemma: either allow the answer to go forward to the CEEC and thus widen the rift with the French, or antagonise Britain's American partners in the Bizone. On 2 August the question was submitted to Bevin, who made it clear that he was not disposed to side with the French.[11] In Paris the difficulty was explained to Alphand and it was decided that, upon receipt, the completed questionnaire from the Bizone would be held in the Delegation Office until a suitable moment for its release.[12] By 8 August it had become clear that consideration of the replies in the technical committees of the CEEC would grind to a halt if the French were not given some degree of satisfaction.[13] It was this impending deadlock which two days later induced the Americans to agree to a tripartite examination of the question in London.[14]

The US government had given early consideration to what their attitude should be in this position and it had been thought that the sure course would be to confront the French with the stark choice of a rise in German production or no American aid for Europe.[15] The Americans had an interest in the stability of Western Europe and were relying on France to play a central role in the forthcoming recovery programme but this gave the French little leverage over US policy in the crucial matter of German industry. Following the London talks, therefore, the 10 million tons of crude steel production for the Bizone was entered in the CEEC report as the official working figure for the final year of the Marshall Plan.[16] Except only for a short footnote recording their reservations, the French had thus been prevailed upon to acquiesce in a level of industry for Germany which they regarded as inflated. Moreover, they were now faced with the prospect of the increase being largely achieved within four years under the stimulus of American aid. With the advent of the Marshall Plan, what had been conceived as a *ceiling* on steel output now assumed the character of a *target*.

The disbursement of American dollars to achieve this goal also raised the question of the status of the beneficiary. The British preference was that the Bizone should be treated in the same way as the member states.[17] From the administrative point of view this was a perfectly workable arrangement which would place the Anglo-American occupation authorities in a similar position to that of the governments of the other participants. On the political level an early indication of the implications was contained in the telegram from Berlin alerting the Foreign Office to the American determination to return a figure of 10 million tons in the completed steel questionnaire. In his cable, the British Military Governor justified the adoption of this figure on the grounds that it was the one which the Germans themselves would have chosen: 'It has to be borne in mind, and we think the Americans realise this, that we are acting as trustees for Germany in replying to an offer to which they attach very great value.'[18] The Marshall Aid programme thus served to recast the role of the military government in terms of German interests. Brought about by the responsibility of overseeing a revival of the country's industrial heartland, this new focus of activity for the Bizonal authorities developed in advance of any decision on the form of the post-war German state, its government, or its relations with its neighbours.

The military government envisaged that the Bizonal permanent delegation in Paris should have an integrated Anglo-American staff assisted by German professional and clerical personnel selected with a view to facilitating the changeover to full German representation at a later date.[19] By July the day-to-day work was in German hands wherever possible, subject only to the availability of suitable candidates proficient in English or French.[20] This process was later complemented by a drive for increased German participation in the statistical and planning support back in Germany.[21] The rise in staffing levels was prompted by the need to fulfil the next stage of the Marshall Plan. Having arrived at a four-year working programme the participants were now charged with the task of demonstrating how the benefits they would derive were in each case consistent with a coherent long-term economic strategy. Individual long-term programmes were to be produced and subjected to examination and criticism by fellow members in the OEEC before being combined into a forecast on the European scale. Like any participant the Bizone intended that its full potential should be harnessed to promote a recovery which would be sustainable beyond the period of American aid, and it was therefore envisaged that coal exports would remain on the basis of the Moscow sliding scale while industrial output would be raised and exports of manufactured goods maximised.[22] It was not anticipated that account would be taken of any outside interests.

In reply, therefore, to a Foreign Office suggestion that the Bizonal long-term programme should be discussed in Britain and the United States, the British Economic Adviser in Germany had no objection to the two governments agreeing a common position in advance of consideration of the programme in the OEEC. If, on the other hand, it was intended that the programme should be subject to prior vetting and approval, he foresaw a violent reaction from General Clay; and not without justification. 'I should sympathize with him myself, even if I could not say so, because the Bizone is a participating country and should be allowed to put forward its case without external pressure.'[23] This view prevailed and the Bizone submitted its programme to the OEEC in the same way as the other participants.

Scrutiny of the programmes took the form of a verbal defence by representatives in front of delegates of other participating countries. In cross-examination, both the British and the French delegates voiced particular concern regarding the feasibility of funding the recovery of the Bizone through a huge rise in exports in the market conditions then prevailing.[24] Nevertheless, with Western Europe engaged in an economic experiment on a scale never before attempted, it was difficult absolutely to refute the Bizonal claim that the plan was within the bounds of possibility. Except for registering certain reservations, therefore, the United Kingdom was powerless to influence the contents of the programme. In anticipation of impending controversy the London Committee decided to take the matter to Cabinet level.[25] The paper submitted expressed doubts that the Bizone's projected increase in exports could achieve sufficient market penetration unless it was intended to adopt unfair trading practices. This, it was argued, would have serious consequences for the plans of all the manufacturing countries of Western Europe, which would be faced with the choice of cut-throat competition or a return to the cartel arrangements which had characterised the stagnation of the inter-war years. 'The United Kingdom long-term programme in particular would thereby be put in danger and the British standard of living threatened.'[26] This was, of course, the very complaint which the French had long expressed in regard to the effect of a resurgent German industry on the Monnet Plan. The London Committee paper did not, however, seek to draw the analogy.

Neither did Ministers dwell on this aspect of the situation when the matter came before them in the Economic Policy Committee on 14 December 1948.[27] Foremost in Bevin's mind was the dilemma with which he was now faced: it was accepted policy that every effort should be made to restore the West German economy, yet it was now proposed to press for the emasculation of a bold plan which had precisely that objective. There was still, however, the possibility that re-examination of the Bizonal programme in the OEEC would present a further opportunity to exercise some influence. In the meantime the Ministers invited the Chancellor of the Exchequer to draft a note to the US Ambassador indicating that the United Kingdom might wish, in due course, to put forward major criticisms of the programme. This message went forward to the Ambassador over Bevin's signature on 20 December.[28] Upon learning of the contents of this communication, General Clay expressed astonishment that the British government should object to a programme which had been prepared by a joint UK/US staff in the best interests of the Bizone.[29] In the final analysis, however, Clay's attitude stemmed from his understanding of the Anglo-American relationship. 'If U.K. Government can oppose Bizonal program in OEEC, then it is not only in opposition to us but is clearly failing to recognize U.S. predominant voice under fusion agreement.'[30] This concession, which Britain had been forced to make in return for financial support in the Bizone prior to the Marshall Plan, could now be invoked to deter British interference in what was increasingly perceived as an internal matter.

The developing conflict of interests eventually came to a head over a question of high policy. The Chancellor of the Exchequer had, through ministerial level channels, pressed for the adoption by the OEEC of the principle that no country should plan on the assumption that it would be possible to earn gold or dollars from other member countries.[31] Since the convertibility crisis of July 1947, one of Britain's main concerns had been to preserve the prestige of sterling in an economic climate dominated by the dollar shortage.[32] There was, therefore, a sense of outrage in Whitehall when it was learned that the Bizone intended to oppose the principle to which the Chancellor attached such importance.[33] A telegram was despatched to Berlin to ascertain whether the British element had reserved its position when the policy was being discussed with the Americans.[34] The reply came back from General Robertson that the policy had been jointly arrived at.[35] Defending himself and his colleagues in a later despatch, the British Economic Adviser in Berlin wrote that their action was based on an objective view of the best interests of the Bizone, and of Europe as a whole.

> In any event, there is hardly any use arguing this matter further since, as a result of the Washington decisions, it will be the Germans and not the Americans or ourselves who will be going to Paris in a few months' time.[36]

This was in anticipation of the establishment of a Federal German government in accordance with the measures agreed between Britain, France and the United States a few days previously.[37] Events were now moving rapidly towards the rehabilitation of West Germany within a Europe still weak in the aftermath of war but poised for a planned recovery on an unprecedented scale. At this critical juncture the ex-enemy was by no means at a disadvantage. Ahead of political developments, the Bizonal authorities had seized the economic initiative with the result that, newly arrived on the threshold of statehood, West Germany was set to take over a functioning system of representation already experienced in the vigorous defence of the German point of view.

That any programme of recovery for Europe would of necessity include the Western zones of Germany had been accepted by both Britain and France as a general principle. The emergence of an ascendant and self-assertive German state to dominate the Marshall Plan was, however, anticipated by neither, and no agreement or informal understanding of any sort covered this contingency. Britain had envisaged a certain independence of action for the Bizone in the OEEC, but in the frustration of almost complete impotence was now relegated to the position of bystander which had for so long been reserved for France. The industrial might of the former British zone now found a natural home at the heart of the European Recovery Programme and, as the Marshall Plan took effect, questions of German economic policy which had bedevilled relations between Britain and France now receded beyond the influence of either.

EUROPEAN STEEL CO-ORDINATION

The French had accepted from the outset that the Marshall Plan would have to include Germany, if only because German coal was essential to European recovery.[38] Of course, the less fuel consumed by the German steel industry, the greater the tonnage which would be available for export to countries such as France. From France's point of view this was a further reason for an agreed plan of development for the European steel industry as a whole. At the Marshall Plan conference in Paris in July 1947 the French delegation approached their British counterparts with the suggestion that the Steel Committee of the conference should make a special study of particular products causing bottlenecks in industrial expansion. It also emerged that:

> For the long-term, the French view is that there should be some integration of the steel development plans of European countries. They suggest that a permanent committee should be established to discuss projects for development and in particular to consider whether these projects overlap each other.[39]

This echoed the proposals for integration of plans which in the recent past had figured in Anglo-French discussions on economic co-operation, but now extended to cover the entire European steel industry.

From the British point of view the fact that the request was framed in the context of the Marshall Plan conference made it difficult to respond with a categorical refusal, as such schemes would be likely to have considerable appeal for the Americans. Moreover, it had to be conceded that steel was the conspicuous case where some measure of European integration including the United Kingdom might be technically possible.[40] The difficulty revolved around the same differences which had been apparent at the Anglo-French discussions in February: while the French anticipated a situation of general over-capacity and were bent on tailoring the European steel industry accordingly, the British were concerned with overcoming what they assumed would be a protracted shortage. The United Kingdom had therefore tended to avoid discussion of steel plans on the assumption that the French would be looking to restrict production.[41]

In readiness for Cabinet consideration of this issue, officials briefed their respective Ministers. At the Treasury it was felt that Britain stood to lose from integration with Western Europe. On the other hand, as European self-help was a key element in the Marshall Plan, it was necessary to 'produce schemes which will look well'.[42] The Lord President was informed that the general consensus favoured a recommendation by the London Committee to offer the French a study group on long-term supply and demand on the understanding that no pressure for adjustment of development plans would arise from its work. It was understood that the Prime Minister was being briefed accordingly, the Ministry of Supply were in agreement and the Foreign Office also supported this line. 'but it is possible that the Foreign Secretary personally may press to go further. If he does we think, in the interests of the U.K. economy, that he should be resisted.'[43] At the Foreign Office, Bevin was advised that informal contacts indicated that the study group option would be acceptable to the French, who were now thinking in terms of expansion rather than restriction of steel production in Europe.[44]

If this was correct, the paper already circulated to Ministers cast the French proposals in a more unfavourable light than was warranted. The Chairman of the London Committee therefore made a point of bringing this possibility to the attention of the European Economic Co-operation Committee of Ministers which met on 31 July 1947.[45] This announcement in effect undermined the central plank of the argument in the paper before the committee. Nevertheless, none of those present sought to reopen the debate, and the meeting, chaired by the Prime Minister, dealt rapidly with the question.

> THE CHANCELLOR OF THE EXCHEQUER said that it was essential that we should enter into no commitment which would prevent us from expanding our steel production as we wished. This was vital to our economy.[46]

The Minister of Supply and the representative of the Ministry of Fuel and Power urged caution but saw no objection to a study group.[47] The Foreign Secretary apparently made no comment and it was agreed that the United Kingdom might offer to participate in a general survey of the European steel situation on the clear understanding that: 'we should not be committed to modify our own steel development programme according to recommendations by the study group'[48] This was a major impediment to the formulation of a comprehensive plan of action for a sector of the European economy which, to the French way of thinking, was fraught with uncertainty and ripe for regulation.

By the end of 1948 French thinking had already developed to the point where it leant towards favouring an arrangement with some of the characteristics of a cartel. In December of that year Sir Oliver Harvey had a conversation with the newly-appointed French *Chargé de Mission* in Germany, André François-Poncet, who felt that a solution along these lines would provide the means of integrating Germany into Western Europe.

> He would like to see, for instance, European Councils for coal, for steel, for wood and other basic materials. These cartels would allot certain

programmes to all the producing countries of Western Europe. In this way the Germans could be given the feeling of being on an equal footing with other Western European countries.[49]

This found an echo in the ideas of the Labour MP Maurice Edelman, who wrote to the Chancellor of the Exchequer enclosing a reprint of an article he had written for the *New Statesman*. Edelman envisaged that the cartel principle would be developed so as to be consistent with the requirements of public policy, and imagined that from the starting-point of an Anglo-French Iron and Steel Organisation might be formed a European Iron and Steel Authority.[50] A similar suggestion arose the following month in the course of a discussion between Sir Stafford Cripps and his French counterpart on the subject of the co-ordination of investment programmes within the OEEC. Cripps observed that any agreement would be worthless without the means to ensure its enforcement.

> M. Petsche agreed, but thought that it would be possible to secure an adequate control through cartels – not the old, devitalizing and restrictive kind which we all wanted to abolish, but new and useful cartels.[51]

Cripps confessed to a lack of enthusiasm for the means proposed but nevertheless accepted the principle that co-ordination of investment should be examined by the OEEC. It was agreed that the oil and steel industries were suitable cases for study. Cripps, however, remained sceptical of anything which smacked of 'integration' and was determined not to be 'rushed into a lot of impractical follies to suit our more volatile friends'.[52]

Still there remained a school of thought in French political circles which embraced the possibility of a *modus vivendi* with a revived Germany. Though not fully developed, the ideas expressed by François-Poncet and Petsche indicated an acceptance that it was difficult to take a constructive view of the European steel industry in which German participation was defined only in terms of the blanket restrictions deriving from the Allied occupation. On the other hand, Britain was content to take the narrow view of Germany's place in the overall picture. In March 1949, by way of illustrating to an American audience the genuine spirit of European co-operation which had been engendered amongst the OEEC countries, Stafford Cripps cited the example of the 'common programme for steel development' which had just been decided upon.[53] This was true only in a limited sense. Before approving the first applications for funding, the Office of the United States Special Representative in Europe had requested, and been supplied with, a report on the individual projects in relation to overall demand for steel.[54] It had also been agreed that the OEEC would examine the co-ordination of steel investment programmes, though the terms of reference were only established the following month.[55] To which of these instances Cripps was alluding in his broadcast is unclear but in both cases the lack of formal ties to a continuing pattern of interrelationship characterised action of an essentially *ad hoc* nature.

Neither did these examples of European co-operation have any relevance to the future of the German steel industry, which at that very moment Britain and France were fighting to dismantle in the face of American opposition.[56] It was in this respect that British policy diverged from enlightened French thinking. While both countries remained unswerving in their determination to strip Germany of any capacity in excess of that required for the Level of Industry agreement, the feeling clearly existed in France that this alone did not amount to an adequate conception of Germany's place in the post-war European steel industry.

In Britain, though the French desire to bind German steelmaking into a wider association of producers was understood, it was nevertheless felt that a Steel Cartel, pure and simple, would not recommend itself to American opinion. In the analysis of the Foreign Office, the idea would need to be developed to encompass some form of inter-governmental co-ordination.

> This might lead in turn to the creation of an international control body with far-reaching powers over production, development, sales and management superimposed upon a varying pattern of ownership in the different countries.[57]

There was no indication of how far France would be prepared to travel along that path. It was, however, apparent that certain elements in high political circles in France were uneasy with the prospect of even a residual German steel industry without a clearly-defined niche in the European network of supply and demand.

This was not a preoccupation which was shared by the British, who were quite prepared to let Europe go its own way as long as the policy of His Majesty's Government was not affected. As early as July 1947, the French proposal that steel development plans be compared in the CEEC gained Cabinet approval only on the understanding that the United Kingdom should not be committed to modifying its own programme. Nearly two years later the Ministry of Supply echoed this reaction in its appraisal of the implications of the OEEC long-term programmes.[58] The same report also referred to the finding of the OEEC Steel Committee that by 1952/53 there was likely to be a substantial surplus of steel available for export to outside the OEEC area, but concluded that Britain should be able to hold her own in established markets, such as the Dominions, where she had a considerable advantage.

The work on the long-term programmes had not, therefore, induced Britain to consider steel from the European perspective. The idea that co-ordination of investment among the participating countries might serve as an example of European integration was conceived as a gesture which Britain could comfortably make in the circumstances. Even as a fact-finding exercise this work was overtaken by events as development projects were submitted for urgent approval in advance of completion of the preliminary study. In its report of October 1949 the OEEC Steel Committee concluded that this piecemeal approach had 'seriously, perhaps irretrievably, prejudiced any useful work in the future'.[59] As so many of the schemes to be funded under Marshall Aid were now under way, the Steel Committee felt that little scope remained for co-ordination in any meaningful sense. In the circumstances, and in the light of a similar report from the Oil Committee, the Secretary-General of the OEEC, Robert Marjolin, came to question whether any effective co-ordinating action could in fact be taken under the auspices of the OEEC.[60]

In London, the Ministry of Supply took the view that the role of the OEEC would in future be limited to that of a clearing-house for information.[61] Nevertheless the continuing statistical work of the OEEC was cited in the House of Commons as an example of the efforts of the members to co-ordinate their industrial and economic systems.[62]

This minimalist British view was not commensurate with developing French ideas, nor did it answer France's abiding concerns. In January 1947 the case put forward by Hervé Alphand for a lower level of German production had been based on the premise that the overall outlook for European steelmaking was one of eventual over-supply.[63] Two years later, there was every indication that by 1952, if all plans were fulfilled, the steel produced within the OEEC for export to non-participating countries would exceed by at least 1.5 million tons the amount which could reasonably be expected to be marketable.[64] Even with this glut in prospect, however, the exercise on co-ordination of investment was overtaken by a scramble for Marshall Aid funding, with the result that the majority of the proposed development projects went ahead regardless. Over this scene of expanding capacity loomed the German steel industry, its future beyond the power of France to influence except through increasingly uncertain instruments of control and restriction.

BRITISH COAL

It was early realised that Britain's commitment to the principle of mutual assistance inherent in the Marshall Plan would be largely judged on her willingness to contribute substantial supplies of coal to the common effort. To this end it was proposed to increase production by all possible means, including the recruitment of extra labour, an end to restrictive practices, and an expansion of open-cast mining.[65] This was welcomed by Ernest Bevin, who was certain that his task in relation to the Marshall Plan would be facilitated if the United Kingdom were able to export coal on anything approaching the pre-war scale.[66] In particular, he felt that it was necessary to restore adequate fuel supplies to France without the French share of Marshall Aid being used to import coal from the United States when food and machinery were more important.[67] In the opinion of the Minister for Fuel and Power, it would be just possible to schedule 7 million tons for export to participating countries during 1948, and then 13 million tons in 1949, 21 million tons in 1950, and 29.5 million tons in 1951.[68] Bevin was disturbed to learn that this was the best that could be done but accepted that it was essential to quote targets which could be fulfilled. In order to allow the British delegation a degree of latitude, Ministers therefore agreed to present a figure of 6 million tons for 1948 to the Paris Conference.[69] Even this amount was in contrast to the current situation, in which Britain, far from supplying the needs of Europe, was importing coal from the United States after an unseemly wrangle in the European Coal Organisation to obtain French approval for the allocation.[70] The advent of Marshall Aid was thus set to mark a turning-point in the United Kingdom's response to the fuel shortage in Europe. This was the primary reason why, despite a precarious stock situation, it was thought inappropriate to apply through the ECO for one last allocation of American coal for 1947.[71]

The ECO was wound up in December and its functions transferred to the Coal Committee of the Economic Commission for Europe in Geneva. It was thus to this body that the announcement was made in January 1948 that the United Kingdom was about to resume coal exports. This news was accompanied, however, by the rider that, instead of declaring the entire tonnage for inclusion in the pool, Britain intended to avail herself of the option to make such bilateral deals as were to her advantage.[72] One arrangement which had been in mind was a scheme to exchange British coal for supplies of steel from France. Of the six million tons destined for export during 1948, it was intended to reserve 1.04 million tons for this purpose.[73] British hopes in this respect received a setback, however, when negotiations began and the French delegation dismissed the proposal on the grounds that it would involve refusing American coal, which could be obtained free of charge under Interim Aid.[74] Resumed discussions in Paris closed with an alternative agreement that, as French production rose, increasing quantities of semi-finished steel would be made available to Britain on a commercial basis, in consideration of which France would also obtain some steel strip from Britain.[75]

This was the first indication that in the climate of the Marshall Plan the promise of British coal did not offer unlimited scope for bargaining. The danger that free coal from the United States might detrimentally affect British exports to Europe was a source of concern at the National Coal Board, where it was felt that, if informal pressure failed to resolve the matter, an approach should be made to the US government.[76] Rumours that the French had declined to purchase UK coal had already reached the State Department through contact between the British and American delegates in Geneva and had been denied in Paris.[77] This denial was, strictly speaking, founded on fact: the French had turned down the proposal of a straight exchange of coal for steel, and were merely displaying no haste to take up the option on any other basis. With the benefit of American coal as grant-in-aid, and having recently acquired the rights to the Saar coalfields, France was faced with an embarrassment of riches. Nevertheless, Harry Lintott was informed in Paris that, although requirements were covered for 1948, it was likely that France would take some British coal in order to re-establish a trading relationship for the future. Lintott's source envisaged, however, that this would cause difficulties with the Americans, who were pressing strongly for the French to take up their full quota of US coal.[78] This ran counter to the sympathetic attitude displayed by the United States representatives on the Coal Committee in Geneva, who undertook to recommend that American shipments be reduced by an amount corresponding to the tonnage available from Britain.[79]

The problem to some extent was that, in concentrating on mining the maximum tonnage possible, Britain had neglected the question of quality. This was recognised by the London Committee, who were informed that participating countries, especially France but also Belgium and Denmark, were reluctant to take the inferior qualities on offer, with the effect that the full weekly tonnage allocated for export was not being sold.[80] It was felt that if traditional European markets were not regained in the near future they might be lost for ever. The difficulty lay in the increase of American production from 440 million tons per year to 600 million tons, which was expected to result in pressure to include coal in Marshall Aid with a view to disposing of the surplus and opening up new markets for the post-reconstruction period. An aide-mémoire for the attention of the

US Ambassador had already been proposed and the London Committee had before them a draft prepared by the Ministry of Fuel and Power.[81] The Committee therefore agreed that the draft should be revised in line with the discussion and that it should then be considered by the Overseas Negotiations Committee (ONC).[82] At its next meeting the ONC also examined the extreme solution of restricting coal deliveries to France from the Ruhr in order to dispose of British production. This was rejected mainly on the grounds that Ruhr coal was well suited to the French steel industry, from where it was hoped to obtain supplies.[83]

On 3 March 1948 Bevin met with the US Ambassador in the company of Hugh Gaitskell.[84] The Ambassador was handed an aide-mémoire which drew attention to the difficulties being experienced in exporting British coal. The solution proposed in this document was that there should be a 'quality budget', whereby European availabilities and requirements would be matched, and only after the deficit *in terms of qualities* had been ascertained would US coal of the appropriate types be brought in to make up the shortfall.[85] After a perusal of the document, the Ambassador, Lewis Douglas, said that he fully accepted the British view that US coal must be marginal and gave an assurance that there was no need for anxiety in the matter. Gaitskell also touched upon the possibility that countries might deliberately ask for qualities which Britain was not offering in order to justify indenting for supplies under Marshall Aid. Once delivered, this coal could then be used for quite another purpose instead of suitable coal from the UK which would have to be paid for. Douglas agreed that any plan would have to take this into account.[86]

As far as France was concerned, however, it was clear that the offer of coal would not secure any special favours, and it was accepted that 1.3 million tons should be offered for delivery during 1948 with no strings attached.[87] This course of action was shown to be appropriate to the circumstances when the American response was eventually received to Gaitskell's aide-mémoire. In his reply Ambassador Douglas held to the principle that participating countries should decide for themselves the most effective use of resources, but expressed the view that the US Administrator would be reluctant to authorise any expenditure for the supply of American coal when suitable qualities were available for purchase on equitable terms in Europe.[88] Despite the diplomatic language in which the reply was couched, it was immediately clear to the London Committee that the Ambassador was at pains not to commit the US authorities to any positive action to meet the specific points raised by Britain. In particular it seemed to infer that the Administrator would not necessarily be bound by the recommendations of the Coal Committee of the Economic Commission for Europe, nor would the machinery of US export licences be invoked to prohibit the despatch of qualities already in adequate supply.[89]

This was the crux of the matter for Britain, where the drive for greater production was having an effect but it appeared that there would be an unsold surplus of 3.5 million tons of a quality known as 'uncleaned smalls'.[90] The problem of obtaining a corresponding reduction in supplies from the United States was, in one respect, of a technical nature in that American coal was not sorted before despatch but was loaded straight from the mine. This 'run-of-mine' coal would then be screened on arrival in Europe and separated into various qualities, of which only a certain proportion would be inferior grades. Even these were superior to British uncleaned smalls in that they had a lower ash content.[91] Irrespective of cost, therefore, Britain was faced with the problem of reducing the flow of good quality coals under Marshall Aid in order to market her own less desirable qualities. This was a complete reversal of the situation the previous year when European countries had been clamouring for coal of any type whatsoever. In those conditions of shortage not only had all British production been retained for home use but Britain had been glad to take American coal in the face of French opposition.

This was no longer the prime concern of British policy in the changed circumstances of May 1948 when the Cabinet Production Committee considered a further approach to the United States authorities with a view to reducing shipments.[92] An aide-mémoire was subsequently prepared for the attention of Avrell Harriman, the United States Special Representative in Europe.[93] In this it was requested that American exports of coal be reduced forthwith and that consignments be screened before despatch to eliminate the lower qualities.[94] After discussion in the London Committee it was decided to impart the contents of this message in the first instance to the London representative of the US Economic Co-operation Administration, Mr Finletter, with a view to early discussion.[95] The Minister of Fuel and Power, accompanied by Hector McNeil, Minister of State at the Foreign Office, met with Finletter on 5 July 1948 and received a sympathetic hearing.[96] As with the earlier approach to the Ambassador, however, this sympathy failed to be translated into positive action. The episode nevertheless demonstrated how, in surplus as in shortage, the crucial role of American coal supplies in European recovery continued to be viewed in terms of British national interest.

All the same, efforts to market the poorer qualities of British coal resulted in an indirect benefit for France and other countries. By March 1948 a scheme was being examined whereby British coal would be shipped to North Germany, and superior German coal released through the Economic Commission for Europe in exchange.[97] This proposal was presented to the House of Commons as a resumption of the traditional trade with North Germany, where the long haul by rail made supplies from the Ruhr uneconomical.[98] In fact the bulk of the coal was destined for consumption in electric-power and gas-production plants in Hamburg, which, before the war, had been specifically designed to utilise these inexpensive qualities.[99] The scheme came into force in July 1948 with France as the major beneficiary in terms of enhanced fuel allocations.[100] There was also a corresponding benefit to Germany, where the operation was not only financially profitable, but yielded additional fuel as the exported tonnage was, by agreement, lower than that received. An examination of a proposal to renew the arrangement for 1949/50 gave a projected gain to the Bizone of 160 000 tons of coal, 171 724 German marks and 123 502 dollars.[101]

The resumption of British coal exports, originally seen as the United Kingdom's main contribution to the Marshall Plan, did not finally provide the medium for an Anglo-French accord within the context of the European Recovery Programme. On the contrary, French nonchalance with regard to a commodity which one year earlier had been a prize almost beyond value, provoked British moves to restrict its flow under Marshall Aid. Even in a field which the United Kingdom could reasonably have expected to dominate, the surge in supplies left British coal marginalised and demanded remedial action by any means. Attempts to unload poorer qualities of British coal onto the European market then resulted in the development of a triangular pattern of trade which, far from linking Britain and France, had Germany at the apex and France as the recipient of coal from the Ruhr. The progress of the Marshall Plan thus left Anglo-French relations trailing in its wake, dwarfed by the forces of supply and demand in a Europe of reviving fortunes.

7 The Schuman Plan

THE BRITISH REACTION

The brusque announcement of what rapidly became known as the Schuman Plan came as a surprise to most of those concerned. On Sunday afternoon 7 May 1950 a telephone call to the French Ambassador in London requested his presence in Paris on Monday morning. Not in the best of health, Massigli sent his right-hand-man, Philippe Baudet, in his stead. This latter returned at 7.30 in the evening with a draft of the joint Franco-German declaration which was to be published the following day and the information that the preparations had been made in the greatest secrecy and masterminded by Jean Monnet.[1] The concept of a supranational organisation with authority over coal and steel, which this announcement was to put forward, was near enough to ideas which had been in the wind not to astonish Massigli. What did alarm him, however, was the fact that the proposal emphasised the benefits to France and Germany but took no special account of Britain's position either as a major coal and steel producer or as an occupying power. It was immediately apparent to the Ambassador that Ernest Bevin, even had he been the most modest and accommodating of men, would have difficulty in swallowing such an affront.[2]

Asked for his first reactions, in Paris, Sir Edmund Hall-Patch offered the opinion that the Schuman Plan was a crystallisation of ideas which the French had been airing for some years.[3] In London, Roger Stevens (now Supervising Under-Secretary of the German General Economic Department) was reluctant to commit himself to an assessment of the intrinsic merits of the scheme on the scant information available but had no hesitation in classifying it as the latest chapter in a history of French moves to establish a permanent influence over the heavy industry of the Ruhr.[4] This view was developed in an interdepartmental paper prepared for Ministers, which explained that it had been increasingly evident that the main concern of the French was competition from the German steel industry.[5] It was suggested that the object might be in effect to freeze German production by implementing the Schuman Plan on the basis of the *status quo* while controls remained in force.

There was thus no difficulty in grasping the logic of the French action, which fell naturally into the context of those enduring preoccupations with which British political circles had been made amply familiar over the years. From the earliest days of work on the Monnet Plan it had been clear that inherent in France's drive for modernisation was a certain conception of the post-war pattern of production and trade in Europe. Over three years later Britain still remained uncomfortable with the prospect of being a cog in this machine. Reviewing the United Kingdom's overseas obligations in March 1950, a paper prepared for the Permanent Under-Secretaries Committee took the view that, stretched as she was economically and militarily, Britain could not undertake any irrevocable commitment to European unity.[6]

This order of priorities was reflected the following month when the brief for the British delegation to the London Conference was circulated under a caveat by Bevin to the effect that great caution should be exercised in dealing with any proposals for a surrender of sovereignty which might be unacceptable to the Commonwealth.[7] After the unexpected turn of events on 9 May this guiding principle encountered French intransigence with regard to the terms of the proposed coal and steel organisation. On 16 May, Monnet explained to a group of British officials that nothing yet existed of the Schuman Plan except the communiqué of the previous week. Two points were paramount, however: France and Germany would go ahead even if no other country chose to join, and the establishment of the High Authority would indeed entail a loss of national sovereignty for member states.[8]

This proved to be the stumbling-block. Though leaving everything else open to discussion, the French continued to insist on the acceptance of this principle as a *sine qua non* for entry to the talks. Unwilling to concede the substance of their position merely to obtain a seat at the negotiating table, His Majesty's Government declined to participate.[9] Ernest Bevin, who had been unwell, asked for it to be made known in Washington that he had nevertheless kept in touch with developments and wished to be fully associated with this decision. Expressing the view that Anglo-French relations would not suffer unduly, he felt sure that his American counterpart, Dean Acheson, would understand that in matters of such vital importance Britain could not 'buy a pig in a poke'.[10] Britain and France thus reached deadlock on the fundamental question, and the negotiations of detail which opened on 20 June 1950 were consequently confined to the 'six': France, the Federal Republic of Germany, the Benelux countries and Italy.

The British government nevertheless set up a working party to consider the likely effects of the scheme.[11] Furthermore, a stand-by British proposal for a European Coal and Steel Authority operating on inter-governmental lines was prepared.[12] It was by no means certain, however, that an opportunity would arise to put forward this alternative. In Washington, Sir

The Schuman Plan

Oliver Franks, who had been following events from the British Embassy, confided, in a personal letter to Roger Makins, that he did not imagine that the French would ever consent to any dilution of the principle of supranationality. In the Ambassador's view, the French were now willing to stake all in an effort to obtain a share in the control of the Ruhr. The proposed High Authority was therefore a reflection of the permanent preoccupation of the French; the beginning and the end of their concept. Without it they had nothing.[13] Agreeing with this analysis, Makins explained that it had nevertheless been felt that, in view of the hopes which had been aroused by the Schuman Plan, Britain should be ready to step in with her own proposals if the talks encountered difficulties. The advantages of this approach had been weighed against the risk of the plan succeeding despite British non-participation.[14]

As time went by this seemed ever more likely. Though accepting that the issue at stake was essentially political, the Ministry of Fuel and Power nevertheless had an interest in the matter and were beginning to fear that the day-to-day progress of the talks would soon undermine the credibility of the British alternative. 'We are in appreciable danger of missing the bus and, unless we are indifferent as to whether or not we catch it, this danger should, I feel, be carefully considered.'[15] In the Economic Policy Committee, the Chancellor of the Exchequer was forced to concede that the chances were indeed remote that Britain would have the opportunity to present her proposals and that the time might be ripe to consider to what degree His Majesty's Government could associate themselves with the Schuman Plan as it stood. For his part, Ernest Bevin was not inclined to accept that the matter was settled until the negotiations were finally concluded and the agreement ratified by the French parliament.[16] In the event, the treaty establishing the European Coal and Steel Community was signed in Paris on 18 April 1951, four days after Bevin's death, but not debated in the *Chambre des députés* until 13 December. Even by mid-August 1950, however, it was evident that any idea of presenting British counter-proposals was behind the times.[17] At the end of September the French let it be known informally that the stage at which the outcome of the talks might have been affected was now passed and that Britain need have no further inhibitions about putting forward any comments.[18]

To all intents and purposes the die was now cast. Henceforth the commanding heights of the European economy were out-of-bounds to any understanding of an essentially Anglo-French complexion. Given the obvious political implications, it was also inconceivable that Britain would attempt to undermine the French plan. As the Foreign Office absorbed its significance, the view of Sir Ivone Kirkpatrick was that they should certainly not be placed in the position of seeming to 'torpedo a promising move towards Franco-German rapprochement'.[19] Nevertheless, Britain still occupied the Ruhr and thus retained custody over the major part of the German resources on the negotiating table. France had provided the inspiration but the idea of a community of equals crystallising round a Franco-German reconciliation presupposed a change in the treatment of Germany which could only come through tripartite agreement between the Western Allies. The Schuman Plan thus held out the prospect of a new age in Europe but could not, of itself, fulfil that promise. At the heart of the matter was the question of sovereignty over basic industries. On these terms active British participation was problematic from the outset but, as the West German steel industry chafed and fretted under residual Allied control, Britain's interests were involved alongside those of France.

THE PLAN IN CONTEXT

Although unwilling to envisage the development of the European steel industry in terms of a formalised system of regulation, Britain nevertheless had hitherto shown sympathy for France's desire to control Germany's potential as a producer. At the Paris meetings in November 1949 which prepared the way for the Petersberg Protocol, Bevin did not dissent from Schuman's view that over-production carried the risk of unemployment throughout Europe but expressed the opinion that the policy of dismantling German steelworks was no longer practicable.[20] It was to be made clear, however, that plant already dismantled would not be re-erected and that any proposal to re-equip from other sources would be subject to approval by the Military Security Board.[21] On the subject of one of Schuman's major anxieties, the August Thyssen steelworks at Hamborn, the British High Commissioner assured him that this would not be restored to its full capacity of about 2.25 million tons of steel per year but would, at his discretion, be allowed to reactivate sufficiently to achieve an output of 117 000 tons only.[22]

To some extent the question would turn on whether a particular item of equipment could be said to have been dismantled or not. For example, in order to save double handling, machinery was often unbolted from the floor but left in its usual position awaiting transport. In a secret despatch to the Commissioner of North Rhine-Westphalia, the High Commissioner stressed that the decision was one for the British authorities alone and that he would tolerate no argument from the Germans. In particular, under no circumstances was the Hamborn works to be permitted a capacity in excess of the figure which he had personally quoted to Schuman in Paris.[23]

Arrangements were accordingly made for the agreement with the French to be adhered to but not published.[24] Although not attributed to any source, this figure was subsequently leaked to the management of the works concerned in an unguarded moment by a British officer who, with the best of intentions, was attempting to convey to the Germans that it would be pointless to go to the trouble of preparing plans for a return to normal working.[25] Subsequent discussions revolved around the anomalies inherent in imposing a reduced regime on a massive, integrated steelworks where resumption of crude steel production would presuppose bringing into service rolling capacity and ancillary equipment requiring a minimum level of activity to justify reactivation. In conformity with General Robertson's instructions, however, all German proposals for a viable operation based on combinations of existing plant were returned for revision if they entailed ingot capacity in excess of 117 000 tons per year.[26]

Not only in this particular instance did British and French policies coincide. The application of the Petersberg Protocol posed the general question of what to do in the case of equipment which was in undisputed working order when dismantling was halted but which could not be used due to the inoperability of the plant where it was situated. One option was to move the item concerned to another works where the loss of a similar machine had created a bottleneck in the normal production process. When this matter came before the Industrial Division of the Military Security Board, the American opinion was that such transfers should be approved where they would lead to greater efficiency. The French and British representatives, however, were united in the view that the criterion should be that relocation would not result in an increase in overall capacity in the steel industry.[27] In the weeks before the Schuman Plan there thus remained an afterglow of the fiery Anglo-French resistance to American moves to relax restrictions in line with the Humphrey Report.[28]

Whatever scope could be found for interpretation, the Petersberg Protocol had nevertheless established the principle that a *quid pro quo* might be offered for German co-operation. Much remained to be settled but it was clear that the state reconstituted from the British, French and American zones of occupation was to be enticed away from the Soviet orbit. The wooing of this Germany for the West would have implications beyond bloc politics, raising also the question of the rehabilitation of the new republic among the comity of European nations. The weaving of these two threads into the fabric of a common policy was the challenge which faced British and French statecraft if continued co-operation in

German matters was to amount to anything more than the persistence of old habits.

The French fear was that German influence would be restored in Europe before a durable framework for peaceful co-existence had been established. This was a problem to which statesmen of many countries had already turned their attention. Even before the end of hostilities a feeling had grown that intra-European relations must henceforth be conducted on a more rational basis than the perpetual cycle of confrontation and mistrust between nation-states. Blum, de Gasperi, Spaak; the familiar roll-call of the movement for change resounds with the names of influential figures of the day. In Britain, Winston Churchill spoke out for a United States of Europe. There was no sign, however, that this would become a reality at an early date; certainly not before the resumption of a healthy level of economic activity throughout the countries of the Marshall Plan. In these circumstances the burning question was how Germany's reviving industrial base might be harmoniously accommodated among those nations to whom it had long represented an arsenal of destruction. This problem had been addressed even before it could be foreseen that a reprieve of the steelmaking capacity of the Ruhr basin would one day be the price paid to turn a newborn German Republic westwards.

In early 1948 the President of the French Republic, Vincent Auriol, envisaged exploitation of the Ruhr basin to the benefit of Europe as a whole under a scheme along the lines of the Tennessee Valley Authority.[29] Elsewhere in Europe thinking was moving along similar lines. By mid-1948 enlightened opinion within the British Labour Party tended to the view that control of the Ruhr should be but the first step to a wider control of European resources.[30] This conclusion was shared in Germany, where the Minister President of North Rhine-Westphalia revealed his thoughts on the matter in a radio broadcast on New Year's Day 1949.[31] The main thrust of his message was that the controls imposed on Germany should be superseded by the setting up under international law of a utility association based on co-operation. To this, Germany would contribute the Ruhr, France the ore deposits of Lorraine, both countries the Saar, and Belgium and Luxembourg their heavy industries; powers over production and distribution being vested in the members collectively. Although the French did not share such a clear conception, the proposal was not far removed from the vague ideas involving some form of refined cartel arrangement which began to find expression at about this time.[32]

The idea that controls over Germany might form the nucleus of a wider system for the management of Continental resources was taken up the following year by the Federal Chancellor. Speaking at a press conference following 'purely informatory' talks with Robert Schuman in January 1950, Adenauer took the view that every good European would support the extension of the Ruhr Statute to the Saar mines and, perhaps, to the ore mines of Lorraine.[33] To the British Ambassador in Paris, it was apparent that Franco-German relations were also in the process of being re-examined from the French side in the light of the current situation in Europe. With this in mind he set out his appraisal of developments in a series of long reports to his Secretary of State which, on Bevin's instructions, were printed for circulation to the King and the Cabinet. In the first of his despatches the Ambassador expressed the opinion that a new atmosphere had been introduced by the replacement of Georges Bidault as Minister for Foreign Affairs. Although the new incumbent belonged to the same party, Sir Oliver felt that Schuman's calmer personality and special competence in German matters would enable a more constructive policy to be pursued. Fear of Germany remained, and there was a deep anxiety that, left alone to contend for supremacy, France would quickly become the under-dog. A wider framework would provide support for France and a legitimate outlet for German energy.[34] In subsequent despatches, Harvey developed the view that, whatever the difficulties, the French government would continue to aim for a workable relationship within a European context.[35]

At that moment preparations were in hand for a tripartite conference in London to tackle the question of future relations between the Western Allies and Germany. At the Foreign Office it was suggested to Bevin that he might take the opportunity to remind his French and American colleagues that the problem of the level of German steel production would, sooner or later, have to be faced.[36] A brief was prepared for the UK delegation putting forward the view that there were arguments both for and against an alleviation of restrictions.[37] It was recommended that the UK delegation should initiate an exchange of views on the question and raise the possibility of removing the ceiling on production at a not too distant date as part of an agreement which would anchor the Federal Republic firmly in the Western security system. In this regard, on 2 May 1950, Roger Stevens made it clear to a tripartite working party at the London Conference that a precondition for the removal of restrictions was a solid association of the Federal Republic with the Western powers.[38]

Announcing the Schuman Plan on 9 May, therefore, the French were safe in the knowledge that their prospective German partner had this hurdle to jump before quantitative restrictions were lifted. Even then the level of output attainable would still depend on the amount of productive capacity actually brought back into service: a question upon which the British had so far held the line. In particular, with production at the giant

August Thyssen works reduced to a dribble, the French home industry would at least be spared the discomfort of operating under the same High Authority as the largest integrated steelworks then in Europe. To the Foreign Office, however, it seemed that the maintenance of restrictions was incongruous if the Schuman Plan was to be a true association of equals, though it was expected that the French would offer at least a tactical resistance to any formal relaxation.[39] This ploy would demand a fine balancing of France's interests and a sure touch with allies whose priorities were shifting towards wider considerations of collective security. Months of negotiations lay ahead if the outline principles of the Schuman Plan were to be transformed into a functioning Coal and Steel Community. Meanwhile, for West Germany, the Atlantic community also beckoned.

THE BACKGROUND TO THE NEGOTIATIONS

Three days after the announcement of 9 May 1950 burst upon the London Conference, Schuman had the opportunity to explain to his British and American colleagues that his coal and steel plan was only a starting point from which to tackle the normalisation of West Germany's position in Europe.[40] On this wider question the Ministers approved a paper recommending that an Intergovernmental Study Group be set up in London with a view to producing a report by the end of September.[41] In the meantime Schuman made it known that he did not envisage any change to the existing system of control, but implied that this might function in tandem with his proposed High Authority.[42] The same day the three Ministers approved a paper which took the view that, as supplies of steel in Germany were sufficient to cover demand, there was no need to relax the limit on production. It was recognised, however, that with output already running at the permitted maximum, there was likely to be some agitation for an upward revision. With this in mind the High Commission was instructed to carry out a secret review of the situation. If, in the meantime, the Germans made a formal request for a higher ceiling, they were to be asked to submit a justification for close analysis.[43]

Approached by the Federal Chancellor in August with an informal suggestion that the steel quota might require modification, the British High Commissioner therefore based his reply on the letter of his instructions and gave no encouragement. In his personal opinion, however, German co-operation had become so important that, without pandering to every desire, it should be possible to demonstrate some flexibility.[44] Certainly, the outbreak of the Korean War on 24 June had put a new complexion on matters. In the Intergovernmental Study Group on Germany the United States delegate expressed the hope that agreement might be reached in principle to relax restrictions on non-military capacity in order that this might contribute to Western defence programmes. The French delegate asked for time in which to obtain instructions.[45] These were long in coming but, with time running out, it was agreed to report that the American and British members of the group recommended that the question of the Prohibited and Limited Industries be included on the agenda for the next meeting of the three Foreign Ministers.[46] It was not envisaged that Germany would produce finished ordnance items, but rather, various commodities which would be of general use to the defence effort. Chemicals, ball bearings and aluminium were cited as examples but the need was particularly underlined for steel.[47]

The French attitude soon seemed to be softening and some guarded comments by Schuman were seized upon by the German press as clear evidence that the raising of the steel quota was inevitable.[48] To Sir Ivone Kirkpatrick, who was aware of French reticence in the Intergovernmental Study Group, the impression that France was an outspoken champion of the German steel industry was somewhat galling.[49] In the Allied High Commission the review set in motion by Ministers at the London Conference had also revealed wide differences of opinion with regard to the amount of steel which should be allotted to export, with the French adhering to their familiar line that foreseeable needs would be covered by new capacity in other producing countries. The French element conceded, however, that the prevailing situation of international tension might give rise to abnormal demands for steel which would have to be assessed elsewhere.[50] Time did not permit any further elaboration. Originally requested by the end of September, the report of the International Study Group was now required for the tripartite talks which had been arranged for 12–14 September in New York in order to take advantage of the presence of all three Foreign Ministers for meetings of the North Atlantic Council and the General Assembly of the United Nations. The findings of the High Commission were therefore submitted as they stood, with no attempt to reconcile the differences of opinion.[51]

The New York Conference was to be a turning-point in relations with West Germany. Drawing the analogy with Korea, the Foreign Ministers and High Commissioners were concerned for the Federal Republic to assume willingly the role of a front-line state in the resistance to communist expansionism. Steps were agreed towards a formal end to hostilities, the Federal government was recognised as the sole embodiment of legitimacy pending a final settlement with a united Germany, and it was announced that any act of aggression against the Federal Republic or Berlin would be treated as an attack upon the three Western Allies.[52] The subject of a German military contribution to the defence of the West was broached, but left in abeyance due to French sensitivity. On the possibility of the Western powers availing themselves of German industrial capacity, however, it was agreed that, pending a full review, steel production should be allowed to rise so that tonnages exported to allies or otherwise devoted to defence would not reduce the amount available to domestic consumers.[53] This was only accepted by the French on the understanding that cases of deviation from existing limits were to be authorised by unanimous approval of the three High Commissioners. At the same time Schuman assured his British and American colleagues that he was not insisting on unanimity with any intention of applying the rule obstructively.[54]

With German production already nudging the maximum permitted level, the French attitude was on the point of being put to the test. As output for the 11 months ending 31 August 1950 reached 10 142 100 tons, it was anticipated that the ceiling of 11.1 million tons would be attained before the end of the accounting year in September, necessitating a close-down for two or three days at the end of the month in order not to exceed the limit.[55]

An alternative put forward by the Federal Minister of Economics was that the excess should be condoned on condition that it would be deducted from the quota for the following twelve-month period. This proposal was considered by the Industrial Division of the Military Security Board, who were willing to accede to the German request on the understanding that it was an extraordinary measure which would not constitute a precedent.[56] In the High Commission that day, the United States member recommended an immediate favourable reply but was opposed from the French side, who wished to defer a decision pending word from the New York Conference. The British member declined to press the matter when it became clear that his French colleague, apparently against his own judgement, was under firm instructions that the question was to be postponed.[57] The question was resolved the following week when all agreed to accept the German proposal.[58] By this time, of course, the Foreign Ministers had announced that German steel production would be allowed to rise in line with the needs of the Western defence effort. In the light of that decision the US representative asked if France was going to insist on the surplus produced during the last days of September being offset against the quota for the following year. His French colleague, refusing to be drawn, replied that he insisted on nothing but was merely agreeing to the suggestion as put forward.[59]

Though not actually obstructive, neither did this demonstrate an enlightened attitude on the part of the French. The British member did not, however, feel that the point was worth arguing, and the meeting moved on to the next item on the agenda: the proposed partial rehabilitation of the August Thyssen steelworks. This had first been put forward in June of the same year, when it had been envisaged that DM 20 million would be raised by the federal and *land* authorities for investment in the plant at Hamborn.[60] Recognising that important political considerations were involved, the Combined Steel Group had referred the matter to the Economics Committee of the High Commission.[61] Members of this body felt that the political aspects placed a final decision outside their competence but produced a memorandum which was circulated to the General Committee. Here the British and American members took the view that, within the permitted limits, the Germans were at liberty to utilise any plant not expressly forbidden by the Petersberg Protocol. The French, on the other hand, wished to put off any decision pending the outcome of the conference then in progress in New York. In the meantime, the question was passed to the Council of the High Commission.[62]

The meeting of the Council on 21 September thus had before it the memorandum of the Economics Committee. This concluded that, on purely economic grounds, permission for the investment should be denied. For the moment the Hamborn plant was inoperable and a tacit understanding between Britain and France limited eventual production to 117 000 tons of steel per year, DM 20 million being the funding for those repairs essential for restoration to this level of activity. In the view of the Committee, however, the plant was not a viable proposition at such a low output and reactivation therefore had no merit from the economic point of view.[63] This was seized upon by the French member of the Council in support of his opinion that the proposed investment was merely the thin end of the wedge; the first phase of a hidden agenda leading to major refurbishment. From another angle he also felt that a premature decision would prejudge the future assessment of Thyssen's place in the European picture by any organisation which might emerge from the Schuman Plan negotiations then in progress.[64]

To the British member this was hardly in keeping with the spirit of the new relationship with the Federal Republic which he had supposed they were fostering. On the subject of viability he knew of examples in his own country of uneconomic plants being operated under government subsidy purely for socio-political reasons. If the authorities in North Rhine-Westphalia wanted to make a gesture towards safeguarding employment in the steel industry, the High Commission could not react by forbidding them to activate capacity which they were already authorised to use. This point of view was supported by his American colleague, who further recalled that it had been the High Commission itself which had granted the Germans full powers to act on their own behalf in the Schuman Plan discussions. He now shrank from the idea of undermining their position at the negotiating table by what would be seen as an act of bad faith and an abuse of power in support of France.[65]

The French member denied that there was any intention of making a pre-emptive move against the growth of competition from Germany but said that his government nevertheless felt that a question as important as the reactivation of August Thyssen Hütte should fall within the framework of the Schuman Plan. He informed his colleagues frankly that his instructions were to press for a postponement of the decision. If the matter went to a vote and he found himself in a minority, he was to invoke the appeals procedure under section 7(b) of the Agreement on Tripartite Controls. This provided means for a High Commissioner who considered that a decision was in fundamental conflict with any international agreement to refer the question to his government. Such an appeal would serve to suspend action for 30 days, and thereafter unless two of the governments indicated that continued suspension was not justified.[66] The British were far from convinced that the Schuman Plan negotiations provided a case for appeal on these grounds but drew an appropriate conclusion as to where French preoccupations lay.[67]

Rather than go to appeal immediately, the US member suggested that they adopt a form of words establishing a clear link between the proposed investment and the 117 000 tons of steel which was the accepted annual level of production for the plant. The French member would seek the approval of his government on that basis and, if this was not forthcoming, they would take the matter to a vote at the next meeting.[68] In the event, at the next session, the French member was able to report that the American formula was acceptable subject to close supervision to ensure that reactivation of the Hamborn works remained within the prescribed limits.[69] This decision was passed down to the Combined Steel Board, who noted that permission was granted to undertake such repairs as would enable production of 117 000 tons of steel per year.[70] Nearly a year after this figure had been the subject of a 'gentlemen's agreement' at the Paris talks, only combined Anglo-American pressure had persuaded the French to unblock the necessary investment. Even at an advanced stage the Schuman Plan negotiations had clearly failed to usher in a new era of Franco-German brotherhood. On the contrary, the tactics of the French were apparently to take

The Schuman Plan

advantage of their position as an occupying power by withholding for as long as possible a concession already agreed.

While oblivious to the full extent of French machinations in the High Commission, the Germans were nevertheless aware in a general way of the source of the opposition to those projects which they held dear. In a letter to Ernest Bevin in October 1950, Ivone Kirkpatrick told of the bad feeling which this had engendered.[71] On taking up his appointment as British High Commissioner in June, he had encountered a warmth of feeling for France and an expectation that the Schuman plan would open a new chapter in relations. This had now been replaced by a litany of complaints, among which was Schuman's insistence at the New York Conference that the limit on steel output should be maintained but that production for defence would be permitted above this ceiling; the problem being that nobody knew for certain how the formula could be applied in practice. The whole subject of the Prohibited and Limited Industries was, however, about to be tackled afresh by the Intergovernmental Study Group, which was due to reconvene on 25 October on instructions from the New York Conference.[72]

In advance of the first meeting, the French delegation circulated a note which took the view that it was difficult to determine the scope of Germany's industrial contribution to Western defence until the requirements of the various rearmament programmes had been properly defined by the NATO countries. In the meantime the arrangements for steel should be continued on the existing interim basis. The note closed with an assurance:

> The French Government wish to make it clear that it is not the object of the above suggestion to delay the solution of the problem but to enable it the more thoroughly to be studied and to allow of the achievement of more efficacious results.[73]

This note was considered by a meeting of the Heads of Delegations on 27 October. Holding to the line that a decision should be deferred on the grounds that the subject could only be dealt with in the overall context of Western defence, the French Ambassador encountered an insistence on the part of his British and American colleagues that there was nothing to prevent preliminary work beginning immediately.[74] Having consulted Paris, Massigli finally indicated on 3 November that he was now authorised to proceed with discussions.[75] At the Foreign Office, however, difficulty was expected in persuading the French to agree to any practical steps.[76]

Such did not prove to be quite the case. In November 1950, the French proposed that the ceiling should be raised to 12.4 million tons per year with *no* extra allowance for steel exported for the defence programme.[77]

This would in effect fix a new maximum at a figure which German output was even then approaching, thereby immediately raising the question of enforcement at a time when German co-operation was being sought. Bevin, reluctant to ask the French to 'swallow too much at once', suggested starting at their figure and raising the limit by 1 million tons in each subsequent year.[78] Nothing came of this proposal and the following month the Intergovernmental Study Group announced that no agreement had been reached due to French immobility.[79] The question thus reverted to one of what percentage of German production could be regarded as a contribution to defence under the interim arrangements. This was still a sticking-point in the High Commission in March of the following year; opinion being divided between the United States and Britain on one hand and France on the other.[80]

By April it was apparent that the argument had become academic. It had already been reported in the press that the lifting of restrictions was implicit in the Schuman Plan and that the French government would urge the appropriate steps as soon as the treaty had been initialled.[81] On the other hand, at a press conference given by the Ruhr Authority the French Chairman had revived the idea of retaining the organisation and perhaps extending it to the rest of Europe. On expressing surprise to his Belgian colleague, the British representative heard that:

> the French had one foot on the Ruhr Authority and the other on the Schuman Plan. Depending on progress in negotiations over the latter, the French shifted their weight from one foot to the other.[82]

Such manoeuvres could not be continued indefinitely and, as the Schuman Plan negotiations approached their conclusion, the French were obliged to come down unequivocally on the side of abolition of controls. For its part, the Federal government was at pains to make it known that without a firm assurance on this in advance its representatives at the talks were empowered to sign nothing.[83] Briefing his Secretary of State, Roger Stevens accepted that it was, at first sight, paradoxical and irritating that the French should now take this line after a policy of consistent obstruction in the Intergovernmental Study Group. All the same, he doubted that the Germans had left them any choice and, in any case, an early announcement of concessions would ease the passage of the Schuman Plan ratification through the Federal Parliament.[84]

The Cabinet were nevertheless of a mind to dissuade the French from precipitate action before the matter could be discussed in the forum of a meeting between the Allied powers.[85] The French, however, were under pressure to enter into a moral engagement to move towards the removal of remaining controls, and intended, on completion of the signature of the treaty, to hand to the Germans a letter to this effect.[86] Following British representations Schuman agreed to amend the wording to convey that any action would be subject to Allied approval, but regretted that he could not delay delivery of the letter as this would undoubtedly result in a German refusal to proceed with the signature. The Foreign Office bowed to the inevitable and issued a statement to the effect that any overlap between existing controls and the machinery set up under the Schuman Plan was something which His Majesty's Government would discuss sympathetically.[87] In Paris the French made light of the matter by presenting the offending letter as merely an expression of their opinion, committing nobody but themselves. In reply to which, William Hayter of the British Embassy asked how they would react 'if the British Government in a letter to the Germans expressed their opinion that the Germans ought to have an army of 20 divisions "subject of course to French approval" '![88] To this jibe, the French retorted by reproaching Britain for being overly formalistic.

This was ironic, considering that the French had embarked upon the Schuman Plan with the attitude that controls were to remain in place, and had since used every device behind the scenes to prevent any relaxation until they judged the moment appropriate. Even as the international situation demanded a mobilisation of all available industrial capacity, France had used her position in the councils of the Western powers to thwart practical steps towards a monitored expansion of German steel output. Finally, faced with a German ultimatum, the French government accepted the abolition of all controls without reservation. With the same abruptness which had characterised the announcement of 9 May 1950, Britain was thus informed that the bodies on which she was represented: the Steel Control Group, and the International Authority for the Ruhr, were to be wound up as the Schuman Plan came into effect. Only the courtesies remained to be observed, and Britain and the United States were therefore invited to discuss how a transfer of functions might best be achieved to coincide with the eventual ratification of the treaty.[89]

In the United Kingdom, however, the surrender of control over German resources was viewed as rather more than a mere formality, particularly on account of the privileged access which this had allowed to convenient supplies of scrap metal for use in British steelmakers' furnaces. The Foreign Office was not convinced that it was worth making an issue of this point but the new Secretary of State, Herbert Morrison, obtained Cabinet approval to stand firm.[90] Following protracted negotiations, an agreement was finally concluded in September 1951, enabling the withdrawal of

British reservations regarding the elimination of all controls over the German steel industry upon the entry into force of the treaty of the European Coal and Steel Community.[91] Whether Morrison's predecessor, Ernest Bevin, would have thought the effort worthwhile for the sake of a few thousand tons of scrap metal is open to conjecture. Bevin had been dead for five months, however, and the Labour government whose foreign policy he had guided for the last five-and-a-half years of his life was coming to the end of its term in office. Within a month, a General Election had returned the Conservatives under Winston Churchill as the Schuman Plan treaty finally went forward for ratification by national parliaments. With that process complete in the French *Chambre des députés* in December 1951 and in the German *Bundestag* in January 1952, future British Foreign Secretaries would find economic relations with Federal Germany or France increasingly subsumed under a European heading.

On hearing the news of the German ratification, Jean Monnet sent a telegram to Konrad Adenauer: 'The Community is born, long live Europe.'[92] Certainly, the conclusion of the treaty was ripe with political significance and prefigured the establishment of a wider Community which would eventually become synonymous with Europe itself. The dawn of this new age had not, however, come about through a selfless sacrifice of French interests. On the contrary, France had used her position as an occupying power to hold the German steel industry prostrate while she extracted the most favourable deal.

Moreover, as a symbol of Franco-German rapprochement, the Schuman Plan was marred by the fact that France maintained an economic hold over the Saar in the face of German irredentism. While, under the Franco-Saar Conventions of 3 March 1950, the area had gained a wide measure of autonomy, links with France had been established on a firm contractual basis.[93] In particular, the Saar coal mines were to remain under French control for fifty years, subject to the payment of a royalty on every ton produced. Rather than remove this bone of contention as part of the Schuman Plan, the French chose to stand on the provisions for economic annexation sanctioned by the Western Allies. Under German pressure to make a formal statement of intent, to coincide with the signature of the treaty in April 1951, France took refuge in the formula employed in the tripartite Saar Agreement of February 1948.[94] Thus, an exchange of letters annexed to the treaty reiterated that the fate of the territory remained a subject for an eventual peace settlement.[95] In other words, the Saar would be run for the benefit of the French economy for the foreseeable future.

For the moment the Germans refrained from pursuing the matter further. The atmosphere was, however, soured in May 1951 by the banning by the Saar government of a political party committed to reunion with Germany.[96] Suspecting that France was pulling the strings, the Federal Chancellor, Konrad Adenauer, addressed a memorandum to the Allied High Commission, condemning the move and questioning the legal grounds for the political status of the Saar.[97] A French reply was ready within a few days.[98] While sound at the juridical level, it was thought in London that the general tone of this draft was 'somewhat abrupt and likely to be unnecessarily wounding to German susceptibilities'.[99] In the words of the Political Director of the Office of the UK High Commissioner, it sent the Chancellor away 'with a flea in his ear'.[100] A further two months' work was required to arrive at a reply which was sufficiently anodyne not to excite German opinion while still conveying that the matter was not open to discussion.[101]

In Paris the British Embassy learned that the process was so protracted due to the fact that every small drafting change had to be submitted to Schuman, who was taking the closest personal interest.[102] By this time Britain was increasingly torn between previous assurances of support, and recognition that what had been expedient in early 1948 was inappropriate to the new situation. In the appraisal of the British High Commissioner, Sir Ivone Kirkpatrick, the policy pursued by France was no longer tenable and the time had come to advise the French government accordingly.[103] Sir Ivone's concern was that the reopening of the controversy over the Saar might imperil ratification of the Schuman Plan treaty by the *Bundestag*. This would be to the detriment of Adenauer's avowed policy of building a new Europe on a solid Franco-German foundation.[104]

At a critical moment it was thus the British who were more mindful of this pitfall on the road to European union. The matter was a delicate one, however. After long deliberation a meeting was arranged in Paris between Schuman and the British and American Ambassadors on 26 October 1951 as an opportunity to suggest tactfully, as friends and allies, that the situation could not continue indefinitely. Schuman agreed that the political status of the Saar should be re-examined in the near future but made it clear that the policy of his government was that the territory should remain economically part of France.[105] There the matter rested. In the event, ratification by the Bundestag of the treaty establishing the European Coal and Steel Community was achieved without further concessions and it was not until 1957 that the Saar was returned to Germany.

For the last year of the Attlee government, however, it had been clear to Britain that France's hold over the economic life of the area was out of step with the reality of Europe in the 1950s. The French, despite having clothed the Schuman Plan in the rhetoric of European idealism, saw no incongruity in their position and remained wedded to the principle of economic attachment. This was in marked contrast to their view that the loss to Britain of supplies of steel scrap was a mere detail which should not be allowed to stand in the way of the Schuman Plan. On the scrap question Britain eventually arrived at a negotiated agreement with the Federal government. On the other hand, the French claim to the coal mines of the Saar for the next fifty years, in the face of German opposition, was tantamount to levying reparations from current production until the year 2000.

In his memoirs, published in 1976, Jean Monnet denounces French policy prior to May 1950 as being based on the outmoded notion of the rights of the victor over the vanquished.[106] Monnet does not, however, dwell on the point that, in the case of the Saar, France remained set to continue in this very style for a further fifty years even after the Schuman Plan. This is not to impute any cynicism to Monnet himself, who was the force behind the plan but did not have absolute control over the circumstances of its signature or ratification. The intention is, rather, to illustrate that the web of issues surrounding the genesis of the Coal and Steel Community did not resolve neatly into a choice between high ideals and base national interest, or between Europeanism and isolation. Nothing so simple. The first moves towards European integration were bound up with attempts by the French to procure the maximum material advantage, even to the extent of maintaining in the Saar a position which was an affront to their major partner and an embarrassment to their allies.

Even minus the Saar, the strength of West Germany's industrial base, for the moment lying dormant, was enormous. Writing some twenty-five years later, Monnet admits the sense of foreboding which the prospect of a revived German steel industry had aroused in him in 1950.[107] To the author of the French national plan for reconstruction and modernisation it was clear that, given a free hand, Germany would eventually resort to dumping production surpluses on export markets while France's steelworks languished behind protectionist barriers. According to Monnet the Schuman Plan was conceived as a framework in which the rival industries could be placed on an equal footing and thereby become the catalyst of European union. For the two founder members this would be a liberation: France would be free from the fear of German economic domination, while Germany would cast off the discrimination which was the legacy of defeat and occupation.

Committed to paper a quarter of a century later, this rationale overlooks the point that the restrictions imposed on the German steel industry would clearly have had to be lifted in any case. In fact such was the pressure for a relaxation of controls that the French were obliged to resort to every device at their disposal in order to delay the inevitable while the Schuman Plan came into effect. Nearer the event, it was a connection between the plan and the French obsession with the industrial power of the Ruhr basin which came to mind in the Foreign Office in May 1950.[108] In the British analysis it was this perennial concern which had culminated in what was, in Monnet's own account, a desperate intervention at the eleventh hour to prevent France from slipping back into the stagnation of the inter-war years.[109]

Rather than leave French economic planning at the mercy of the market, thoughts had already turned to some form of international organisation with powers of control. Monnet's stroke of genius was to give away the icing with the recipe for the cake. Thus, the announcement of 9 May 1950 promised a lasting peace between France and Germany, in token of which each would relinquish a degree of sovereignty to a High Authority. Presented in this light, an end to the free play of comparative advantage in the European coal and steel industries was a first step on the road to a saner world. On the other hand, this agenda postponed a general normalisation of relations with West Germany pending the satisfaction of pressing French interests. If Britain saw the Schuman Plan in these terms from the outset, neither was there anything in the circumstances surrounding the negotiation, signature and ratification of the eventual treaty which would tend to put a different complexion on matters.

From these muddy waters, however, arose the foundations of a new order. With the benefit of hindsight, a chapter was opening in which Britain's influence would come to be measured on a European scale and the prevailing creed of British parliamentary politics judged against the yardstick of Community orthodoxy. That much was still to come, however, and belonged to a Europe as yet still half-imagined and intangible. At the time, the reluctance of a Labour government to gamble with the future of Britain's basic industries was excusable. More significant was the confident identification of an underlying motive in the French enthusiasm for European integration. In the years since the war no-one had been made more aware of France's preoccupation with German coal and steel than His Majesty's Government. Throughout the search for the elusive quadripartite settlement; as Western Germany underwent its mutations through Bizone into Trizone and Federal Republic; while the Marshall Plan set the Ruhr at the heart of European recovery, this had been implicit in the French quest for an understanding with Britain on the broad economic questions of the day. Regardless of the wider implications of the Schuman Plan, therefore, it marked the end of a period during which Britain had dallied with the idea of building a post-war economic partnership with France yet had persistently skirted the question of German industrial recovery. As the Labour government ended, it was those very issues which had lain unheeded in the neglected corners of Anglo-French co-operation which were now addressed under the banner of European unity.

8 The Parting of the Ways

THE LIMITS OF INTEGRATION

As progress towards the formation of the Coal and Steel Community gathered momentum it was clear that a watershed had been reached in Anglo-French relations. After years of looking across the Channel for inspiration France had seized the reins of her own destiny, leaving Britain only the choice of whether to come along for the ride. This was perhaps expressed most cogently by David Butt of the Economic Section of the Cabinet Office, who recalled attention to the central issue in a letter to the Foreign Office: 'Surely we are not debating whether the Community is a good or a bad thing, but whether we should or should not join it.'[1] This was from the same official who had, in the early weeks of 1947, been occupied with in-depth analyses of the possibility of co-ordinating British and French economic policies on the basis of the Monnet Plan.[2] Four years later Monnet's latest creation was a far cry from the vision of Europe which had given rise to that early work by Butt and his colleagues.

It was the belief that a close relationship between Britain and France would form the cornerstone of post-war Europe which had led the Foreign Secretary of the day, Ernest Bevin, to establish the Anglo-French Economic Co-operation Committee in 1946 as a forum in which the economic plans of the two countries might be opened to examination. The original aim was that the recovery programmes of the two countries should be 'helpfully related' to each other, but at the request of the President of the Board of Trade, Stafford Cripps, these terms of reference were diluted to seeking to 'prevent conflicts' between the respective plans.[3] From the outset, therefore, Bevin's policy was susceptible to the conflicting pressures of Cabinet government even as he contrived to keep relations with France abreast of developments.

In January 1947 during Cabinet consideration of the proposed visit by Léon Blum, it was again Cripps who was wary of being drawn into discussion of the Monnet Plan. Bevin, however, was anxious that the visit should go ahead, if only as a gesture of solidarity with a fellow moderate Socialist.

> We should do anything we could to strengthen the position of his Government; for France was now at the crossroads and if his Government could survive, this would be very valuable not only for France but for the whole future of social democracy in Europe.[4]

This objective was not, however, foremost in the minds of all present, as is witnessed by the fact that the extract of these minutes circulated in the Board of Trade omitted the above passage on Cripps's instructions.[5] Nevertheless, despite the reservations expressed in Cabinet, officials later that month left for Paris to have an account of the Monnet Plan.

At this moment Bevin returned to the charge with a Cabinet Paper urging a study of the practicability of either a customs union or some other special economic arrangement between the United Kingdom and either France or Western Europe as a whole.[6] The Cabinet felt that such an exercise would take up too much time and preferred to commission a general appraisal of the options by economists outside the government service.[7] This group, which was recruited mainly from the staff of Cambridge University at the start of term, did not report until late October.[8] By this time the work had been overtaken by events, becoming absorbed in a yet wider study of the possibility of a customs union between the countries of the Marshall Plan.[9] Following the deliberations of the Cambridge dons the question was passed to an interdepartmental group under the leadership of the Board of Trade, whose officials decided on the unusual step of starting work on their report in advance of the first meeting. In the words of Sir Edmund Hall-Patch, the Board seemed to be 'trying to strangle this baby fairly early in life'.[10]

In the meantime Bevin's speech on the occasion of the exchange of ratifications of the Treaty of Dunkirk in September 1947 had envisaged an ever closer economic partnership between the two countries.[11] These same sentiments resurfaced later that month in a conversation with the French Premier, Paul Ramadier, during which Bevin proposed that they should set in train an examination of measures aimed at closer understanding and ultimate union between the two countries.[12] This was a source of satisfaction to the francophile British Ambassador, Duff Cooper, who recorded in his diary: 'The conversation went very well and I was glad to have been present. As we came away Bevin said to me "We've made the union of England and France this morning".'[13] It was clear that the Anglo-French relationship retained its hold on Bevin's imagination even as the economic landscape of Western Europe was about to be transformed by the Marshall Plan.

Not that Europe was uppermost in the minds of officials taking part in a preliminary examination of the issues arising from Bevin's conversation with Ramadier. In Paris, Duff Cooper was dismayed to learn that much of the time at this interdepartmental meeting had been taken up with the implications for Britain's relations with Eire.[14] Even when discussion returned to the matter in hand, the question of combining British and

French resources was dealt with solely in the context of what the two Empires had to offer by way of agricultural produce and raw materials. Rice from Indo-China and oil from the Middle East were mentioned but the development of industrial assets in the European area did not enter into the discussion.[15]

Undaunted, Bevin began 1948 with a Cabinet Paper: 'The First Aim of British Foreign Policy', urging the consolidation of Western Europe.[16] Requested as soon as possible, this paper had been hurriedly prepared, providing no opportunity for comments by the Economic Section of the Foreign Office, much to the irritation of its experts.[17] On this occasion Bevin carried his Cabinet colleagues, however, and regardless of the sensibilities of his officials, was able to forge ahead and cable to the Paris Embassy:

> In this enterprise it is essential that there should be close Anglo-French co-operation in every field and I am resolved to do all in my power to foster the closest relationship between our two countries.[18]

This was to be but the beginning. Bevin explained to the Embassy in Brussels that the next step would be to invite the Benelux countries to join Britain and France in a treaty on the Dunkirk model. This was advance notice of a parliamentary speech he intended to make two days later.[19] Meanwhile, in response to the complaint that the Economic Section had not been consulted, Sir Orme Sargent revealed that Bevin's idea was to create a 'spiritual union' of all countries believing in certain common principles; economic and political aspects being subsidiary.[20] To Roger Makins this seemed nothing but vacuous nonsense. Assuring that he was in no way leading a mutiny, he nevertheless felt obliged to put his feelings on record before Bevin spoke.[21]

There is nothing to indicate that Sir Orme Sargent conveyed the full force of these opinions to the Foreign Secretary. Bevin was, in any case, not usually disposed to let the tail wag the dog. Opening for the government in the Foreign Affairs Debate on 22 January 1948, he unashamedly employed the expression 'spiritual union' which had so disgusted Makins.[22] With a warm reference to France, he said that, although no formal political union was proposed for the moment, Britain would maintain the closest possible contact and work for ever closer unity between the two nations. Western Europe would spring from the Treaty of Dunkirk, extended to embrace, in the first instance, the Benelux countries.[23] With regard to the consequences of the Marshall Plan, Bevin had neither any objection to the element of European interdependence implied, nor any fear of being in thrall to the United States, upon whose economic support he counted.[24]

In all this Bevin could see that Germany would have a part to play, but he remained convinced that her recovery should not take precedence over that of her former victims.[25] The conception of Western Union presented to Parliament was thus an essentially Anglo-French view of post-war Europe underwritten by the United States. It remained to be seen to what extent these elements were compatible. In the meantime the Treaty of Brussels between Britain, France, Belgium, Luxembourg and the Netherlands was signed on 17 March 1948.[26] This departed from the pattern of the Treaty of Dunkirk in that it provided for mutual assistance in the event of military aggression from any quarter, whereas the original had committed Britain and France only in the case of hostilities involving Germany.[27] For their part, Britain and France would have preferred to follow the same formula for the new treaty, but the Benelux countries felt that to identify Germany as the major threat would not reflect the reality of the situation.[28] Clearly, however, in Bevin's mind the Anglo-French relationship remained the pivotal one. The 'grand design' which he had formulated upon taking office had survived until 1948 but the Europe in which it was coming to fruition was not the Europe of 1945. The new facts of life included not only a bipolar Europe where Germany was no longer the principal threat, but also a Europe founded on American aid and forged in the heat of the Marshall Plan.

As implied by its official name: the European Recovery Programme, this was envisaged as a combined effort. The United States gave assistance on the understanding that the projects funded in each recipient country would interlock to form a coherent whole. The eyes of His Majesty's Government were on wider horizons, however. It was early decided that, while Britain would co-operate as far as possible with other OEEC countries, the use of Marshall Aid should be planned to free her as rapidly as possible from outside support.[29] In effect this meant that advantage had to be taken of the opportunities presented by traditional trade links in preference to forming new relationships with partners in Europe. This strategy bore fruit and, in January 1949, the London Committee Working Party on Long-Term Programmes reported that: 'We are in a position where our export trade stands to lose more than it could possibly gain from "co-operative action".'[30] In fact Britain was able to dispense with Marshall Aid ahead of schedule, and before her European neighbours, by the end of 1950.[31]

Nevertheless, all of the Marshall Plan countries were prevailed upon to submit long-term programmes compatible with a sustainable recovery on the European scale. From the early days the British delegation in Paris recognised the French lead in the techniques of economic planning and took care to familiarise themselves with the Monnet Plan.[32] It was left to the French, however, during a session of the Anglo-French Economic Co-operation Committee at the end of August 1948, to suggest that it might be desirable to hold bilateral discussions on the two long-term programmes before their submission to the OEEC.[33] This proved difficult to arrange, in part because of the reluctance of the Treasury to have the matter dealt with through the medium of the Anglo-French Committee, which was under Foreign Office chairmanship.[34] It was eventually agreed that a meeting should be arranged between the British and French delegations in Paris on 29 October 1948, the day before the British were due to give an account of their programme in the OEEC.[35]

During that discussion it emerged that of most concern to the French was the pattern of international trade envisaged by the British programme. At a time when currencies were not generally convertible, European reserves of the most useful medium of exchange, the US dollar, were depleted by large purchases of American goods for which no alternative source of supply existed. Some essential raw materials were, however, available where British influence lingered; so that wool from Australia, rubber from Malaya, or oil from the Middle East could be bought for pounds sterling. The problem was to generate enough revenue in that same currency to pay for those purchases. Examination of the long-term programme revealed that Britain herself intended to be the major supplier to the Sterling Area; a plan which would exclude France from any post-war boom in sales of capital equipment, leaving her the trade in wine and perfume in a world avid for machinery. Worse still, the programme also precluded any possibility that France might earn sufficient sterling from exports across the Channel to the United Kingdom.

In these circumstances the British and French intentions were far from compatible and the examination of the British programme in the OEEC on 30 October 1948 was thus the occasion of a strong attack by the French, who criticised it for being likely to make the pound sterling as scarce as the dollar, to the detriment of all Europe.[36] The British defence revolved around possibilities which existed for members to earn sterling through multilateral trade; France, for example, could profit from the export of rice from Indo-China to Hong Kong and Malaya. This was far removed from the role which the French had imagined themselves playing in the post-war world and was scarcely in keeping with the level of economic activity implicit in the Monnet Plan.

In his new posting to the OEEC in Paris, Bevin's economic adviser over the last three years, Sir Edmund Hall-Patch, was quick to grasp the significance. Sir Edmund was a hard-headed pessimist not given to excessive francophile tendencies.[37] Nevertheless he now sought authorisation to press ahead with a determined effort to achieve co-ordination between the British and French long-term programmes. He acknowledged that this meant staking Britain's recovery on the success of the French programme but feared that to hold back would make its failure a self-fulfilling prophesy. While eliciting from the French such tokens of good faith as might circumscribe the risk, he felt that the time was ripe to throw in Britain's lot with that of France.[38] This logic ran counter to that put forward by Sir Edmund's successor back at the Foreign Office, Roger Makins, who saw no reason why the French should expect the British to 'carry them on our backs for the next four years'.[39] The issues could not have been presented with greater clarity. Europe was on the threshold of a general revival and the future interaction of the national economies involved would be determined by the directions taken during that process. If the Anglo-French relationship was to encompass integration of production or co-ordinated use of resources, a full commitment could not be delayed indefinitely.

Hall-Patch suggested that some 'straight talking at a Ministerial level' might be the order of the day.[40] The Chancellor of the Exchequer was now Sir Stafford Cripps, who during his term as President of the Board of Trade, had shown little enthusiasm for closer Anglo-French economic relations. This was not, however, in the nature of an attack on the Foreign Secretary but merely reflected a different priority. Despite marked differences of character, Bevin and Cripps recognised in each other a sense of duty which transcended personal ambition, so that by the time the latter was ensconced in the Treasury, mutual trust was firmly established.[41] In any case, the fateful decision did not belong to Cripps alone but was discussed at a session of the Economic Policy Committee chaired by the Prime Minister, Clement Attlee. At this meeting, on 25 November 1948, there was general agreement that the French long-term programme did not inspire sufficient confidence to permit an adjustment of British plans to accord with its assumptions. Ernest Bevin was not present but it was his Parliamentary Under-Secretary, Christopher Mayhew, who in fact took the lead in casting doubts on the viability of the French economy in the absence of far-reaching reforms.[42]

The next day Hall-Patch himself attended a discussion at the Treasury. After hearing that Mayhew had kept Bevin informed by telephone, this meeting concerned itself with the practical steps to be taken. It would be presumptuous to lecture the French on the measures required to put their house in order but it was hoped that the Chancellor might arrange to be invited to Paris for a review of the situation in general terms.[43] Meanwhile it was decided to be brutally honest. Accordingly a letter went, over Cripps's signature, to the French Minister of Finance, Henri Queuille.[44]

> I should be less than frank with you if I were not to let you know that under existing circumstances we are bound to have hesitation in placing reliance upon the fulfilment of the programme which you have forecast for France. This hesitation arises entirely from our fear that the financial and fiscal conditions which exist are not such as to make the realization of this programme possible.[45]

The reply from Queuille was equally frank and reiterated the charge that the British programme was biased towards the Sterling Area, heedless of European concerns.[46]

This note of discord sounded the death knell for an idea which had been in the air since 1946, when the Monnet Plan had first raised the question of Anglo-French integration. There was now no longer any need to meditate on the form that this might take. Either Britain put her faith in the French long-term programme or she did not. Unlike the situation in 1947 when attempts to align British policy with the Monnet Plan had eventually fizzled out, this was a decision which did not go by default. Whatever the academic appeal of interlocking economies, faced with a stark choice in these circumstances His Majesty's Government came down on the side of caution. Nor was this a case of civil servants foisting the Foreign Office line on an unwary Secretary of State. The open difference of opinion between two senior figures, Makins and Hall-Patch, precluded any fudging of the issues, and Bevin, through his Parliamentary Under-Secretary, thus participated in the decision of the Cabinet Committee in the full knowledge of what was at stake. With this turn of events the vision of a post-war Europe turning on an Anglo-French axis was effectively consigned to the realm of might-have-been.

Not that the needs of France were a matter of indifference. In early 1949 Stafford Cripps undertook a number of visits to Paris to explore those areas where import controls might be relaxed to admit increased quantities of specific goods to the benefit of the French balance of trade.[47] Nor did the Chancellor object when an *ad hoc* session of the Anglo-French Economic Co-operation Committee in February 1949, augmented for the occasion by members of the respective planning staffs, led to direct contact between Jean Monnet and Sir Edwin Plowden.[48] Monnet was eager for his *Commissariat au Plan* and Plowden's Central Economic Planning Staff to work together in transcending narrow national interests and was disappointed to learn that Plowden's position allowed him considerably less scope for deviation from the official line than did his own.[49] Nevertheless the cordial relations which were established between the two planners proved a useful adjunct to the normal lines of communication between London and Paris and formed the background to an invitation by Monnet for Plowden to join him at his home in France where they would explore the possibilities in the company of a small group of their close associates.[50]

Plowden arrived at Monnet's house on 21 April 1949 accompanied by Alan Hitchman, the member of his team at the CEPS most closely involved with the long-term programmes, and Robert Hall, the head of the Economic Section of the Cabinet Office. Over the next four days the three Englishmen remained closeted with Monnet and his two colleagues, Étienne Hirsch and Pierre Uri. It was Uri who provided the inspiration for the idea that, rather than waste money on subsidies to British farmers, advantage should be taken of the more favourable conditions in France, where agriculture could be developed to specialise in meat production for the British market. This would be offset against assured deliveries of British coal to France, making each country dependent on the other for those commodities in which the partner enjoyed natural advantages of production. Whatever the economic merits of the scheme, however, the political will for its implementation did not exist in the United Kingdom, where Bevin's indifference was clear evidence of the change which had taken place. From the time he took office until November 1948, the Foreign Secretary had time and again promoted unity between Britain and France as the very engine-room of a new Europe. With the decision of the Cabinet Committee on the French long-term programme, however, the die had effectively been cast. When Plowden met Monnet the time for acts of faith was already past.

THE GERMAN QUESTION

For Monnet, economic partnership with the United Kingdom had implications beyond beefsteak and coal. Proposing to Plowden that they should hold the famous talks at his home, he was sure of the direction in which the discussion must inevitably turn.

He felt that those taking part would quickly find they were discussing the relationship of Germany to Western Europe. In his view neither England nor France had any positive policy towards Germany and that unless they soon developed a common one, they would find themselves disputing about the line to be taken towards a resurgent Germany, economically the equal of either.[51]

As part of the preparatory work for Plowden's trip, the Central Economic Planning Staff accordingly decided to ask the Foreign Office for their appraisal of those factors which would determine the scope for joint action.[52] It emerged, however, that this request entailed breaking new ground in analysis; an enormous task to which the Foreign Office felt unable to do justice at such short notice.

Plowden's brief before leaving for France consequently amounted to little more than advice from Roger Makins to steer clear of any commitment to grandiose schemes and confine the discussions as far as possible to the bread-and-butter issues of bilateral agreements and tariff reductions.[53] Monnet recalls that as the talks progressed he raised the subject of Germany but, while Plowden accepted that this was a question which ought to be jointly addressed, the impression given was that it was not for the moment one of burning importance to the British.[54] This lukewarm response was understandable given that the Foreign Office had been unable to provide a coherent expression of British policy in this respect.

In a conversation with Robert Hall later that year Monnet again bemoaned the fact that neither Britain nor France seemed to have any sense of purpose or any idea of what to do with Germany. Developing the theme that the key to European stability lay in Anglo-French relations, he returned to the idea of a gesture of mutual confidence based on the exchange of coal for meat. Hall sympathised with Monnet but recorded in his diary: 'But I don't think anyone in the Foreign Office cares about all this, or cares that there is no German policy.'[55] After consultation with all concerned, it was Plowden who wrote to Monnet with the news that he was nursing a forlorn hope.[56]

Plowden, who later developed an enduring friendship with Monnet, identifies this as the moment when he turned his attention to the possibility of a Franco-German understanding.[57] This opinion is borne out by a comment two days after the announcement of the Schuman Plan when Sir Edmund Hall-Patch contrived to exchange a few words with Jean Monnet and found him uncharacteristically reticent regarding the origins of the scheme. It nevertheless seemed obvious that Monnet had been closely involved and this news was sent back to London with an indication of the tenor of the conversation:

> Incidentally you should know that there was a hint of 'Well, you had your chance' in his attitude and a sly reference or two to the talks with Plowden last year which we were not very keen about at the time and which came to nothing.[58]

The time had been when Hall-Patch had himself advocated a joint Anglo-French basis to long-term planning.[59] Good civil servant that he was, Sir Edmund had seemingly accepted being overruled without rancour, though he saw to the heart of the matter probably better than anyone. By the Autumn of 1948 there was already a noticeable shift in French political opinion towards some form of international control over basic materials, such as coal and steel, which would embrace a revived Germany.[60] In early December Sir Edmund became aware that the French were drawing the logical conclusion from British reluctance to be involved in co-ordination of investment or specialisation within the OEEC. Rather than wait for Britain and other laggards, it seemed that there might be a move afoot in France to form a working party with the Benelux countries, Italy and the Bizone. The French official floating this idea was obviously only thinking aloud, but, in view of his influence, Sir Edmund felt that the possibility should be taken seriously. 'In particular we shall need to consider the political as well as the economic implications of the organisation of this work on a basis which separates the continent from the U.K.'[61] It was foreseen that this might entail cartel-like arrangements such as were already being mooted. The difference now was that British participation was not being canvassed and the target membership had been reduced to a select club of six.

If this was a foretaste of things to come the idea still lacked the Monnet touch. Monnet was otherwise occupied, however, and it was not until Plowden's letter at the end of 1949 that the future architect of the Coal and Steel Community came to accept that it was not the course of Anglo-French co-operation which would determine the agenda for the consolidation of Europe.

In the meantime there was reason enough to believe that the core issues were amenable to the combined influence of Britain and France. In a conversation with Robert Schuman in January 1949, Ernest Bevin said that it was essential that there should be a day-to-day collaboration between the two countries on matters relating to Germany. A community of interests was recognised which transcended Britain's relations with

The Parting of the Ways

the United States, whose policy was regarded as being overly concerned with the revival of German industry. In a warm spirit of Anglo-French solidarity, Bevin assured Schuman that: 'together His Majesty's Government and the French Government should be able to guide the United States Government aright.'[62]

Other factors were in play, however. In June 1948 the Soviet Union had begun a blockade of the Western zones of Berlin which lasted for nearly a year. During that period the city was supplied entirely by air; a mammoth task involving thousands of tons each day, with planes arriving and departing every thirty seconds at peak-time. An operation on such a scale could not have been mounted without the participation of the US Air Force. Also of importance was the contribution of the German population, who gave their labour willingly to build new runways and endured whatever hardships were necessary to stand firm against the Soviet action. The Germans were becoming, to all intents and purposes, the allies of the West.[63]

Not that British policy underwent an immediate conversion. The Berlin Airlift was in its eighth month when, true to Bevin's promise, the United Kingdom stood alongside France to resist American pressure for a reprieve of German steelworks on 31 March 1949.[64] Four days later the signing of the North Atlantic Treaty marked a formal commitment by the United States to the security of Western Europe. That September it was announced that the Soviet Union had exploded its first nuclear device, yet it was November before Ernest Bevin came out in favour of the American view that a few blast furnaces was a price worth paying to bring West Germany into the fold.[65] Even then, Britain's interpretation of the Petersberg Protocol was less than generous and it was only over the following months that a softening British attitude diverged from the continuing hard line taken by the French.[66]

All the same, a shift in priorities was apparent as Britain gave back the very steelworks which she had been intent on destroying earlier in the year. From closing ranks with France to falling into line behind the United States had taken the eight months between March and November 1949. The period during which Monnet pursued his quest for Anglo-French unity with Plowden and Hall thus coincided with a turning-point in British policy towards Germany. Unable to give any indication of their government's intentions in this respect, the two Englishmen were hamstrung in their response. Born of frustration, Hall's comment that there was 'no German policy' was the complaint of an economist. The impression of inertia was deceptive, however. Seemingly hanging motionless, the pendulum was merely at the end of its swing. With the next tick of the clock the sleeping giant of German industry would stir at the sound of a new voice calling from the West.

THE NEW EUROPE

If the rehabilitation of the Federal Republic had yet to reach its logical conclusion, the scene was none the less set. In the post-war balance sheet, East German real estate on the Soviet side was offset against West German capital assets on the account of the Atlantic powers. Nothing in an Anglo-French partnership could re-write this equation. The only unknown quantity was the extent to which life in such a bipolar world would be a shared experience.

On the economic level, the answer had already emerged as American dollars flowed into Western Europe. Conceived in a bleak time of shortage, the vision of Britain and France drawing closer together through mutual support on the road to recovery did not adapt well to the hot-house conditions of the Marshall Plan. The sudden influx of aid faced both countries with decisions which allowed no time for the slow and sure building of confidence day by day and year by year. The paths of Britain and France thus diverged, although to the American way of thinking the idea of integration was inherent in the European Recovery Programme (ERP). Still awaited, however, was a coherent expression of what this might entail. Lunching with the Administrator of the ERP in January 1949, Sir Edmund Hall-Patch noted that 'the same woolly concept of "integration" still exists in Mr. Hoffman's mind as when he visited Europe in July 1948'.[67]

In any case it had been decided that the first priority for Britain was to achieve independence from outside assistance as soon as possible.[68] The Marshall Plan was thus seen more as a stepping-stone out of the morass than as the first foundation of a bridge between nations. Yet although the annals of the European Recovery Programme abound with examples of a pervading British antipathy to economic integration, in the absence of clearly defined objectives this hardly broke any promises. On the other hand, the failure to harness British recovery to the French long-term programme consigned to the same limbo an option which had been high on the agenda for Ernest Bevin and those of like mind since the early days of the Monnet Plan. Unlike the evasion of entanglements linked to American aid, the discarding of this piece of political baggage marked the end of a singularly British approach to the consolidation of Europe.

The Parting of the Ways

Moreover, in the months which followed, relations with Germany became increasingly dictated by the iron logic of bloc politics. While Britain adjusted to the political and economic consequences with fluent pragmatism, the transition from war to peace, from occupation to co-operation, was seen from a different perspective in France. To the French, the crude rationale of the Cold War did not provide an adequate conceptual frame work for co-existence with their West German neighbour. With British interest at a low ebb, it was consequently a French initiative which eventually formed the basis of an acceptable *modus vivendi* in May 1950.

This is not to imply that there was no more to the Schuman Plan than is recorded in the foregoing pages. Certainly, there was in Europe a widespread desire for change which the Coal and Steel Community fulfilled. For many, the war had left an abiding sense of weariness and disgust with the endless futility of it all. In France, there were senior citizens who had lived through the previous war with Germany, and the one before that. Those in their eighties would have seen their homeland devastated three times since Krupp developed breech-loading artillery. Enough was enough. Even as the conflict ground to a bitter end, in the Resistance movements and the prison camps men and women lived in hope of breaking the perpetual cycle of aggression and mistrust for all time.

This was the motivation behind the Hague Congress of May 1948 and the formation of the Council of Europe. During these days of hope and idealism, there were many who felt that the system of nation-states in Europe had brewed enough mischief and was in need of a fundamental overhaul. Progress on a wide front lost momentum, however, as the impact of the intellectual surge was absorbed in the channels and backwaters of inter-governmental discussion. While a United States of Europe awaited some bright tomorrow, Jean Monnet resolved to produce a breakthrough which was 'profound, real, immediate'.[69]

That the means chosen should improve the prospects for France's own industrial development is not remarkable. It could hardly have been otherwise. For Monnet's line of action to be readily applicable it had to reflect French aspirations as they stood at that moment. This element of enlightened self-interest, however, detracts nothing from the seminal importance of the Schuman Plan, which effectively ended the speculation as to what European integration might, could or should mean. Before talks began on prices, quotas and subsidies, Monnet insisted that the devolution of sovereignty to a High Authority was one principle which was beyond discussion. The hinge of History turned and the unification of Europe took the 'community' route.

The Schuman Plan was a not, however, Monnet's first attempt to build a new Europe by letting form follow function. Nor was West Germany his first choice of partner for the pilot scheme. Early in 1948 Monnet was convinced that Britain would turn towards Europe through the medium of an Anglo-French Union rather than become 'another star on the American flag'.[70] Neither was this just some fanciful notion of his own; there was every reason to believe that, though such a union might not be imminent, the possibility occupied British thinking in the highest political circles.[71]

The hope that something might be made of economic relations between Britain and France which would establish a European framework for the re-emergence of Germany as an industrial power figured prominently in Monnet's contacts with Plowden and Hall during 1949.[72] Such was not to be, however, and years later Monnet remained haunted by the suspicion that the British had understood his purpose better than they had revealed at the time.[73] In fact, there is no evidence to suggest that anyone on the British side followed Monnet's train of thought to what he saw as its logical conclusion. On the other hand, Robert Hall displayed considerable prescience in his assessment of what would be the ultimate challenge of a purely Anglo-French economic partnership.

> To my mind this can only be successful if there is a kind of federation, and the minimum required is to have a common monetary system, which requires a common central bank and common exchange control regulations.[74]

An Anglo-French Union which successfully tackled this question would already have cleared a hurdle which remains insurmountable to the countries of the European Union over forty years later. In the event, the Anglo-French relationship proved unequal to the task of leading Europe down this path. Even Monnet's proposal for a trailblazing project limited to an exchange of British coal for French beef failed to gain any support in London.

It was this British indifference which spurred Monnet to employ whatever other means presented themselves. The road down which he took Europe thus began in a certain set of circumstances, a particular balance of interests. So, although the Schuman Plan was in one respect a triumph of reason over nationalism, it could not be other than a product of its times. Of course, the goal of a European federation had an enduring appeal which still retains the power to inspire. On the other hand, the conviction expressed in the famous declaration of 9 May 1950 that one of Europe's main tasks was to develop the continent of Africa was long ago discred-

The Parting of the Ways 139

ited. If, in retrospect, the seeds of modern Europe are discernable in the Schuman Plan, so also is evidence of an attitude on the part of the French which was later to bring them so much grief in Algeria.

It is obviously beyond the scope of these pages to dwell on events in French North Africa and the constitutional crisis which they eventually provoked. The intention is merely to illustrate the pitfalls of judging the Schuman Plan solely on its success in capturing the spirit of the age. Such an approach inevitably leads to the question of Britain's refusal to participate in the manifest destiny of the European nations. Stripped of rhetoric and considered objectively, however, the Schuman Plan occupies a frame of reference which relegates this familiar question to a postscript. Coal requirements in France, steel production in Germany, and the long-term pattern of supply and demand in Europe were subjects which had preoccupied the French for five years. Throughout most of this period there had been an expectation that, despite setbacks and misunderstandings, these matters would somehow fall into place as Europe reformed around a nucleus of Anglo-French unity. Brutally disabused of this notion in the autumn of 1949, Jean Monnet had found an alternative point of departure by the following spring.

Thus, the Schuman Plan, rather than precipitating Britain's rejection of a role in Europe, was symptomatic of a divergence which had already occurred. The Coal and Steel Community was in this respect a French response to the fading of an older dream: a vision of Britain and France united. That was not now to be. A beacon of hope in times of adversity, the torch passed from Churchill to Bevin burned less brightly in peacetime until the flame lit by Jean Monnet in 1939 shone too faintly for even this most far-sighted of Frenchmen to see the way forward. Allies but not partners, Britain and France had fallen short of an ideal to which only they could aspire. For the want of this paradigm of political and economic symmetry, Europe was condemned to limp from makeshift to makeshift in search of an identity. It need not have been so. Between Europe of the heroes and Europe of the clerks, something had been lost. Among the flotsam and jetsam of those turbulent years lay the Anglo-French heart of the Europe that never was.

Notes

Notes to the Introduction

1. Jean Monnet, *Mémoires* (Paris: Fayard, 1976) pp. 13–36.
2. *Hansard*, HC DEB, vol. 408, col. 769, 21 February 1945.
3. *Hansard*, HC DEB, vol. 410, col. 84, 25 April 1945.
4. FO 371/49066, Z.2029, personal note from Churchill to Eden, 5 February 1945.
5. Of the many commentaries on the Potsdam Conference, see in particular the relevant pages in: Alan Bullock, *Ernest Bevin: Foreign Secretary 1945–1951* (Oxford University Press, 1985) pp. 25–30; John W. Young, *France, the Cold War and the Western Alliance* (Leicester University Press, 1990) pp. 58–63. At the Public Record Office, records of meetings are in CAB 99/38–40; miscellaneous files occupy the class FO 934.

Notes to Chapter 1: The Road from Ruin

1. FO 371/49069, Z.9196, press cutting of an article by Hubert Beuve-Méry in *Le Monde*, 31 July 1945.
2. FO 800/464, Fr/45/1, letter from Cooper to Bevin, 31 July 1945; letter from Bevin to Cooper, 4 August 1945.
3. FO 371/49069, Z.9501, notes on a conversation with Bevin by P. Dean. 8 August 1945.
4. BT 13/220A, President's Morning Meeting no. 7, 13 August 1945, minutes of daily briefing by Sir Stafford Cripps to his officials at the Board of Trade, during which he gave an account of his discussion with Bevin and the Chancellor, Hugh Dalton.
5. FO 371/49069, Z.9595, record of meeting, 13 August 1945. See also: John W. Young, *Britain, France and the Unity of Europe, 1945–51* (Leicester University Press, 1984) p. 14.
6. Duff Cooper, *Old Men Forget: The Autobiography of Duff Cooper (Viscount Norwich)* (London: Rupert Hart-Davis, 1953) p. 361.
7. FO 371/49069, Z.9595, note from P. Dean to Mr Hoyer-Millar, 17 August 1945.
8. FO 371/59978, Z.7069, record of a conversation between Ashley Clarke and Hervé Alphand, 26 July 1946.
9. Ibid., letter from Harvey to Hoyer-Millar, 31 July 1946.
10. FO 371/59954, Z.6814, minute by Hebblethwaite.
11. Ibid.
12. FO 371/59954, Z.6814, minute by Hoyer-Millar, 3 August 1946.
13. CAB 129/9, CP(46)197, 17 May 1946, record of conversation at the Canadian Embassy the previous evening printed as a Cabinet paper for circulation to Ministers.
14. FO 371/59978, Z.7116, record of meeting, 8 August 1946.

15. CAB 129/10, CP(46)218, 'The Cost of the British Zone in Germany', 4 June 1946.
16. Ibid.
17. CAB 129/10, CP(46)223, 7 June 1946.
18. CAB 134/596, ORC(46)52, 17 June 1946, paper circulated to the Overseas Reconstruction Committee: a Cabinet Committee of which the Foreign Secretary was Chairman.
19. Ibid.
20. FO 371/59978, Z.7116, letter from Dixon to Hoyer-Millar, 11 August 1946.
21. BT 11/2631, letter from Cooper to Bevin, 21 August 1946.
22. Conference to consider draft treaties with Italy, Finland, Hungary, Romania and Bulgaria.
23. BT 11/2631, letter from Bidault to Attlee, 21 August 1946.
24. BT 11/3357, record of meeting at 11.30, 5 September 1946.
25. Ibid.
26. CAB 128/6, CM(46)82, 17 September 1946, Cabinet meeting.
27. FO 371/59982, Z.9438, Lintott to Waley, 15 October 1946.
28. *State Papers*, vol. 145, p. 775, Agreement and Joint Statement, Great Britain and USA, 6 December 1945.
29. FO 371/59982, Z.9438, Lintott to Waley, 15 October 1946.
30. FO 371/59982, Z.9615, 'Anglo-French Economic Collaboration', draft note by the Board of Trade, 14 October 1946.
31. Ibid. Underlining in original.
32. CAB 128/6, CM(46)82, 17 September 1946.
33. FO 371/59982, Z.9615, 'Anglo-French Economic Collaboration', Draft note by the Board of Trade, 14 October 1946.
34. FO 371/59981, Z.9339, Minute by Gandy, 25 October 1946.
35. FO 371/59982, Z.9615, minutes of meeting held on 21 October 1946 at 3 pm to consider Anglo-French economic co-ordination, p. 2.
36. FO 371/59982, Z.9984, minutes of meeting held at the Board of Trade at 3 pm on 8 November 1946, p. 2.
37. Ibid.
38. Jean Monnet, *Mémoires* (Paris: Fayard, 1976) p. 308. Translation by this author.
39. FO 371/59982, Z.10427, letter from Cooper to Foreign Office, 7 December 1946.
40. FO 371/59982, Z.10112, minute by Hebblethwaite, 13 December 1946.
41. BT 13/220A, MM(47)3rd Meeting, President's Morning Meeting, 3 January 1947.
42. BT 13/220A, MM(47)4th Meeting, President's Morning Meeting, 6 January 1947.
43. BT 11/3357, note, Lintott to Brown, 6 January 1947.
44. Cooper, *Old Men Forget*, p. 379.
45. CAB 128/9, CM(47)2, 6 January 1947.
46. PREM 8/516, letter, 8 January 1947 (Bevin's draft is to be found in FO 800/465, file 66, Fr/47/3).
47. BT 11/3357, Rowe-Dutton to Hall-Patch, 2 January 1947.
48. *The Economist*, 14 December 1946, vol. 151, no. 5390, pp. 954–957.
49. BT 11/3357, note by Lintott, 22 January 1947.

50. Published as a White paper: Cmd 6811, May 1946.
51. BT 11/3357, note by Lintott, 22 January 1947.
52. BT 11/3357, note by Sanders, 23 January 1947.
53. BT 11/3357, CRT 130/47, note by Lintott, 30 January 1947.
54. BT 11/3357, letter from James Meade to Lee (Ministry of Supply), 24 January 1947.
55. BT 11/3428, Board of Trade paper: 'Relation of the Monnet Plan to U.K. Economic Planning', 10 February 1947.
56. T 230/24, EC(S)(47)1 (revise), *'The Monnet Plan'*, by D. Butt, 11 January 1947.
57. Ibid.
58. CAB 134/190, ED(47)11, 23 January 1947, Meade's account of the talks in Paris (a copy also exists in BT 11/3357).
59. Ibid.
60. In conjunction with Meade's paper (ED(47)11) a reprint of the article in *The Economist*, 14 December 1946, was circulated to the Committee as ED(47)12.
61. T 230/24, EC(S)(47)4, 'A Note on the Theory of the Integration of the Investment Programmes of France and Britain', by D. Butt, 1 February 1947.
62. Ibid.
63. Ibid.
64. BT 11/3357, note from Meade to Lintott, 6 February 1947.
65. BT 11/3357, note of a meeting on 14 February 1947.
66. BT 64/2268, letter, 4 March 1947, from Mitchell (Ministry of Supply) to Miss Frost (Board of Trade) with his (belated) comments on the record of the meeting: 'I am quite sure that Mr. Nowell agreed that steel was a special case.' Miss Frost's comment: 'Yes, of course! But as the subject was not discussed in detail I did not include a reference in the minutes.'
67. T 273/307, note from Bridges to Pimlott, 15 February 1947.
68. CAB 134/190, ED(47)5th Meeting, Confidential Annex: Item 3, 26 February 1947.
69. BT 11/3357, 'Anglo-French Economic Co-operation: State of Play', by Sanders, 1 March 1947.
70. CAB 130/21, GEN 188/6th Meeting, European Economic Co-operation (London) Committee, 21 July 1947. The paper referred to was probably a note by the Economic Intelligence Department of 5 February 1947, consisting of an assessment of the plan's shortcomings. Copies exist in FO 943/342 and BT 11/3341.
71. *Observer*, 23 February 1947 cutting in BT 11/3357.
72. Roger Makins, returning from a posting to Washington in February, had succeeded Edmund Hall-Patch as Supervising Under-Secretary of the Economic Intelligence and Economic Relations Departments.
73. See, for example, J. Fourastié and J-P. Courtheoux, *La Planification Economique en France* (Paris: Presses Universitaires de France, 1968).
74. Monnet makes the point that, due to political instability, the Plan was in fact adopted by a succession of governments and was able to achieve a higher profile by virtue of its inclusion in every investiture debate. Monnet, *Mémories*, p. 308.
75. Letter from Professor Meade to this author, 10 November 1990.

Notes

76. See Alec Cairncross, *Years of Recovery: British Economic Policy 1945–51* (London: Methuen, 1985).
77. BT 64/2268, CRT 296/47, 14 February 1947, note by Lintott reporting a conversation between Monnet and Hall-Patch.
78. BT 64/2268, CRT 296/47, 14 February 1947, note by Lintott.
79. Cripps papers, Box 385, Nuffield College, Oxford (undated).
80. T 273/307, Gorell-Barnes to Bridges, 25 February 1947.
81. BT 11/3357, note by Sanders (Board of Trade), 'Anglo-French Economic Co-operation: State of Play', 1 March 1947.
82. Edwin Plowden, *An Industrialist in the Treasury: The Post-War Years* (London: Andre Deutsch, 1989) p. 8.
83. T 229/106, Minutes of a meeting chaired by Plowden in the Cabinet Office, 20 May 1947.
84. Cairncross, *Years of Recovery*, p. 325.
85. Below, p. 129.
86. Plowden, *An Industrialist in the Treasury*, chapter 7 (underlining added).
87. Letter from Lord Plowden to this author, 20 March 1991.
88. FO 371/59955, Z 10679, record of conversation, 23 December 1946.
89. Ibid, handwritten comment appended by Bevin.
90. Above, p. 3. The finished paper was circulated as CP(46)386, 18 October 1946 (now to be found in CAB 129/13).
91. CAB 128/6, CM(46)91, Cabinet meeting, 25 October 1946.
92. *State Papers*, vol. 147, p. 844, Treaty of Alliance and Mutual Assistance, 4 March 1947 (original exists in FO 93/33/405).
93. *The Times*, 7 March 1947 (cutting included in BT 11/3357).
94. In February 1947, with a stormy reception expected for the Economic White paper, his public relations adviser was especially anxious to let it be known that Morrison had been too ill to take any active part in the affairs of government. Morrison papers, LSE, Box 1/8, letter from P. H. Boon to Morrison's secretary, Miss Donald, 6 February 1947.

Notes to Chapter 2: Steel

1. FO 943/167, 4A, memorandum, 28 January 1947.
2. BT 11/3360, letter, 8 February 1947, from Ronald Fraser to Lintott describing a meeting between himself, Hall-Patch, and Alphand.
3. FO 943/167, 16A, record of conversation, 18 February 1947.
4. Ibid.
5. Above, p. 3.
6. T 230/76, note for the Lord President of the Council by the Economic Section of the Cabinet Office, 5 June 1946.
7. FO 942/276, EIPS/179/9, 'Draft Directive on Iron and Steel', Economic and Industrial Planning Staff, 25 June 1945.
8. FO 942/390, Allied Control Authority – Directorate of Economics, Memorandum: 'Points of View of the Metals Sub-Committee', 11 December 1945. The figures favoured for steel manufacturing capacity by the representatives of the four powers were, in millions of tons per annum, Soviet Union: 4.6; United States: 7.8; France: 7.0; UK: 10.5.

9. FO 942/390, 29th meeting of the Allied Control Authority Co-ordinating Committee, 31 December 1945.
10. CAB 129/8, CP(46)114, 16 March 1946, 'Level of German Industry', paper by the Chancellor of the Duchy of Lancaster,
11. CAB 129/9, CP(46)186, 3 May 1946, 'Policy Towards Germany', memorandum by the Secretary of State for Foreign Affairs.
12. *Hansard*, HC DEB, vol. 427, col. 1515, 22 October 1946.
13. FO 943/178, record of a meeting at the Waldorf-Astoria Hotel, Washington, between Bevin, General Robertson and Hall-Patch, 3 December 1946.
14. BT 11/3357, note by Lintott, 22 January 1947.
15. CAB 21/2278, M53/47, memorandum from Attlee to John Wilmot, the Minister of Supply, 22 January 1947.
16. AVIA 11/67, note by F. G. Lee, 31 January 1947.
17. AVIA 11/67, note from Lee to Hall-Patch, 20 February 1947.
18. BT 64/2268, note from Lee to Nowell (Board of Trade), 13 February 1947.
19. FO 943/167, 4A, 28 January 1947.
20. CAB 134/598, ORC(47)14, report by Working Party to the Overseas Reconstruction Committee, 24 February 1947.
21. Ibid.
22. Ibid.
23. FO 943/167, 5A, note of conversation between Mark Turner and Hervé Alphand, 28 January 1947.
24. CAB 134/597, ORC(47)3rd Meeting, 26 February 1947.
25. Ibid.
26. CAB 128/9, CM(47)25, 27 February 1947.
27. CAB 134/598, ORC(47)19, report to Overseas Reconstruction Committee, 'Level of German Steel Capacity: Discussions with the French Government', 4 March 1947.
28. Ibid.
29. Ibid.
30. Above, p. 3.
31. CAB 134/598, ORC(47)19, 4 March 1947.
32. FO 943/181, 203A, note by Frank Lee, 3 March 1947.
33. CAB 134/598, ORC(47)14, 24 February 1947, p. 7.
34. FO 943/342, 'The Monnet Plan', report by the Economic Intelligence Department of the Foreign Office, 5 February 1947.
35. FO 943/167, 11A, E1/6/91, letter from Turner to Alec Cairncross, adviser to the Board of Trade, 8 February 1947.
36. CAB 132/5, LP(46)250, 14 October 1946, memorandum by the Ministry of Supply, 'Steel Supplies', over Wilmot's initials.
37. CAB 129/16, CP(47)20, 7 January 1947.
38. BT 13/220A, MM(47)27, Board of Trade, President's Morning Meeting, 2 April 1947.
39. T 229/106, EP(O)(47)2, 12 June 1947, draft papers for the first meeting of the Planning Board, no. 4: 'Steel'.
40. Ibid.
41. BT 11/3631, copy of letter to the Foreign Secretary from the British Embassy in Paris, 3 March 1948.

Notes

42. CAB 134/191, ED(48)2, *Economic Survey for 1948*, 2 February 1948.
43. T 229/173, note from Cairncross to Robinson, 10 March 1948.
44. CAB 134/565, ON(49)218, 20 June 1949.
45. CAB 133/27, CLC(S)(49)14, 13 December 1949, note by the Board of Trade to the Commonwealth Liaison Committee Steel Working Party.
46. CAB 134/598, ORC(47)14, 24 February 1947.
47. T 232/81, GEN 258/23, 18 January 1949, note by the Ministry of Supply to the Working Party on Long-term Programmes.
48. BT 11/3631, letter from Ronald Fraser, Commercial Department, Paris, to Edgar Cohen, Board of Trade, 29 May 1948.
49. BT 11/3631, Mrs P. M. B. James to R. Fraser, 16 June 1948.
50. SUPP 14/117, E/ECE/114, 25 March 1950, *Report of the 5th Session of the Economic Commission for Europe*, Appendix I, p. 19. (The ECE was a United Nations body.)
51. CAB 134/541, OEP(47)6, 'Survey of the Overseas Economic Situation as it affects the United Kingdom', 30 January 1947. (Circulated to members of the Overseas Economic Policy Committee, which was usually chaired by Attlee. The Survey was never considered by a session of the Committee.)
52. The possibility of surplus capacity first figured in an early draft submitted to the Committee on Overseas Economic Information on 29 March 1946, see CAB 134/205, EI(O)(46)1.
53. CAB 129/19, CP(47)163, 'Level of German Industry', Memorandum by the Secretary of State for Foreign Affairs, 19 May 1947.
54. BT 11/3357, note by C. W. Sanders, 23 January 1947.
55. BT 64/2268, note from Lee to Nowell (Board of Trade), 13 February 1947.
56. Cmd 6811, May 1946.
57. *The Times*, 7 March 1947, press cutting in BT 11/3357.
58. CAB 21/2363, letter from Bevin to Morrison, 17 July 1948.
59. FO 371/69216, UE.8896, handwritten comment appended to a memorandum dated 27 September 1948.
60. BT 11/3631, 47A, Agreement between the *Comptoir Français des Produits Sidérurgiques* and the *Chambre Syndicale de la Sidérurgie* on the one hand and the British Iron and Steel Corporation Limited on the other, 11 March 1948.
61. T 236/2168, ON(AG)(48)42, 6 September 1948, Minutes of the session 30 August–2 September 1948, circulated as a paper to the Overseas Negotiations Committee. (For the incorporation of the Saar into the French customs area, see p. 64, below.)
62. T 232/83, 160, GEN 258/A/14th Meeting, 23 February 1949, Working Group on Long-Term Programmes. See note 39, p. 162 below.
63. T 238/227, 88, ON(50)27, 27 January 1950, note by the Ministry of Supply.
64. CAB 129/28, CP(48)181, 'Iron and Steel Bill: Review of Arguments', 15 July 1948, p. 3, para. 7.
65. FO 371/68960, UE.6081, note by H. Trevelyan, 17 July 1948. An attached note reads: 'SoS agrees with the point made in this brief.'
66. CAB 21/2363, letter from Bevin to Morrison, 17 July 1948.
67. René Massigli, *Une Comédie des erreurs 1943–1956: Souvenirs et réflexions sur une étape de la construction européenne* (Paris: Plon, 1978) p. 188.

68. Sir Roderick Barclay, *Ernest Bevin and the Foreign Office 1932–1969* (published by the author, 1975) p. 89. (Barclay was Bevin's Private Secretary from March 1949.)
69. BT 11/3357, record of meeting at the Quai d'Orsay, 5 September 1946.

Notes to Chapter 3: Coal

1. René Massigli, *Une Comédie des Erreurs 1943–1956* (Paris: Plon, 1978) p. 87.
2. FO 371/59955, Z.10679, letter from Bevin to Duff Cooper, 23 December 1946.
3. FO 943/188, 1A, telegram 3290 from Washington to Foreign Office, 18 May 1946.
4. FO 800/465, official translation of letter from Blum to Attlee, 1 January 1947 (typewritten copy of French text is in CAB 21/2278, M13/47; Blum's handwritten original in PREM 8/516).
5. CAB 128/9, CM(47)2, 6 January 1947.
6. CAB 128/9, CM(47)3, 7 January 1947. This Cabinet meeting considered measures such as diverting coal from industry to power stations, calling for restraint from domestic consumers and even, where possible, supplementing the local power supply from the generators aboard submarines. The possibility was also raised of importing coal.
7. Above, p. 10.
8. *The Economist*, 14 December 1946, p. 956. Reprinted and circulated as ED(47)12 (see above, p. 14).
9. FO 371/58410, UR.8122, undated report of a fact-finding mission to the Ruhr, 22–28 August 1946, by Ashley Clarke of the British Embassy in Paris. (Monthly figures in report multiplied by twelve to arrive at the above.)
10. BT 64/2268, 17, note of a conversation between Monnet and Hall-Patch in Paris, 7 February 1947. (Bridges was Chairman of the Steering Committee on Economic Development.)
11. Above, pp. 25–6.
12. FO 943/181, 203A, report by Sir Mark Turner, 3 March 1947.
13. *The Economist*, 1 June 1946, p. 887.
14. PREM 8/516, letter from Massigli to Attlee, 24 March 1947.
15. BT 211/153, TP(I)34, 9 October 1944. (TP(I) was an informal committee of officials under Foreign Office chairmanship.)
16. FO 371/45669, UE.2078 and UE.2141, Foreign Office account of proceedings.
17. Cmd 6732, *Agreement for the Establishment of the European Coal Organisation*, 4 January 1946.
18. Records of the Allocations Proposals Committee are incomplete in FO 371, but an appreciation of the procedure may be obtained by perusal of FO 371/5972–5973, containing minutes of the 14th–23rd meetings.
19. FO 371/57925, UR.4471, handwritten comment by Warner, appended to a note from Crossley to Fraser, 10 May 1946.
20. FO 371/58400, UR.4326, telegram no. 180 from UK delegation to Council of Foreign Ministers to Gen. Robertson, British Deputy Military Governor,

Germany, 15 May 1946. (Félix Gouin headed a Provisional Government from 26 January to 12 June 1946.)
21. CAB 124/1212, letter from Emanuel Shinwell, Minister of Fuel and Power, to Clement Attlee, 15 May 1946.
22. FO 371/58401, UR.4409, letter from Bevin to the Chancellor of the Duchy of Lancaster, 23 May 1946. (The Chancellor, John Hynd MP, was responsible for the Control Office for Germany and Austria.)
23. FO 371/58401, UR.4722, telegram no. 458 from Berlin to Control Office, 21 May 1946.
24. FO 371/58401, UR.4722, telegram no. 565 from Control Office to Berlin, 24 May 1946.
25. FO 371/58402, UR.5010, telegram from Berlin to Control Office, 3 June 1946.
26. FO 371/58402, UR.5008, telegram no. 288 from Duff Cooper to Foreign Office, 3 June 1946.
27. Ibid.
28. FO 371/57942, UR5348, Minutes of 17th meeting of the Allocation Proposals Committee of the ECO, 4 June 1946.
29. Ibid.
30. FO 943/192, 7B, telegram no. 849 from Foreign Office to Political Adviser to Commander in Chief, Berlin, 5 June 1946.
31. FO 371/58402, UR.5008, telegram no. 485 from Foreign Office to Paris, 5 June 1946.
32. CAB 128/9, CM(47)3, 7 January 1947, Consideration of Cabinet paper CP(47)17 (CAB 129/16).
33. CAB 128/9, CM(47)18, 7 February 1947.
34. *Hansard*, HC DEB, vol. 432, cols 2178, 2179, 7 February 1947.
35. *FRUS*, 1947, vol. 3, p. 492, telegram, 13 February 1947, from US Secretary of State to London Embassy transmitting text of a press release by President Truman.
36. PREM 8/449, Prime Minister's personal telegram no. T.33/47, Attlee to Truman, 14 February 1947.
37. FO 371/62457, UE.1575, Minutes of the 26th meeting of the Allocation Proposals Committee, 25 February 1947.
38. *Hansard*, HC DEB, vol. 434, col. 1181, 11 March 1947.
39. CAB 128/9, CM(47)27, 11 March 1947.
40. CAB 134/273, FC(47)47, 13 March 1947.
41. FO 371/62467, UE.1674, text of telegram, 12 March 1947 (transmission copy not in file, but was apparently sent as no. 5).
42. FO 371/62467, UE.1991, telegram no. 68 from Moscow, 14 March 1947.
43. FO 371/62467, UE.2024, Confidential note from the Chairman, Eaton-Griffith, to McNeil. Undated copy under cover of a note of 24 March 1947, by which date the contents of the letter had already been referred to by Gorell-Barnes of the Prime Minister's Office in a note of 14 March (see FO 371/62467, UE.1824).
44. Ibid.
45. FO 371/62367, UE.1892, telegram no. 221 from Moscow, Bevin to Attlee, 20 March 1947.
46. CAB 128/9, CM(47)31, 21 March 1947.
47. Ibid.

48. FO 371/62467, UE.2091, note from Roger Makins to Fergusson (Fuel and Power) reporting a telephone conversation with the US Ambassador at lunchtime, 22 March 1947.
49. CAB 134/272, FC(47)16th Meeting, 16 April 1947.
50. *FRUS*, 1947, vol. 3, p. 504, telegram no. 2643 from Douglas to the US Secretary of State, 8 May 1947.
51. FO 371/62469, UE.3638, record of a conversation between Makins, Hall-Patch and the US Ambassador, 8 May 1947.
52. *FRUS*, 1947, vol.3, p. 504, telegram no. 2643 from Douglas to the US Secretary of State, 8 May 1947.
53. FO 371/62469, UE.3902, account of discussions by Roger Makins, 15 May 1947.
54. CAB 129/19, CP(47)162, memorandum by McNeil, 18 May 1947.
55. FO 371/62469, UE.4140, telegram no. 833 from Foreign Office to Paris, 20 May 1947.
56. *FRUS*, 1947, vol. 3, p. 509, telegram no. 2142 from Marshall to London Embassy, 16 May 1947.
57. FO 934/182, 229A, telegram no. 5105 from Foreign Office to Washington, 22 May 1947.
58. FO 371/62469, UE.4124, report of proceedings by Watkinson (Fuel and Power), 22 May 1947.
59. Ibid.
60. FO 943/182, 298A, telegram no. 858 from Foreign Office to Paris, 22 May 1947.
61. FO 371/62469, UE.4124, report by Watkinson, 22 May 1947.
62. CAB 134/274, FC(47)118, memorandum by the Minister of Fuel and Power, 1 August 1947.
63. CAB 134/274, FC(47)114, 22 July 1947.
64. Above, p. 42.
65. FO 371/62469, UE.4021, Fraser's comments on the meeting between Roger Makins and Alphand on 14 May 1947, 15 May 1947.
66. For an appreciation of the functions and working methods of the NGCC, see FO 1036/774, *passim*, and FO 943/676, 93A.
67. FO 943/1, P. (Terminal)54, 30 July 1945, Annex: text of draft US directive as transmitted in telegram no. 4827, 11 July 1945, from Washington.
68. FO 934/1 (pagination incomplete in this volume), telegram no. 39, Foreign Office to Eden at Potsdam, 16 July 1945.
69. Ibid.
70. FO 942/383 (not paginated but filed between EIPS/321/25 and EIPS/321/26A), letter from Bevin to John Hynd, Chancellor of the Duchy of Lancaster, 10 December 1945.
71. FO 371/58400, UR.3771, record of proceedings, first plenary session, 12 April 1946.
72. Ibid. Sub-committee on German coal consumption, 13 April 1946, Appendix A: Note by British delegation.
73. FO 371/58400, UR.3771, Record of proceedings, Sub-committee on German coal consumption, 13 April 1946. Annex B: Official translation of note by French delegation.
74. Ibid.

Notes

75. FO 371/58400, UR.3771, British record of final plenary session, 14 April 1946.
76. FO 371/58400, UR.3771, Anglo-French Coal Conference, Appendix 8: Joint Communiqué. Press Release, 14 April 1946.
77. *The Economist*, 20 April 1946, p. 633.
78. FO 371/58403, UR.5273, DECO/M(46)30, Minutes of 50th meeting of Economic Directorate, 29 May 1946, Annex A: French memorandum concerning coal allocation.
79. FO 371/58403, UR.5373, note of meeting held at the Treasury, 28 May 1946.
80. CAB 128/5, CM(46)56, 6 June 1946.
81. Ibid.
82. CAB 134/595, ORC(46)9th Meeting, 21 June 1946.
83. FO 371/58405, UR6000, conversation on coal between British, French and American experts, 3rd Meeting, 8 July 1946.
84. FO 371/58405, UR.6170, CFM(46)42nd Meeting, British record of 42nd Meeting, Palais du Luxembourg, Paris, 12 July 1946.
85. FO 943/180, 69A, Hall-Patch's account of interview between Shinwell and Massigli, 17 July 1946.
86. FO 371/58409, UR.7883, CEC/M(46)22, Special issue of the minutes of the Coal Experts Committee, 6 September 1946.
87. FO 371/58410, UR.8168, CORC/P(46)307, 21 September 1946.
88. FO 943/676, 73A, telegram ARGUS 654 from Berlin to Control Office, 23 September 1946.
89. FO 371/58409, UR.7996, telegram no. 1232 from Political Adviser to Commander-in-Chief, Germany, to Foreign Office, 24 September 1946.
90. FO 943/662, 23A, telegram SUGRA 699 from Control Office to Berlin, 7 September 1946.
91. FO 371/58408, UR.7721, telegram no. 752 from UK delegation, Paris, to Foreign Office, 12 September 1946.
92. FO 943/188, 12A, telegram no. 471 from Duff Cooper, Paris, to Foreign Office, 11 September 1946.
93. FO 371/58409, UR.7967, telegram no. 818 from Paris to Foreign Office, 23 September 1946. Transmits record of conversation between Alphand and Hall-Patch.
94. FO 800/464, Fr/46/21, UK Delegation Circular no. 27: Record of meeting at the Quai d'Orsay, 24 September 1946. Sent to London as telegram no. 830. (FO 371/58409, UR.8016).
95. FO 371/58411, UR.8423, letter from Bevin to Bidault, 20 October 1946.
96. Below, p. 67.
97. FO 371/58406, UR.7795, letter from James F. Byrnes (US Secretary of State) to Bevin, 11 October 1946.
98. FO 371/58411, UR.8414, Minutes of meeting in Paris between Bevin and representatives of the Control Office and the British Element of the Allied Control Commission, 11 October 1946.
99. FO 371/58412, UR.8800, record of conversation between Alphand and Hall-Patch, 22 October 1946.
100. Ibid.
101. FO 371/58410, UR.8147, press cutting.

102. Hervé Alpand, *L'Étonnement d'être: Journal de 1939 à 1973* (Paris: Fayard, 1977) p. 195.
103. PREM 8/516, letter from Massigli to Attlee, 24 March 1947 (see above, p. 36).
104. FO 943/181, 278B, sliding scale agreement. Under cover of letter dated 23 April 1947.
105. FO 943/181, 254, note by Sir Mark Turner referring to concern expressed verbally the previous week, 10 April 1947.
106. FO 943/181, 248A, telegram no. 660 from Moscow to Foreign Office, 9 April 1947. Personal for Makins from Hall-Patch, in reply to Makins's telegram no. 554 of 4 April relaying Turner's misgivings.
107. FO 943/181, 268A, telegram no. 257 from Moscow to Berlin transmitting text of letter from Bidault to Bevin, 19 April 1947.
108. Above, p. 30.

Notes to Chapter 4: The Saar

1. FO 943/181, 282C, telegram no. 319 from Duff Cooper to Foreign Office, 25 April 1947.
2. FO 371/45668, UE.1588, telegram no. 594 from Duff Cooper to Foreign Office, 12 April 1945.
3. FO 371/55801, C.2130, typeset translation of note of 19 February, 6 March 1946.
4. Ibid.
5. FO 371/55801, C.2130, Bevin's handwritten comment appended to a note by Oliver Harvey dated 19 February 1946.
6. CAB 130/9, GEN 121/2, 11 March 1946.
7. CAB 128/5, CM(46)23, 11 March 1946.
8. CAB 130/9, GEN121/1st Meeting, 15 March 1946. Present: Attlee (in the Chair), Morrison, Bevin, Dalton, Cripps.
9. CAB 128/5, CM(46)36, 17 April 1946. (The German Industry Committee papers, GEN 121/1 and GEN 121/2, were circulated to the full Cabinet under CP(46)156 of 15 April, now filed in CAB 129/9.)
10. *Hansard*, HC DEB, vol. 423, col. 1845, 4 June 1946.
11. Ibid., p. 127.
12. FO 371/57948, UR.6264, *Weekly Statistical Report of the European Coal Organisation no. 49: 16–22 June 1946*. p. 3.
13. Ibid., p. 1. (week's figure of $148\,270 \times 52 = 7\,710\,040$).
14. Above, p. 47
15. CAB 134/595, ORC(46)9th Meeting, 21 June 1946.
16. FO 1082/9, *French Basic Handbook*, April 1943, p. 1.
17. FO 942/276, EIPS/179/7, SCMT/P(46)1, paper by the French Secretary of the Metals Sub-Committee of the Industry Committee of the Directorate of Economics, 27 February 1946.
18. FO 942/481, SCMT/Misc(46)105, paper by the US Secretary, Metals Sub-Committee, 24 April 1946.
19. The handbook figure was based on *actual output* for 1929, when production of national groups was restricted by the quotas of the *Entente International*

de l'Acier, which in 1927 had fined the Saar for overproduction (see Ervin Hexner, *The International Steel Cartel* (Westport Conn: Greenwood Press, 1971) p. 76).
20. FO 943/331, 35A, EID/10/14, paper by the Foreign Office Economic Intelligence Department: 'The Contribution which the Saar could make to French Economy', 26 July 1946, pp. 1 and 2.
21. Ibid., p. 5.
22. Ibid., p. 3.
23. Above, p. 22.
24. FO 943/331, 36A, telegram no. 823 from Bevin (in Paris) to Attlee, 24 September 1946.
25. FO 943/331, 28A, note from Hall-Patch to Dixon, 25 September 1946.
26. FO 800/464, Fr/46/23, memorandum by Bevin referring to conversation with Byrnes, 25 September 1946.
27. FO 800/464, Fr/46/24, record of conversation between Bevin and Bidault at dinner at the British Embassy, 11 October 1946.
28. *Hansard*, HC DEB, vol. 427, col. 1517, 22 October 1946.
29. FO 371/57411, U.8249, CFM(46)(NY)18th Meeting, 9 December 1946, British record of meeting.
30. FO 371/57414, U.8257, CFM(46)(NY)74 (revised), 13 December 1946, Agenda: item 3(b).
31. FO 371/64214, C.150 (in French), C.881 (in English), 18 December 1946 (NB The English translation of Article 3, Decree 75 does not correspond to the French version. 'Contravention of this decree will be published...' may be a typographical error for 'punished'. Original reads: 'Toute infraction àla présente Ordonnance sera poursuivie et réprimée...').
32. FO 371/64214, C.461, telegram no. 15, Duff Cooper to Bevin, 6 January 1947.
33. Ibid. Bevin's handwritten comment. Transmitted to Paris as telegram no. 83, 11 January 1947.
34. FO 371/64214, C.881, letter to Bevin from British Consulate General, Baden-Baden, 8 January 1947.
35. Established 14 January 1946 at the Paris Conference. Records in FO 371/70970 A and B.
36. CAB 128/5, CM(46)36, 17 April 1946.
37. FO 371/55801, C.2130, note from Massigli to Bevin, 19 February 1946.
38. FO 371/64214, C.256, telegram no. 362 from Foreign Office to Washington, 11 January 1947.
39. FO 371/64214, C.1043, telegram no. 378 from Washington (Lord Inverchapel, Ambassador) to Foreign Office, 20 January 1947.
40. FO 371/64214, C.1043, comment by P. Dean dated 27 January, endorsed by Sir Oliver Harvey on a minute by Jellicoe dated 24 January 1947.
41. *Hansard*, HC DEB, vol. 432, col. 1372, 3 February 1947, reply by Mr Mayhew (Bevin's Parliamentary Under-Secretary) to Mr Edelman.
42. CAB 134/598, ORC(47)7, 21 February 1947.
43. FO 943/331, 41A, Brief for CFM, 27 February 1947.
44. FO 371/64214, C.4849, CFM(47)(M)9th Meeting, 19 March 1947.
45. FO 371/64215, C.5086, record of conversation, 25 March 1947.
46. FO 371/64215, C.5558, record of discussion at the UK delegation meeting, 5 April 1947.

47. FO 371/64199, C.5848, CFM(47)(M)25th Meeting, 10 April 1947, British record of plenary session. FO 371/64215, C.5749 & C.5755, CFM(47)(M)120 and CFM(47)(M)116, Statements submitted by the French and US delegations.
48. FO 371/64199, C.5849, CFM(47)(M)26th Meeting, 11 April 1947, British record of plenary session.
49. FO 943/331, 83A, telegram no. 800 from UK delegation to Foreign Office, 17 April 1947.
50. FO 943/331, 86A, telegram no. 886 from UK delegation to Foreign Office, 21 April 1947.
51. FO 943/331, 85A, telegram no. 846 from Sir Orme Sargent (Permanent Under-Secretary) to UK delegation, 20 April 1947.
52. FO 943/331, 87A, telegram no. 964 from UK delegation to Foreign Office, 28 April 1947.
53. FO 371/64202, C.6416, letter from Pat Dean, UK delegation, to Foreign Office reporting a meeting between Sir William Strang and Freeman Matthews (US delegation), 30 April 1947.
54. Above, p. 42.
55. *FRUS*, 1947, vol. 3, p. 506, telegram no. 2068 from Marshall to London Embassy, 12 May 1947.
56. FO 943/182, 298A, telegram no. 858 from Foreign Office to Paris, 22 May 1947.
57. *Hansard*, HC DEB, vol. 437, col. 1956, 16 May 1947, Bevin's reply to a speech the previous day by his predecessor, Anthony Eden (ibid., col. 1746), who had apparently been briefed by the Foreign Office, presumably with Bevin's knowledge and approval. (see FO 371/64216, C.7328, note by Jellicoe, 13 May 1947.)
58. FO 371/64216, C.7511, record of conversation between Sir Oliver Harvey and René Massigli, 19 May 1947.
59. FO 371/64216, C.7423, minute by Harvey, 19 May 1947.
60. FO 371/64216, C.7423, record of conversation between Harvey and Massigli, 27 May 1947.
61. FO 371/64216, C.7648, note by Bevin, 27 May 1947.
62. FO 371/64216, C.7648, telegram no. 5340 from Foreign Office to Washington Embassy, 31 May 1947.
63. FO 371/64216, C.7701, letter handed to Bevin by Massigli, 4 June 1947.
64. FO 371/64216, C.7648, telegram no. 5478 from Foreign office to Washington, 4 June 1947.
65. FO 371/65422, CK.600, telegram no. 3298 from Washington to Foreign Office, 6 June 1947.
66. FO 371/65422, CK.600, telegram no. 5598 from Foreign Office to Washington, 7 June 1947.
67. FO 371/65422, CK.600, telegram no. 3316 from Washington to Foreign Office, 7 June 1947.
68. FO 371/64216, C.7950, 10 June 1947, aide-mémoire handed to French Ambassador.
69. FO 371/64216, C.8231, record of conversation between W. J. Gallman and Sir Oliver Harvey, 12 June 1947.

Notes

70. BT 211/131, 64, minutes of meeting in Room 25 of the Foreign Office, 16 June 1947, Roger Makins in the Chair.
71. FO 943/182, 324B, note by J. H. Brook (Ministry of Fuel and Power), 3 July 1947.
72. FO 371/65423, CK.614, record of meeting in the Foreign Office, 21 July 1947.
73. FO 371/65197, CJ.1065, record of meeting, 25 August 1947.
74. FO 371/65423, CK.617, note from French Embassy and covering note by Makins, 20 August 1947.
75. FO 371/65420, CK.543, TT/Berlin/47/M/1, 8 September 1947, British record of first meeting.
76. FO 371/65198, CJ.1416, TT/Berlin/47/P/2, 10 September 1947.
77. FO 371/64217, C.12741, telegram no. 4994, Washington Embassy to Foreign Office, 10 September 1947.
78. FO 371/64217, C.12741, telegram no. 183 from Washington Embassy to Foreign Office, 11 September 1947.
79. Ibid.
80. BT 211/131, 82, telegram no. 5378 from Foreign Office to Berlin, 7 November 1947.
81. FO 371/65423, CK.1472, Note delivered to the Foreign Office from the French Embassy, 11 November 1947.
82. FO 371/64219, C.14944, telegram no. 24 REMAC from Paris to Foreign Office, 22 November 1947. (The CAMER/REMAC signals series applied to financial matters only and identified an appropriate distribution list for incoming cables.)
83. FO 371/65341, CJ.3481, CFM/47/L/3rd Meeting, 27 November 1947, British record of meeting.
84. FO 371/65341, CJ.3481, CFM/47/L/4th Meeting, 28 November 1947, Annex A: Statement by Bevin.
85. FO 371/70620, passim. (This file contains all the relevant extracts from the *Journal Officiel*.)
86. BT 211/131, 94, telegram no. 13299 from Foreign Office to Washington Embassy, 25 December 1947.
87. BT 211/131, 101, telegram no. 93 from Foreign Office to Berlin, 17 January 1948.
88. BT 211/131, 102, telegram no. 96 from Berlin to Foreign Office, 18 January 1948.
89. FO 371/71142, CK.453, letter from UK Permanent Delegation to the ECE to the Executive Secretary, 26 January 1948.
90. FO 371/71142, CK.453, E/ECE/COAL/ASC/4, 2 February 1948, French memorandum to the Allocations Sub-Committee of the ECE Coal Committee.
91. *FRUS*, 1948, vol. 2, pp. 73–5, *Economic Agreement between the United States, the United Kingdom, and France Regarding the Saar*, 20 February 1948.
92. Reparations were divided between Category B, comprising items physically removed from Germany, and category A, which encompassed all other forms of reparation. The RM 70 million was a charge against plant

which would remain *in situ* and should therefore not be counted under Category B. On the other hand, if the value were debited to Category A, France could still draw her full Category B quota from the rest of Germany in addition to her Saar acquisitions. For resolution of this issue, which was not a pre-condition to the Saar Agreement, see FO 371/71049 and 71050.

93. *FRUS*, 1948, vol. 2, p. 74, footnote. Agreed draft of a letter from the three governments to the IARA.
94. BT 11/3892, Brief prepared by the Board of Trade for the Chancellor of the Exchequer. Undated but intended for use in talks with French Finance Minister, René Mayer, 16 January 1948.
95. Below, p. 101.
96. FO 371/62434, C.3674, record of negotiations leading to the establishment of the Bizone, Annex K: Memorandum of Agreement, 2 December 1946.
97. Above, p. 24.
98. BT 211/131, BIB/P(47)15, 27 February 1947.
99. FO 1005/81, BIP/M(47)3, 3 March 1947. Considered by the Bipartite Board, comprising Generals Clay and Robertson and members of their staffs, and approved with a minor amendment. (Amended version issued 4 March as BIB/P(47)15/1.)

Notes to Chapter 5: The Ruhr

1. *Hansard*, HC DEB, vol. 427, cols. 1510, 1511, 22 October 1946.
2. FO 371/57366, U.7326, CFM(46)39th Meeting, 10 July 1946, Annex 2: Statement by Bevin.
3. FO 371/57366, U.7326, CFM(46)40th Meeting, 11 July 1946.
4. CAB 129/11, CP(46)292, 'Germany: Results of the Paris Discussions', paper by the Foreign Secretary, 23 July 1946. CAB128/6, CM(46)73, 25 July 1946, Cabinet meeting.
5. FO 371/64234, C.3674 contains an officially compiled and printed summary of events from the American offer to the signing of the Bizone Agreement. For the French attitude, see p. 5.
6. FO 371/58409, UR.8016, telegram no. 830 from Bevin, in Paris, to Foreign Office, 25 September 1946.
7. Above, p. 48.
8. FO 371/58415, UR.10057, telegram no. 2483 from Bevin, in New York, to Foreign Office, 10 December 1946.
9. FO 371/64234, C.3674, Official summary of events, pp. 13–31.
10. *State Papers*, vol. 146, p. 484, 'Memorandum of Agreement between the United Kingdom and the United States concerning the British and American Zones of Occupation in Germany', 2 December 1946.
11. The documents relating to the British notification of inability to meet the conditions of the Bizonal Agreement and the subsequent discussions with the United States are to be found in FO 371/65072–83.
12. *State Papers*, vol. 147, p. 1191, 17 December 1947. (This revised agreement established a board of directors taking its decisions by majority voting

weighted according to the size of the funds made available by members' governments.)
13. Ibid.
14. FO 371/65076, CE.04458, report on the progress of negotiations, 27 October 1947.
15. Ibid., Covering note by Hoyer-Millar, 27 October 1947.
16. Copious American documentation is presented in *FRUS*, 1948, vol. 2, pp. 1–60. British files are in FO 371/70571–2.
17. CAB 128/12, CM(48)2, 8 January 1948.
18. FO 371/70572, C.345, telegram no. 72 from Gen. Robertson to Foreign Office, 14 January 1948, reports a conversation with Noiret in which the latter admits that he had been forewarned and had passed the information to Paris, where the assumption had been that the French government would be consulted in due course.
19. Below, p. 81.
20. FO 371/70571, C.232, telegram no. 20 from the British Ambassador in Paris to Foreign Office, 10 January 1948.
21. FO 371/70571, C.238, record of conversation between Bevin and Massigli, the French Ambassador, 9 January 1948.
22. *FRUS*, 1948, vol. 2, p. 27, letter from the Associate Chief of the Division of Western European Affairs [Wallner] to the Counselor of Embassy in France [Bonbright], 16 January 1948.
23. *FRUS*, 1948, vol. 2, p. 33, telegram Warx 94204 from the US army Civil Affairs Division to Clay, 17 January 1948. (see above, p. 63 regarding change of US attitude to the Saar question.)
24. CAB 128/12, CM(48)5, 19 January 1948.
25. FO 371/70530, C.977, letter from Harvey to Sir Ivone Kirkpatrick, Foreign Office, 29 January 1948.
26. The plan agreed by the Allied Control Authority in Berlin in March 1946 permitting a capacity of 7.5 million tons per annum and an actual production of 5.8 million tons for the German steel industry (above, p. 22).
27. BT 211/6, GEN 155/60, 9 December 1946, Record of interview on 3 December between the British and American Secretaries of State and the British and American Deputy Military Governors (Generals Clay and Robertson; both later promoted to Military Governor).
28. FO 371/64228, C.485, informal note handed to Hall-Patch by the French Ambassador, 9 January 1947.
29. FO 943/180, 58B, letter from Robertson to Sir Mark Turner, head of the Control Office for Germany and Austria, 13 July 1946.
30. FO 371/65038, CE.1345, telegram no. 783 from Bevin to Foreign Office, 16 April 1947.
31. FO 371/65038, CE.1344, telegram no. 777 from Robertson (in Moscow) to Foreign Office, 16 April 1947.
32. Above, p. 30
33. AVIA 11/67, Memorandum by F. Lee (Ministry of Supply), the Chairman of the Working Party, 20 June 1947.
34. CAB 134/597, ORC(47)6th Meeting, 7 July 1947.
35. Below, p. 89.

36. POWE 41/11, 6th meeting of the UK delegation in the Paris Embassy, Hall-Patch in the Chair, 3 July 1947.
37. FO 371/65190, CJ.86, telegram no. 1981 from Foreign Office to Berlin, 10 July 1947.
38. FO 371/65190, CJ.217, telegram no. 6998 from Foreign Office to Washington, 12 July 1947. (Formally approved by Bipartite Board 16 July 1947, see FO 1005/81, BIB/M(47)10, item 201.)
39. FO 371/65191, CJ.322, aide-mémoire from British Embassy in Washington to US State Department, 15 July 1947.
40. FO 371/65191, CJ.333, French record of conversation between Bevin and Bidault, 15 July 1947 (no English version filed).
41. Ibid.
42. FO 371/65190, CJ.259, telegram no. 150 from Bevin, in Paris, to Washington, 15 July 1947.
43. FO 371/65191, CJ.333, record of meeting at the Quai d'Orsay with Jean Chauvel et al., 16 July 1947.
44. FO 371/65191, CJ.331, personal letter to Bevin in Bidault's own handwriting, 17 July 1947.
45. FO 371/65191, CJ.347, telegram no. 4021 from Washington Embassy to Foreign Office, 18 July 1947.
46. CAB 129/20, CP(47)209, 22 July 1947.
47. CAB 128/10, CM(47)63, 23 July 1947.
48. FO 371/65191, CJ.356, telegram no. 7464 from Foreign Office to Washington Embassy, 24 July 1947.
49. FO 371/65195, CJ.832, report of a telephone call from the US Ambassador to Roger Makins on the evening of 10 August 1947.
50. FO 371/65195, CJ.979, TT/47/P/2, Statement by Massigli.
51. FO 371/65196, CJ.994, TT(47)2nd Meeting, 23 August 1947.
52. FO 371/65196, CJ.998, TT/47/P.6, Statement by Alphand, 23 August 1947.
53. FO 371/65197, CJ.1067, TT/47/P.10 Final, Press Communiqué, 28 August 1947.
54. FO 371/65197, CJ.1109, report by Gilmour Jenkins of an informal conversation between the US Ambassador to France and Alphand and Massigli, 25 August 1947.
55. FO 371/65197, CJ.1198, summary of talks prepared for Sir Orme Sargent, Permanent Under-Secretary of State at the Foreign Office, by Hoyer-Millar, 30 August 1947.
56. Above, p. 68.
57. FO 371/65197, CJ.1198, summary by Hoyer-Millar for Sir Orme Sargent, 30 August 1947.
58. FO 1005/85, BIB/P(47)81/1, paper produced for the Bipartite Board, 8 September 1947.
59. FO 1005/136, BIECO/M(47)26, 8 October 1947. FO 371/70943, CJ.354, list of plants (IARA/AS/DOC 322) and covering letter, 14 October 1947.
60. FO 371/59955, Z.9352, record of conversation between Massigli, French Ambassador to the UK, and Hector McNeil, Minister of State at the Foreign Office, 26 October 1946.

61. *FRUS*, 1948, vol. 2, p. 282, letter from the Under-Secretary of State (Lovett) to the Secretary of the Army (Royal), 25 May 1948.
62. Section 115(f), Public Law 472, 80th Congress, quoted in CAB 129/34, CP(49)76, 5 April 1949, Annex.
63. 6 July 1948 in the case of the United Kingdom. See *State Papers*, vol. 151, p. 123.
64. FO 371/71035, CJ.4912, *The Wolf Report*, 14 August 1948.
65. Ibid., p. 31.
66. Ibid., p. 33
67. FO 371/71148, CK.2469, telegram no. 9058 from Foreign Office to Washington Embassy, 16 August 1948.
68. *FRUS*, 1948, vol. 2, pp. 796–798, telegram from Marshall, no. 3408 to London Embassy, no. 3335 to Paris, 26 August 1948.
69. CAB 128/13, CM(48)63, 15 October 1948.
70. FO 371/71102, CJ.5346, letter from Robertson to Sir William Strang, head of German Section, Foreign Office, 26 October 1948.
71. CAB 128/13, CM(48)74, 18 November 1948.
72. FO 371/71102, CJ.5359, minute by Roger Stevens, head of Economic Relations Department, Foreign Office, 29 October 1948.
73. FO 371/71034, CJ.4803, minutes of meeting in Room 245 at the Foreign Office (German Section), 1 October 1948.
74. Ibid.
75. FO 371/71095, CJ.4387, telegram no. 1235 from Paris to Foreign Office, 9 September 1948.
76. FO 371/71095, CJ.4470, telegram no. 1275 from Paris to Foreign Office, 14 September 1948.
77. FO 371/71096, CJ.4576, record of conversation between Bevin and Robert Schuman, 20 September 1948. (Schuman had replaced Georges Bidault in a government headed by Henri Queuille.)
78. The Humphrey Report was formally presented to Paul Hoffman, its commissioner, on 12 January 1949 and released to the press on 14 April. Copy of the full report in FO 371/76829, CE.984.
79. FO 371/71107, CJ.6210, Foreign Office minute by Roger Stevens, 9 December 1948.
80. FO 371/71107, CJ.6234, report by the Foreign Office on the differences between French and British positions, 16 December 1948. The British position was circulated as a Cabinet Paper (see CAB129/31, CP(48)303, 20 December 1948).
81. FO 371/79072, Z.680, record of meeting between Bevin and Schuman et al. at the Foreign Office, 13 January 1949.
82. FO 371/77148, CJ.681, telegram no. 123 from Paris to Foreign Office, 29 January 1949.
83. FO 371/77149, CJ.785, record of a meeting at the Foreign Office for the purpose of briefing J. H. Penson, posted to the Washington Embassy as Adviser on German Affairs, 21 January 1949. Intervention by Roger Stevens, head of the Economic Relations Department.
84. FO 371/77148, CJ.681, telegram no. 234 from Foreign Office to Paris, 2 February 1949.

85. FO 371/77149, CJ.802, telegram no. 669 from Washington to Foreign Office, 3 February 1949.
86. FO 371/77150, CJ.1012, note of a telephone call from the US Ambassador initialled FKR (almost certainly Frank K. Roberts, Principal Private Secretary to Bevin), 8 February 1949.
87. FO 371/77150, CJ.1314, record of conversation between Bevin and US Ambassador, Lewis W. Douglas, 22 February 1949. FO 371/77151, CJ.1447, conversation with Douglas, 2 March 1949. FO 371/77151, CJ.1560, conversation with Douglas, 7 March 1949.
88. FO 371/77151, CJ.1738, note of telephone conversation between Roger Stevens and the US Ambassador, 12 March 1949.
89. FO 371/77151, passim.
90. FO 371/77151, CJ.1738, Brief prepared for Bevin by Stevens, 12 March 1949, Annex C, Handwritten amendments and margin note dated 14 March. In addition to two chemical factories, the list comprised the following steelworks: Bochumer Verein Gusstahlfabrik, Bochum; August Thyssen Hütte, Hamborn; Deutsche Edelstahlwerke, Krefeld; Deutsche Edelstahlwerke (Tiegelstahl), Bochum; Klöckner Werke AG, Düsseldorf; August Thyssen Hütte AG, Niederrheinische, Duisburg; Hoesch AG, Holenlimburg.
91. FO 371/77152, CJ.1855, recommendations, 16 March 1949.
92. *FRUS*, 1949, vol. 3, pp. 553–592. (A report was circulated to the Cabinet; see CAB 129/34, CP(49)76, 5 April 1949.)
93. FO 371/77153, CJ.2040, telegram no. 1397 from Foreign Office to Berlin, 26 March 1949.
94. FO 371/77153, CJ.2132, statement initialled by the three delegations, 31 March 1949.
95. FO 371/77160, CJ.6481, review by German General Economic Dept., 3 September 1949. Estimated capacity at time of Humphrey study = 965 000 tons; restored to full working order = 3 194 000 tons. (NB An aggregate of the individual rated capacities as originally estimated by the Allied Economics Directorate = 3 414 000 tons; see FO 942/481, SCMT/Misc(46)105, 24 April 1946.)
96. FO 371/64633, passim.
97. CAB 128/10, CM(47)90, 15 December 1947.
98. For Bevin's report to the House of Commons on the breakdown, see *Hansard*, HC DEB, vol. 445, cols. 1874–87, 18 December 1947.
99. FO 371/64632, C.16506, letter from Ashley Clarke, Paris Embassy, to Bevin, 23 December 1947.
100. Above, pp. 62–4.
101. A comprehensive and convenient set of documents is compiled in *FRUS*, 1948, vol. 2, pp. 1–374. British documents are filed in FO 371/70571–70603 and FO 371/70625–70634.
102. *FRUS*, 1948, vol. 2, p. 97, telegram no. 772 from US Ambassador in London to US Secretary of State, 27 February 1948.
103. FO 371/70626, C.2440, TRI/7(FINAL), 5 March 1948.
104. FO 371/71112, CJ.2068, Resumed Session, 3rd Plenary Meeting, 22 April 1948.
105. The voting procedure of the JEIA envisaged eventual tripartite operation, see FO 371/65073, CE.04317, Foreign Office note on progress of Anglo-US negotiations, 15 October 1947.

106. FO 371/70627, C.3744, memorandum from Sir Willian Strang to Bevin, 6 May 1948.
107. FO 371/70627, C.3745, memorandum from Strang to Bevin, 6 May 1948. (The other heads were: Douglas (US), Massigli (France), and Hirschfeld, who represented the three Benelux countries.)
108. FO 371/70627, C.3747, memorandum from Sir William Strang to Bevin, 12 May 1948.
109. *FRUS*, 1948, vol. 2, p. 286, TRI/16 (Final), 26 May 1948 (also: FO 371/70627, C.4286).
110. The OEEC and the Economic Commission for Europe both had Steel Committees and the ECE had taken over the functions of the European Coal Organisation. In respect of coal exports from the Ruhr, the Moscow Sliding Scale still applied.
111. See, for example, R. Poidevin and J. Bariety, *Les Relations franco-allemandes 1815–1975* (Paris: Armand Colin, 1977) ch. 15.
112. The situation was summarised in a paper for the Bipartite Board, see FO 1005/86, BIB/P(48)43, 25 March 1948. See also, historical memorandum: FO 371/71148, CK.2140, 16 July 1948.
113. FO 371/71149, CK.3398, BIB/P(48)186, 11 November 1948.
114. Sometimes referred to in the plural as 'Military Laws no. 75' on account of differences in drafting for use in the British or US zones. Both versions are printed side-by-side for comparison in FO 371/76912, CE.4423.
115. FO 371/70630, C.9336, record of conversation between René Massigli and Sir Orme Sargent, 12 November 1948.
116. The French President committed this view to his diary on 25 November 1948, see V. Auriol, *Journal du Septennat 1947–1954* (Paris: Armand Colin, 1970) vol. 2, p. 542.
117. FO 371/70631, C.9489–C.9507. This was an American proposal which took the British delegation by surprise. Cf. the unexpected US concession on the Saar question, January 1948 (above, p. 63). The following year, Bevin had noticed the pattern and was wary of US calls for backing on the Humphrey Report: 'And then in the end, when the matter had blown up in the Paris press, I had no doubt that there would be a change of attitude' FO 371/77151, CJ.1560, Conversation with US Ambassador, 7 March 1949.
118. FO 371/70631, C.9550, telegram no. 115 from Paris to Foreign Office, 22 November 1948, transmits text of memorandum from Schuman.
119. *FRUS*, 1948, vol. 2, pp. 577–81, Communiqué, 28 December 1948.
120. FO 371/76584. C.3517, record of meeting of Foreign Ministers of US, France, and Great Britain, 6 April 1949. (For a convenient compilation of documents relating to the Washington Agreements see *FRUS*, 1949, vol. 3, pp. 1–186.)
121. FO 371/76912–76914, passim.
122. FO 371/76914, CE.5433, note by Sir Ivone Kirkpatrick, 28 December 1949.
123. For events leading to the establishment of the Federal Republic, see FRUS, 1949, vol. 3, pp. 187–504.
124. FO 1005/1094, HICOM/M(49)3, 20 October 1949. The meeting considered three letters circulated as HICOM/P(49)22, 25 and 28. (The High Commissioners had assumed the authority of the Military Governors. For the UK, General Robertson remained in post under the new title. Generals Clay and Koenig were replaced by John J. McCloy and André François-Poncet respectively.)

125. For pamphlets arguing against dismantling, see FO 371/70935, passim. For examples of graffiti and threatening letters to German demolition contractors, see FO 1013/395, *passim*.
126. In addition to the documents cited below, the background to the meeting and its conclusions were summarised in a Cabinet Paper, see CAB129/37, CP(49)237, 16 November 1949.
127. FO 371/76600, C.8615, telegram no. 1217 from Paris to Foreign Office, 9 November 1949.
128. FO 371/76601, C.8780, record of restricted session of Foreign Ministers and High Commissioners only, 10 November 1949.
129. FO 371/76600, C.8646, telegram no. 281 from Paris to Foreign Office, 10 November 1949.
130. Ibid.
131. Ibid.
132. FO 371/76601, C.8812, 10 November 1949.
133. *State Papers*, vol. 156, p. 584. An account of the negotiations is in FO 371/76603, C.9819.
134. Based on the 24 April 1946 assessment by the Allied Control Authority, in FO 942/481, SCMT/Misc(46)105.
135. Above, p. 78.
136. These plants were: August Thyssen Hütte, Hamborn; Hüttenwerke Niederrhein AG, Duisberg (Thyssen); Klöckner Werke AG Düsseldorf; Bochumer Verein Gusstahlfabrik, Bochum. From the 'last ditch' list, Deutsche Edelstahlwerke (Tiegelstahl), Bochum, was not offered for retention. (Capacity based on the estimates in FO 371/77152, CJ.1855, and including 99 000 tons of ingot production for Klöckner Werke not forming part of the Humphrey proposals and therefore omitted from the total on p. 79, above.)
137. *Humphrey Report*, p. 79. (Copy in FO 371/76829, CE.984.)
138. FO 371/77149, CJ.825, memorandum by the Ministry of Supply under cover of note dated 4 February 1949.
139. FO 371/76602, C.8909, telegram no. 1264 from Paris to Foreign Office reporting conversation between Bidault and Sir Oliver Harvey, 21 November 1949.
140. FO 1005/1461, CSG/M(50)4, 31 January 1950, noted at meeting of the Combined Steel Group.
141. FO 1005/1461, STEELCO/M(50)18, 7 June 1950 ('STEELCO' had replaced 'CSG' as the designation of the Combined Steel Group).
142. Below, p. 105.

Notes to Chapter 6: The Marshall Plan

1. CAB 129/19, CP(47)188, memorandum by Bevin, 23 June 1947.
2. FO 371/62408, UE.5665, documents typeset as Foreign Office Library Print no. 17326, p. 38, French statement of 27 June 1947.
3. CAB 129/20, CP(47)197, 5 July 1947.
4. Above, pp. 70–2.
5. Documents relating to the Paris Conference, 12–15 July 1947, were compiled and typeset on blue paper as Foreign Office Library Print no. 17377. See FO 371/62589, UE.9384.

6. CAB 133/42, ER(47)13th Meeting, 29 July 1947. ('ER' designated the committee of UK officials in Paris which was the counterpart of the 'London Committee': GEN 188, later ER(L).)
7. Retained capacity was divided as follows: 5 600 000 tons in the British zone, 1 210 000 tons in the French zone, 300 000 tons in the US zone, 390 000 tons in the Soviet Zone. See FO 942/481, SCMT/Misc(46)105, 24 April 1946, Allied Economic Directorate, Industry Committee, memorandum by the Metals Sub-Committee.
8. Although not a member, a questionnaire was to be sent to the Soviet zone, see CAB 133/42, ER(47)13th Meeting, 29 July 1947. In any case, production could not exceed the capacity remaining.
9. FO 371/65193, CJ.630, telegram no. 1 from Berlin to UK delegation in Paris, 1 August 1947.
10. FO 371/65193, CJ.633, telegram no. 1140 from Berlin to Foreign Office, 2 August 1947.
11. FO 371/65193, CJ.630, Foreign Office minute for the record, 5 August 1947.
12. CAB 133/42, ER(47)19th Meeting, 4 August 1947.
13. FO 371/65194, CJ.744, telegram no. 101 from Paris to Foreign Office, 8 August 1947.
14. Above, p. 73.
15. *FRUS*, 1947, vol. 3, p. 332, memorandum by G. F. Kennan, Director of the Policy Planning Staff, 18 July 1947.
16. FO 371/65201, CJ.1660, *General Report*, CEEC, September 1947, vol. 1, p. 53.
17. FO 371/65191, CJ.348, telegram no. 59 from Foreign Office to Paris, 24 July 1947.
18. FO 371/65193, CJ.633, telegram no. 1140 from Berlin to Foreign Office, 2 August 1947.
19. FO 1005/86, BIB/P(48)72, 20 May 1948, Bipartite Board paper. (The Board consisted of Clay, Robertson and a secretariat.)
20. FO 1030/138, letter from E. S. Jackson of the Bizonal delegation to Roger Stevens, Assistant Under-Secretary at the Foreign Office, 4 July 1948.
21. FO 1005/114, BICO/ERP/MEMO(48)20, 17 August 1948. (The BICO/ERP series designated the Bizonal organisation set up in Frankfurt to deal with matters relating to the European Recovery Programme.)
22. FO 1005/114, BICO/ERP/MEMO(48)19, 11 August 1948.
23. FO 1030/137, 54A (pagination in this file runs from 1A to 77A, and then from 42B to 68A, giving two pages 54A), telegram no. 1939 from Sir Cecil Weir to Foreign Office, 28 September 1948.
24. CAB 133/62, ER(P)(48)95, UK record of the 11th meeting of the Executive Committee Working Party, 5 and 6 November 1948.
25. CAB 124/1052, GEN 258/1st Meeting, 12 November 1948, Working Group on Long-Term Programmes. See note 39.
26. CAB 134/236, ER(L)(48)206 (revised), 9 December 1948.
27. CAB 134/216, EPC(48)40th Meeting, 14 December 1948.
28. FO 371/76843, CE.30, telegram no. 1670 from Foreign Office to UK delegation in Paris transmitting text of Bevin's message, 23 December 1948.

29. J. E. Smith (ed.), *The Papers of General Lucius D. Clay: Germany 1945–1949* (Bloomington: Indiana University Press, 1974) Book 4, p. 968, Clay to Draper, 27 December 1948.
30. Ibid., Book 5, p. 975, Clay to Voorhees, 6 January 1949.
31. FO 371/76844, CE.1461, Résumé prepared in the Treasury, 25 March 1949.
32. For a full treatment of the effect on foreign policy, see , C. C. S. Newton, 'Britain, the Dollar Shortage, and European Integration, 1945–50', PhD thesis, University of Birmingham, 1981.
33. CAB 134/237, ER(L)(49)20th Meeting, 23 March 1949.
34. FO 371/76844, CE.1338, telegram no. 1342 from Foreign Office to Berlin, 24 March 1949.
35. FO 371/76844, CE.1339, telegram no. 1120 from Berlin to Foreign Office, 26 March 1949.
36. FO 371/76844, CE.1775, letter from Sir Cecil Weir to Roger Stevens, Assistant Under-Secretary in charge of the Economic Relations Department of the Foreign Office, 11 April 1949.
37. *State Papers*, vol. 155, p. 490, 8 April 1949. See also, the White Paper: *Memorandum on the Measures Agreed by the United Kingdom, United States and French Foreign Ministers on the Programme for Germany.* Cmd. 7677 (filed at the PRO in ZHC1/8936). See also above, p. 159, note 120.
38. POWE 41/11, draft record of 4th meeting of the Conference of Foreign Ministers of France, the United Kingdom and the USSR in the 'Salle des Perroquets' at the Quai d'Orsay, 1 July 1947.
39. CAB 130/23, GEN 188/40 (Otherwise: GEN 191/6), 30 July 1947. (GEN 188 denoted the European Economic Co-operation (London) Committee, almost invariably referred to simply as the 'London Committee': an inter-departmental committee under Treasury chairmanship which co-ordinated Marshall Aid business. GEN 191 applied to the *ministerial* committee which met on two occasions to consider matters related to the European Recovery Programme.)
40. Ibid.
41. Ibid.
42. T 236/808, note by R. W. B. Clarke, 31 July 1947. ('Otto' Clarke was chairman of the London Committee.)
43. Ibid.
44. FO 371/62593, UE.6875, note by Roger Makins, 30 July 1947.
45. CAB 130/27, GEN 191/1st Meeting, 31 July 1947.
46. Ibid.
47. Ibid. (Remark ascribed to the Parliamentary Secretary, though according to the list of those present the Ministry was represented by the Minister himself, Emanuel Shinwell.)
48. T 236/808, GEN 191/7, 7 August 1947, note by Sir Edward Bridges: 'European Economic Integration'.
49. FO 371/70530, C.10578, letter from Harvey to Sir William Strang, Permanent Under-Secretary, Foreign Office, 15 December 1948. The letter covers a number of points and carries Bevin's handwritten comment: 'This is very important' (François-Poncet became French High Commissioner in Germany the following year).

50. T 238/225, 227, copy of article under cover of letter dated 7 February 1949 from Edelman to Sir Stafford Cripps.
51. T 232/83, 183, GEN258/A/42, 5 March 1949, note of meeting held at the home of Maurice Petsche in Paris, 3 March 1949. (Petsche had taken over the Finance portfolio from the Prime Minister, Henri Queuille.)
52. T 232/162, 31, handwritten comment appended to an internal Treasury memorandum on the subject, 13 December 1948.
53. Cripps Papers, Box 1042, Nuffield College, Oxford, text of a radio broadcast for the Voice of America, 29 March 1949.
54. CAB 133/63, ER(P)(49)14, British record of the 70th meeting of the OEEC Executive Committee, 17 March 1949.
55. T 232/163, CE(49)76, Draft Directive to the Iron and Steel Committee, 16 April 1949.
56. Above, pp. 78–9.
57. T 232/236, ER(L)(49)120, Paper prepared for the London Committee by the Foreign Office, 6 April 1949.
58. CAB 130/42, GEN 258/23, report by the Ministry of Supply to the Working Group on Long-Term Programmes, 14 January 1949.
59. T 232/163, 120. IS(49)21, 'Some Reflections by the Steel Committee on Co-ordination of Investment in the Steel Industry'. report to the Executive Committee and Council, 7 October 1949.
60. CAB 133/64, ER(P)(49)93, UK record of the 100th meeting of the Executive Committee, 11 October 1949.
61. SUPP 14/322, 13, *Progress report on ERP, Summary Number 37*, 18 October 1949.
62. *Hansard*, HC DEB, vol. 470, col. 1128, 30 November 1949, Christopher Mayhew, Bevin's Parliamentary Under-Secretary, in reply to a question from Mr M. Philips Price.
63. Above, p. 24.
64. CAB 130/42, GEN 258/23, report by the Ministry of Supply, 14 January 1949.
65. CAB 134/274, FC(47)111, memorandum by the Lord President of the Council circulated to the Fuel Committee, 23 July 1947.
66. CAB 134/274, FC(47)116, memorandum by Bevin, 24 July 1947.
67. CAB 134/272, FC(47)21st Meeting, 24 July 1947.
68. CAB 134/274, FC(47)114, 22 July 1947.
69. CAB 130/127, GEN 191/1st Meeting, European Economic Co-operation Committee of Ministers, 31 July 1947, Attlee in the Chair.
70. Above, pp. 42–4.
71. CAB 134/274, FC(47)118, memorandum by the Minister of Fuel and Power, 1 August 1947. (This paper was not taken in committee because of difficulty in scheduling a meeting but was circulated for written comments. See Lord President's papers: CAB 124/735.)
72. FO 371/68946, UE.1112, telegram no. 56 from UK delegation to Foreign Office, 27 January 1948.
73. BT 11/3631, 35. Brief prepared in the Board of Trade for the Chancellor of the Exchequer in his discussions with the French Minister of Finance (René Mayer) in January 1948, undated.
74. BT 11/3631, 29, UK record of meeting held at Steel House, Tothill Street, SW1 at 3 pm on Wednesday, 21 January 1948.

75. BT 11/3631, 47A, Agreement between the *Comptoir des Produits Sidérurgiques* and the *Chambre Syndicale de la Sidérurgie* on the one hand and the British Iron and Steel Corporation Limited on the other, 11 March 1948.
76. COAL 21/4, 177th Meeting of NCB, 13 February 1948.
77. FO 371/71749, UR.006, telegram no. 751 from Washington to Foreign Office, 14 February 1948.
78. T 236/1976, telegram no. 141 from Paris, 19 February 1948, report of a conversation between Lintott and Monsieur Nathan.
79. COAL 21/4, 179th Meeting of NCB, 17 February 1948.
80. CAB 130/22, GEN 188/50th Meeting, 23 February 1948.
81. CAB 130/25, GEN 188/139, 21 February 1948.
82. The ONC was an interdepartmental committee of officials which oversaw the progress of bilateral negotiations.
83. CAB 134/555, ON(48)14th Meeting, 27 February 1948.
84. Minister of Fuel and Power since the Cabinet reshuffle of October 1947, replacing Emanuel Shinwell.
85. FO 371/71800, UR.145, record of conversation between Bevin and US Ambassador, 3 March 1948, includes text of aide-mémoire dated 24 February 1948.
86. FO 371/71800, UR.628, record of conversation, 3 March 1948.
87. CAB 134/558, ON(48)126, note by the Treasury and the Board of Trade, 12 March 1948.
88. FO 371/71800, UR.678, message from Ambassador Douglas to Bevin, 27 March 1948.
89. CAB 130/26, GEN 188/187, 14 April 1948.
90. CAB 134/638, PC(48)61, memorandum for the Production Committee by the Minister of Fuel and Power, 8 May 1948.
91. Ibid.
92. CAB 134/636, PC(48)10th Meeting, 14 May 1947.
93. Appointed under the Foreign Assistance Act of 1948 with the rank of Ambassador-at-Large.
94. FO 371/71800, UR.2412, aide-mémoire, 15 June 1948.
95. CAB 134/232, ER(L)(48)4th Meeting, 18 June 1948.
96. FO 371/71800, UR.3045, record of conversation, 5 July 1948.
97. FO 371/71192, CK.981, letter from Val Duncan, National Coal Board, to George Derbyshire, Director of UK/US Coal Control Group, Essen, 12 March 1948.
98. *Hansard*, HC DEB, vol. 451, col. 188, 11 June 1948, written answer to a question by Mr Granville Sharp (Labour).
99. FO 1028/327, explanatory note by the Joint Export–Import Agency, 19 September 1949.
100. FO 371/71193, CK.2494, Table of loadings for export. Under cover of letter from US/UK Coal Control Group ref CC/INF/22, dated 14 August 1948. (Of 33 408 tons despatched in consideration of British imports during July, 14 010 tons went to France in the form of steam coal, anthracite, domestic coke and 'other coal'.)
101. FO 1028/327, memorandum from the Bipartite Control Office to the Joint Export–Import Agency, 3 May 1949.

Notes to Chapter 7: The Schuman Plan

1. René Massigli, *Une Comédie des Erreurs 1943–1956* (Paris: Plon, 1978) p. 185.
2. Ibid., p. 191.
3. FO 371/85841, CE.2322, telegram no. 217 from Paris to Foreign Office, reporting a conversation between Hall-Patch and M. D. Stikker, Dutch chairman of the OEEC Council, 10 May 1950.
4. FO 371/85841, CE.2141, memorandum by R. B. Stevens, 10 May 1950.
5. CAB 130/60, GEN 322/3, 11 May 1950.
6. T 236/2481, 2. PUSC(79) Final, 9 March 1950.
7. T 236/2483, 22, UK Delegation Brief no. 18, 27 April 1950.
8. FO 371/85841, CE.2297, notes of a meeting at the Hyde Park Hotel between Jean Monnet, Roger Makins, Edwin Plowden, and E. A. Hitchman, 16 May 1950.
9. The events leading to this decision were detailed in a White Paper: Cmd 7970, June 1950. Many of the relevant documents are published in: Roger Bullen (ed.), *Documents on British Policy Overseas, Series 2*, vol. 1, (London: HMSO, 1986) ch. 1. The originals of these are to be found in FO 371/85841–6.
10. FO 371/84847, CE.2826, telegram no. 2634 from Foreign Office to the Ambassador, Washington, reporting a conversation between Bevin and Sir William Strang at the London Clinic, 5 June 1950.
11. First meeting held on 25 May 1950. Documents were in the series FG(WP)(50)1 *et seq.* (FG for Franco-German), see CAB 134/295.
12. CAB 129/40, CP(50)149, 1 July 1950, report by the FG Committee (Ministerial *not* (WP)). Final form circulated to the Cabinet Economic Policy Committee on 24 July 1950 under cover of a note by Stafford Cripps, see CAB 134/226, EPC(50)81.
13. FO 371/85859, CE.3718, letter from O. Franks to R. Makins, 14 July 1950.
14. Ibid., letter from Makins to Franks, 17 July 1950.
15. POWE 41/16, memorandum by C. H. de Peyer, 20 July 1950.
16. CAB 134/224, EPC(50)20th Meeting, 28 July 1950.
17. T 229/751, letter from Roger Stevens at the Foreign Office to William Hayter in Paris, 16 August 1950.
18. T 229/751, letter from Hayter to Stevens reporting an interview with Bernard Clappier, 30 September 1950. (Clappier had replaced Alphand as liaison with the British.)
19. FO 371/85841, CE.2330, memorandum by Sir Ivone Kirkpatrick, 11 May 1950. (Kirkpatrick later succeeded General Robertson as British High Commissioner in Germany.)
20. Above, p. 85.
21. CAB 129/37, CP(49)237, Annex, 16 November 1949.
22. FO 371/76603, C.9623, record of meeting at the Quai d'Orsay, 9 November 1949.
23. FO 1013/869, 70B, HC/813, from General Robertson to Major-General Bishop (retired), 23 November 1949.
24. FO 1013/869, 71, extract from meeting in the office of the *Land* Commissioner, North Rhine-Westphalia, 1 December 1949.

25. FO 1030/230, 169A, letter from Bishop to General Robertson, 3 December 1949.
26. FO 1013/869, 83, NRW/LC/3001, memorandum from Bishop to Robertson, 17 December 1949.
27. FO 1005/1255, MSB/IND/P(50)11, 27 January 1950.
28. Above, pp. 78–9.
29. FO 371/70530, C.2151, letter from Sir Oliver Harvey to Ernest Bevin reporting a conversation, 20 February 1948. (The Tennessee Valley Authority was a model which much appealed to Jean Monnet, see Jean Monnet, *Mémoires* (Paris: Fayard, 1976) p. 327.)
30. FO 371/70627, C.3746, memorandum to Ernest Bevin from Lord Pakenham, Chancellor of the Duchy of Lancaster since the Cabinet reshuffle of October 1947, 7 May 1948.
31. FO 1013/343, 30A, telegram RC 34 from Dusseldorf to Berlin. 31 December 1948, transmits translated advance copy of broadcast. (Minister President: Karl Arnold (CDU – Adenauer's party) became President of the Bundesrat in 1949.)
32. Above, pp. 96–8.
33. FO 371/85147, C.372, telegram no. 79 from Wahnerheide to Foreign Office, 16 January 1950.
34. FO 371/85147, C.1476, despatch no. 127 from Sir Oliver Harvey to Ernest Bevin, 22 February 1950.
35. FO 371/85147, C.2149, despatch no. 201 from Harvey to Bevin, 24 March 1950. FO 371/85148, C.2848, no. 272, 27 April 1950.
36. FO 371/86034, CJ.2133, Foreign Office memorandum to Bevin, 27 April 1950. (Drafted by A. H. Lincoln, approved by R. Stevens, Assistant Under-Secretary, and Sir Ivone Kirkpatrick, Permanent Under-Secretary. Carries Bevin's handwriting: 'Remind me'.)
37. FO 371/86033, CJ.2114.
38. T 236/2484, record of meeting of Working Party A (Economic Questions) of Sub-Group B (German Problems), 2 May 1950. See also, *FRUS*, 1950, vol. 3, p. 918, telegram no. Secto 104 from the US delegation to US Secretary of State, 3 May 1950.
39. FO 371/86034, CJ.2434, minute by A. D. Wilson, 18 May 1950. (This analysis found favour with the Permanent Under-Secretary, Sir William Strang, who appended the comment: 'A useful minute'.)
40. *FRUS*, 1950, vol. 3, p. 1045, telegram no. Secto 243 from US delegation to Acting Secretary of State, 12 May 1950.
41. *FRUS*, 1950, vol. 3, p. 1050, footnote. Terms of reference were approved as document MIN/TRI/P/12. With a preamble indicating this approval, issued as TRI/MIN/P/12 Final, 22 May 1950, and finally circulated to the Study Group as IGG(50)8, 6 July 1950 (see FO 371/85329, C.4455).
42. *FRUS*, 1950, vol. 3, p. 1045.
43. T 236/2488, 63, TRI/MIN/P/15 Final, 22 May 1950. Agreed at the afternoon session, 12 May 1949.
44. FO 371/85330, C.5404, telegram no. 1211 from Wahnerheide (Sir Ivone Kirkpatrick) to Foreign Office, 15 August 1950.

Notes

45. FO 371/85330, C.5305, IGG(50)UKDEL 13, UK record of 5th plenary meeting, 16 August 1950.
46. FO 371/85331, C.5576, IGG(50)116, record of 7th plenary meeting, 30 August 1950.
47. FO 371/85331, C.5667, IGG(50)108, 30 August 1950. (Included in papers for tripartite Foreign Ministers' meeting under omnibus cover: TRI/B/12, 5 September 1950).
48. FO 371/85027, C.5692, telegram no. 1326 from Wahnerheide to Foreign Office, 7 September 1950.
49. FO 371/85027, C.5693, telegram no. 1327 from Wahnerheide to Foreign Office, 7 September 1950.
50. FO 371/86036, CJ.3900, AGSEC(50)1885, 31 August 1950, report circulated by the Allied General Secretariat.
51. FO 371/86035, CJ.3808, telegram no. 1285 from Wahnerheide to Foreign Office, 31 August 1950.
52. The New York Conference is covered in *FRUS*, 1950, vol. 3, pp. 1108–1301. A summary of the proceedings and conclusions were contained in two memoranda circulated to the Cabinet by Ernest Bevin, see CAB 129/42, CP(50)222 and CP(50)223, 6 October 1950.
53. CAB 129/42, CP(50)222, 6 October 1950, Annex: 'Communiqué on Germany', released at 1 pm New York time on 19 September 1950. (Also FO 371/85027, C.5965, telegram no. 1104 from New York to Foreign Office, 18 September 1950)
54. FO 371/85028, C.6302, UK record of Ministers' discussion on Germany, afternoon, 18 September 1950.
55. FO 371/86035, CJ.3882, telegram no. 1314 from Wahnerheide to Foreign Office, 5 September 1950.
56. FO 1005/1250, MSB/IND/M(50)18, 14 September 1950, item 452.
57. FO 1005/1104, 185, verbatim report of an informal meeting of the Council of the High Commission, 14 September 1950. (The High Commissioners being absent in New York, those present were: M. Berard (Chairman), Mr. Steel and Gen. Hays.)
58. FO 1005/1095, HICOM/M(50)32, minutes of the 40th meeting of the Council of the High Commission, 21 September 1950. The text of the reply was circulated as AGSEC(50)2071 (see FO 1005/16).
59. FO 1005/1104, 166, verbatim record of 40th meeting of the Council of the High Commission, 21 September 1950.
60. Above, p. 87.
61. FO 1005/1461, STEELCO/M(50)18, 7 June 1950, item 412.
62. FO 1005/1114, HICOM/P(50)144, 18 September 1950, note by the General Secretariat covering the memorandum of the Economics Committee and outlining the action taken up to that point.
63. Ibid., memorandum of the Economics Committee.
64. FO 1005/1104, 166, verbatim record of the 40th meeting of the Council of the High Commission, 21 September 1950.
65. Ibid.
66. Cmd. 7677, Annex 2, Clause 7(b).

67. T 229/751, telegram no. 478 from Wahnerheide to Foreign Office, 24 September 1950.
68. FO 1005/1095, HICOM/M(50)32, minutes of the 40th meeting of the High Commission, 21 September 1950, item 624.
69. FO 1005/1095, HICOM/M(50)33, minutes of the 41st meeting, 28 September 1950, item 636.
70. FO 1005/1461, STEELCO/M(50)27, 3 November 1950.
71. FO 371/85148, C.7090, letter, 23 October 1950.
72. FO 1030/265, 78A, telegram no. 2549 from Washington to Foreign Office, 22 September 1950.
73. FO 371/85334, C.6899, IGG(50)140, Annex A: French note on Prohibited and Limited Industries (translation), 23 October 1950.
74. FO 371/85334, C.6854, telegram no. 1054 from Foreign Office to Wahnerheide, 28 October 1950.
75. FO 371/85334, C.7176, IGG(50)151, 4 November 1950, record of meeting of Heads of Delegations, 3 November 1950.
76. FO 371/85334, C.7205, telegram no. 1082 from Foreign Office to Wahnerheide, 7 November 1950.
77. FO 371/86038, CJ.4721, telegram no. 1857 from Foreign Office to Wahnerheide, 18 November 1950.
78. FO 371/86038, CJ.4831, note of a conversation between Roger Stevens and Bevin, 28 November 1950.
79. FO 371/85334, C.8112, IGG(50)194, 'Report to Governments', 16 December 1950.
80. FO 371/94105, HICOM/P(51)37, 26 March 1951.
81. POWE 41/16, cutting from *The Times*, 6 February 1951.
82. FO 371/93720, CE(W)1103/13, letter from Edward Warner to R. S. Swann (German Section, Foreign Office), 20 February 1951.
83. POWE 41/16, cutting from the *Manchester Guardian*, 21 February 1951.
84. FO 371/93828, CE(W)1543/110, memorandum from Stevens to Herbert Morrison, 13 April 1951. (Morrison had replaced Bevin on 9 March. Bevin died 14 April.)
85. CAB 128/19, CM(51)28, 16 April 1951, Cabinet meeting. FO 371/93828, CE(W)1543/109, memorandum by Stevens, 17 April 1951.
86. FO 371/93828, CE(W)1543/108, telegram no. 140 from Paris to Foreign Office transmitting text of letter, 16 April 1951.
87. FO 371/93829, CE(W)1543/117, telegram from Foreign Office to Wahnerheide transmitting text of statement, 19 April 1951.
88. FO 371/93830, CE(W)1543/154, letter from Hayter to Roger Stevens, 19 April 1951.
89. FO 371/93834, CE(W)1543/215, undated memorandum handed to Roger Stevens by M. Mattei of the French Embassy on 5 May 1951.
90. CAB 128/19, CM(51)44, 18 June 1951. See also Bullen (ed.), *Documents on British Policy Overseas*, chapter 3, which is largely devoted to this question.
91. FO 371/93841, CE(W)1543/435, letter from Foreign Office to Paris, informing the Ambassador, 20 September 1951.
92. Monnet, *Mémoires*, p. 426.

93. For a summary by the Foreign Office Research Department dated 20 June 1951, see FO 371/93421, C.10112/59.
94. Above, note 91, Chapter 4.
95. *State Papers*, vol. 158, p. 630.
96. The Saar Democratic Party (DPS). For a history and policy appraisal prepared by the Research department of the Foreign Office and dated 29 May 1951, see FO 371/93420, C.10112/42.
97. FO 1005/37, AGSEC/Memo(51)24, 4 June 1951, translation of Adenauer's memorandum of 29 May 1951.
98. FO 371/93420, C.10112/48, French text handed to Sir William Strang by the Ambassador, Massigli, on 9 June 1951.
99. FO 371/93420, C.10112/39, telegram no. 2987 from Foreign Office to Washington, 16 June 1951.
100. FO 371/93421, C.10112/55, letter from C. O'Neil to W.D. Allen, Foreign Office, 15 June 1951.
101. FO 1005/22, AGSEC(51)1274, 2 August 1951, final version of letter to Adenauer. (For copies of successive drafts and related correspondence, see FO 371/93420–93423, *passim*.)
102. FO 371/93424, C.10112/108, letter from William Hayter to W. D. Allen, 3 August 1951.
103. FO 371/93421, C.10112/49, letter from Sir Ivone Kirkpatrick to Herbert Morrison, Foreign Secretary, 8 June 1951.
104. Ibid.
105. FO 371/93424, C.10112/127, telegram no. 628 from Paris to Foreign Office, 28 October 1951 (documents relating to Anglo-US discussion in the preceding three months are in attached files).
106. Monnet, *Mémoires*, pp. 345–7.
107. Ibid., p. 346.
108. Above, pp. 105–6.
109. Monnet, *Mémoires*, p. 346.

Notes to Chapter 8: The Parting of the Ways

1. FO 371/93833, CE(W)1543/198, letter from Butt to Duncan Wilson, 3 May 1951.
2. Above, pp. 13–14.
3. Above, p. 6.
4. CAB 128/9, CM(47)2, 6 January 1947.
5. BT 11/3357, amended extract initialled R.S.C.
6. CAB 129/16, CP(47)35, 18 January 1947.
7. CAB 128/9, CM(47)13, 28 January 1947.
8. CAB 134/47, BP(ON)(47)40, 21 October 1947, report to the Balance of Payments group of the Overseas Negotiations Committee.
9. CAB 128/10, CM(47)77, 25 September 1947. For related files, see FO 371/62554, *passim*.
10. FO 371/62554, UE.9411, comment by Hall-Patch appended to a minute by Roger Stevens, 9 October 1947.
11. FO 371/67673, Z.8028, Speech on 8 September 1947.

12. FO 371/67673, Z.8461, British record of the conversation, 22 September 1947 (for French record, see FO 371/67673, Z.8652).
13. Duff Cooper, *Old Men Forget* (London: Rupet Hart-Davis) p. 377, diary entry for 22 September 1947.
14. Duff Cooper, *Old Men Forget*, p. 379.
15. FO 371/67673, Z.9053, record of meeting at the Foreign Office 8 October 1947. Also present were representatives of the Commonwealth Relations Office, Treasury, Board of Trade, Colonial Office, Bank of England, Ministry of Fuel.
16. CAB 129/23, CP(48)6, 4 January 1948.
17. FO 371/73045, Z.809, memorandum from Hall Patch to Sir Orme Sargent, 15 January 1948.
18. CAB 128/12, CM(48)2, 8 January 1948. FO 371/73045, Z.273. telegram no. 52 from Foreign Office to Paris, 13 January 1948.
19. FO 371/73045, Z.459, telegram no. 50 from Foreign Office to Brussels, 20 January 1948.
20. FO 371/73045, Z.809, minute by Sir Orme Sargent, Permanent Under-Secretary at the Foreign Office, 19 January 1948.
21. FO 371/73045, Z.809, memorandum from Makins to Sir Orme Sargent, 21 January 1948.
22. *Hansard*, HC DEB, vol. 446, cols 383–409, 22 January 1948.
23. Ibid., cols 396, 397.
24. Ibid., col. 392.
25. Ibid., col. 405.
26. *State Papers*, vol. 150, p. 672.
27. *State Papers*, vol. 147, p. 844.
28. FO 371/73047, Z.1256, report by the Minister of State, Hector McNeil, of his talks in Brussels with representatives of the Benelux countries, 7 February 1948. (For associated files, see FO 371/73045–73047, *passim*.)
29. CAB 134/216, EPC(48)2nd Meeting, 9 January 1948. (Economic Policy Committee: Attlee (in the Chair), Morrison and Cripps.)
30. CAB 124/1053, GEN.258/A/15, 17 January 1949, paper circulated to the European Economic Co-operation Committee Working Party on Long-Term Programmes by the Board of Trade.
31. *Hansard*, HC DEB, vol. 482, col. 1162, 13 December 1950. Announcement by Hugh Gaitskell, Chancellor of the Exchequer.
32. CAB 133/42, ER(47)6th Meeting, 21 July 1947. Also: ER(47)8th Meeting, 22 July 1947.
33. T 238/225, 8, letter from Roger Makins, Foreign Office, to Leslie Rowan, Treasury, 2 September 1948.
34. T 238/225, *passim*, exchanges of memoranda between Treasury officials on the subject.
35. CAB 133/62, ER(P)(48)85, 29 October 1948, British record of meeting in Hervé Alphand's room at the Quai d'Orsay.
36. CAB 133/62, ER(P)(48)87, 30 October 1948, British record of the 7th meeting of the Executive Committee Working Party. Dag Hammarskjöld in the chair. Alphand led the examination in the presence of representatives of Switzerland, the Netherlands, Italy, and Turkey.

37. This is apparent from the documentary record. For the appraisal of those who knew him, see Eric Roll, *Crowded Hours* (London : Faber & Faber, 1985) and Roderick Barclay, *Ernest Bevin and the Foreign Office 1932–1969* (published by the author, London, 1975).
38. FO 371/71983, UR.7332, telegram no. 41 from Paris to Foreign Office, 8 November 1948.
39. FO 371/71983, UR.7100, Makins to Bevin, 1 November 1948.
40. FO 371/71983, UR.7332, telegram no. 41, 8 November 1948.
41. Colin Cooke, *The Life of Richard Stafford Cripps* (London: Hodder & Stoughton, 1957) p. 358; Alan Bullock, *Ernest Bevin: Foreign Secretary 1945–1951* (Oxford: Oxford University Press, 1983) pp. 456, 457.
42. CAB 134/216, EPC(48)37th Meeting, 25 November 1948.
43. T 238/225, 96, record of discussion, 26 November 1948.
44. Queuille was *Président du Conseil* (= Prime Minister) and also his own Minister of Finance in a government in which his own Radical Party held only four out of fifteen ministerial posts.
45. T 238/223, 99, letter from Cripps to Queuille, 27 November 1948.
46. T 238/223, 42, letter from Queuille to Cripps, 2 December 1948.
47. FO 371/77932, *passim*.
48. T 229/163, record of meeting, 11 February 1949.
49. T 229/207, note for the record of a conversation between Plowden and Monnet at lunch on 17 February 1949.
50. A wealth of published material covers this well-documented episode. See in particular: E. Plowden, *An Industrialist in the Treasury: The Post-War Years* (London: Andre Deutsch, 1989) pp. 74–6; J. Monnet, *Mémoires* (Paris: Fayard, 1976) pp. 330–332; A. Cairncross (ed.), *The Robert Hall Diaries 1947–53* (London: Unwin Hyman, 1989) p. 57. For preparatory work, see T 229/207. For Foreign Office documents, see FO 371/77933.
51. FO 371/77933, UR.3322, summary of four conversations with Monnet between 3 and 7 March 1949.
52. T 229/163, Meeting in Plowden's room, 15 March 1949.
53. Plowden, *An Industrialist in the Treasury*, p. 74.
54. Monnet, *Mémoires*, p. 331.
55. Cairncross (ed.), *The Robert Hall Diaries 1947–53*, p. 94. Entry for 16 November 1949.
56. Plowden, *An Industrialist in the Treasury*, p. 75. Monnet, *Mémoires*, p. 332.
57. Plowden, *An Industrialist in the Treasury*, p. 76.
58. FO 371/85841, CE.2332, letter from Hall-Patch, at the OEEC in Paris, to Roger Makins at the Foreign Office, 11 May 1950.
59. Above, p. 130.
60. Above, pp. 96–7. (Milward gives June 1948 as the month when the Quai d'Orsay began preparing a shift towards a Franco-German economic association – A. Milward, *The Reconstruction of Western Europe 1945–51* (London: Methuen, 1984) p. 468.)
61. T 232/162, 28B, letter from Hall-Patch to E. A. Berthoud, Assistant Under-Secretary at the Foreign Office, reporting a conversation between Gore-Booth and Baraduc, 7 December 1948.
62. Above, p. 77.

63. This point is made in R. Mowat, *Ruin and Resurgence, 1939–1965* (London : Blandford Press, 1966) p. 191.
64. Above, p. 78.
65. Above, p. 85.
66. Above, pp. 112–18.
67. T 232/162, 156, note of discussion at the Wardman Park Hotel, Washington, on 18 January 1949, Dated 20 January 1949.
68. Above, p. 128.
69. Monnet, *Mémoires*, from the title of chapter 12.
70. V. Auriol, *Journal du Septennat*, vol. 2: *1948* (Paris: Armand Colin, 1970) p. 144, diary entry for 11 March 1948 recording a conversation with Monnet.
71. Above, pp. 127–8.
72. Above, p. 133.
73. Monnet, *Mémoires*, p. 332.
74. T 229/207, paper by Hall in preparation for the talks at Monnet's house: 'First thoughts about M. Monnet', 5 April 1949.

Bibliography

PUBLIC RECORD OFFICE, KEW

Classes of records consulted, with brief descriptions of the most important files:

Foreign Office

FO 371: General Files. Where an extended reference is given, the prefix indicates the department concerned according to broad subject area:

    Z   Western Department [Responsible for French affairs]
    UR European Recovery
    UE Economic
    U   Peacemaking
    CK German Industry
    CJ German General Economic
    CE German Trade
    C   German

FO 800/434–522: The Bevin Papers. These consist of files kept by Bevin's Principal Private Secretary. Where material is duplicated in FO 371, that reference has been preferred if related files are attached.

FO 935–946: Control Office for Germany and Austria.

FO 1005: Control Commission for Germany Records Library.

FO 1013: Control Commission for North Rhine-Westphalia.

FO 1023–1039: Control Commission for Germany.
   In particular:

    1023 Allied General Secretariat
    1030 Military Governor's Private Office
    1032 Headquarters Secretariat, Berlin
    1036 Office of the Economic Adviser
    1039 Economic Divisions

Cabinet Records

CAB 21: This class consists mainly of briefs for the Prime Minister on a variety of subjects. Also of interest are the carbon copies of Attlee's outgoing memoranda in piece numbers 2277–2279.

CAB 124: Lord President's Papers.
CAB 128: Minutes of Cabinet Meetings.
CAB 129: Cabinet Papers.
CAB 130: *Ad hoc* Cabinet Committees
CAB 134: Standing Cabinet Committees.

Treasury

T 229: Central Economic Planning Staff.
T 230: Economic Section.
T 232: Papers relating to the European Recovery Programme.
T 236: Overseas Finance Division.
T 238: Overseas Negotiations Committee Division.
T 273: The Papers of Sir Edward Bridges.

Board of Trade

BT 11: Commercial Relations and Treaties.
BT 64: Industries and Manufactures Division.
BT 211: German Division.

Ministry of Fuel and Power

POWE: Various files in no particular sequence.

Ministry of Supply

SUPP [Also some files under AVIA]

National Coal Board

COAL 21: Meetings of the NCB.

PREM 8

Correspondence of the Prime Minister, Clement Attlee.

OTHER UNPUBLISHED MATERIAL

Collections of Papers

James Meade, London School of Economics.
Herbert Morrison, London School of Economics.
Stafford Cripps, Nuffield College, Oxford.

Doctoral Theses

Colebrook, Mulford J., 'Franco-British Relations and European Integration 1945–50', University of Geneva, 1971.
Lynch, F. M. B., 'The Political and Economic Reconstruction of France, 1944–1947, in the International Context', University of Manchester, 1981.
Mitchell, Joan, 'Economic Planning and the Long-Term Programme', University of Nottingham, 1956.
Newton, C. C. S., 'Britain, the Dollar Shortage, and European Integration 1945–50 University of Birmingham, 1981.

PUBLISHED SOURCES

Official Publications

Foreign Relations of the United States [*FRUS*], US Government Printing Office, Washington.
State Papers, Her Majesty's Stationery Office, London.
Hansard.
Command Papers.

Periodicals

The Economist.

BOOKS

Published in London unless otherwise stated.

Acheson, Dean, *Present at the Creation: My Years in the State Department* (Hamish Hamilton, 1970).
Alphand Hervé, *L'Etonnement d'être; journal de 1939 à 1973* (Paris: Fayard, 1977).
Auriol, Vincent, *Journal du Septennat 1947–1954* (Paris: Armand Colin, 1970).
Barclay, Roderick, *Ernest Bevin and the Foreign Office 1932–1969* (published by the Author, 1975).
Balfour, Michael and Mair, John, *Four-Power Control in Germany and Austria 1945–1946* (Oxford University Press, 1956).
Beugel, Ernst H. van der, *From Marshall Aid to Atlantic Partnership: European Integration as a Concern of American Foreign Policy* (Amsterdam: Elsevier Publishing, 1966).
Bidault, Georges (translated by Marianne Sinclair), *Resistance: The Political Autobiography of Georges Bidault* (Weidenfeld & Nicolson, 1967).
Bullen, Roger (ed.), *Documents on British Policy Overseas*, Series 2, vol. 1 (HMSO, 1986).

Bullock, Alan, *Ernest Bevin: Foreign Secretary 1945–1951* (Oxford University Press, 1983).
Burn, Duncan, *The Steel Industry 1939–1959: A Study in Competition and Planning* (Cambridge University Press, 1961).
Cairncross, Alec, *Years of Recovery: British Economic policy 1945–51* (Methuen, 1985).
Cairncross, Alec, *The Price of War: British Policy on German Reparations 1941–1949* (Oxford: Basil Blackwell, 1986).
Cairncross, Alec (ed.), *The Robert Hall Diaries 1947–53* (Unwin Hyman, 1989).
Cairncross, Alec and Watts, Nita, *The Economic Section 1939–1961: A Study in Economic Advising* (Routledge, 1989).
Carmoy, Guy de, *Les Politiques Étrangères de la France 1944–1966* (Paris: La Table Ronde, 1967).
Clay, Lucius D., *Decision in Germany* (Westport, Connecticut: Greenwood Press,1950).
Cooke, Colin, *The Life of Richard Stafford Cripps* (Hodder & Stoughton, 1957).
Cooper, Duff, *Old Men Forget: The Autobiography of Duff Cooper (Viscount Norwich)* (Rupert Hart-Davis, 1953).
Dalton, Hugh, *High Tide and After: Memoirs 1945–1960* (Frederick Muller, 1962).
de Gaulle, Charles, *Mémoires de guerre,* vol. 3: *'Le Salut' 1944–1946* (Paris: Plon, 1959).
Deighton, Anne, *The Impossible Peace: Britain, the Division of Germany, and the Origins of the Cold War* (Oxford: Clarendon Press, 1993).
Eden Anthony, *Full Circle* (Cassell, 1960).
Fourastié, J., and Courtheoux, J-P., *La Planification Economique en France* (Paris: Presses Universitaires de France, 1968).
Gillingham, John, *Coal, Steel, and the Rebirth of Europe, 1945–1955: The Germans and French from Ruhr Conflict to Economic Community* (Cambridge University Press, 1991).
Gimbel, John, *The American Occupation of Germany: Politics and the Military, 1945–1949* (Stanford California: Stanford University Press, 1968).
Gorce, Paul-Marie de la, *L'Après-Guerre: 1944–1952* (Paris: Bernard Grasset, 1978).
Grosser, Alfred, *La Quatrième République et sa politique extérieure* (Paris: Armand Colin, 1972).
Hennessy, Peter, *Never Again: Britain 1945–51* (Jonathan Cape, 1992).
Hennessy, Peter and Arends, Andrew, *Mr Attlee's Engine Room: Cabinet Committee Structure and the Labour Government 1945–51* (Strathclyde University, 1983).
Jewkes, John, *The New Ordeal by Planning: The Experience of the Forties and the Sixties* (Macmillan, 1968).
Jones, Joseph Marion, *The Fifteen Weeks (February 21–June 5, 1947)* (New York: Harcourt, Brace & World, 1955).
Kindleberger, Charles P., *Marshall Plan Days* (Winchester, Mass.: Allen & Unwin, 1987).
Marjolin, Robert, *Le Travail d'une vie: Mémoires 1911–1986* (Paris: Robert Laffont, 1986).
Martin, James Stewart, *All Honorable Men*, (Boston: Little, Brown, 1950).
Massigli, René, *Une Comédie des erreurs 1943–1956: Souvenirs et réflexions sur une étape de la construction européenne* (Paris: Plon, 1978).

Mayne, Richard, *The Recovery of Europe: From Devastation to Unity* (Weidenfeld & Nicolson, 1970).
McLellan, Davis S., *Dean Acheson: The State Department Years* (New York: Dodd, Mead, 1976).
Milward, Alan S., *The Reconstruction of Western Europe 1945–51* (Methuen, 1984).
Monnet, Jean, *Mémoires* (Paris: Fayard, 1976).
Morrison, Herbert, *Herbert Morrison: An Autobiography by Lord Morrison of Lambeth* (Odhams, 1960).
Mowat, R. C., *Ruin and Resurgence 1939–1965* (Blandford, 1966).
Nutting, Anthony, *Europe Will Not Wait: A Warning and a Way Out* (Hollis & Carter, 1960).
Ovendale, Ritchie (ed.), *The Foreign Policy of the British Labour Governments, 1945–1951* (Leicester University Press, 1984).
Pelling, Henry, *Britain and the Marshall Plan* (Macmillan, 1988).
Pimlott, Ben (ed.), *The Political Diary of Hugh Dalton 1918–40, 1945–60* (Jonathan Cape in association with the LSE, 1986).
Plowden, Edwin, *An Industrialist in the Treasury: The Post-War Years* (Andre Deutsch, 1989).
Poidevin, Raymond and Bariety, Jacques, *Les relations franco-allemandes 1815–1975* (Paris : Armand Colin, 1977).
Roll, Eric, *Crowded Hours* (Faber & Faber, 1985).
Smith, Jean Edward (ed.), *The Papers of General Lucius D. Clay: Germany 1945–1949* (Bloomington: Indiana University Press, 1974).
Turner, Ian D. (ed.), *Reconstruction in Post-War Germany: British Occupation Policy and the Western Zones 1945–55* (Oxford: Berg, 1989).
Urwin, Derek W., *The Community of Europe: A History of European Integration since 1945* (Longman, 1991).
Waites, Neville (ed.), *Troubled Neighbours: Franco-British Relations in the Twentieth Century* (Weidenfeld & Nicolson, 1971).
Werth, Alexander, *France 1940–1955* (Robert Hale, 1956).
Wexler, Imanuel, *The Marshall Plan Revisited* (Westport, Connecticut: Greenwood Press, 1983).
White, Theodore H., *Fire in the Ashes: Europe in Mid-Century* (New York: William Sloan Associates, 1953).
Williams, Francis, *A Prime Minister Remembers: The War and Post-War Memories of the Rt Hon. Earl Attlee* (Heinemann, 1961).
Williams, Francis, *Ernest Bevin: Portrait of a Great Englishman* (Hutchinson, 1952).
Williams, Philip M., *Crisis and Compromise: Politics in the Fourth Republic* (Longman, 1958).
Willis, F. Roy, *France, Germany, and the New Europe 1945–1967* (Stanford California: Stanford University Press, 1968).
Young, John W., *France, the Cold War and the Western Alliance 1944–49: French Foreign Policy and Post-war Europe* (Leicester University Press, 1990).
Young, John W., *Britain, France and the Unity of Europe 1945–51* (Leicester University Press, 1984).
Zametica, John (ed), *British Officials and British Foreign Policy 1945–50* (Leicester University Press, 1990).
Zink, Harold, *The United States in Germany 1944–1955* (Princeton, New Jersey: D. Van Nostrand, 1957).

Index

Acheson, Dean, 85, 106
Adenauer, Konrad, 84, 85, 120
   and Franco-German relations, 120–1
   talks with Schuman, 111
Allied Coal Committee, 44
Allied Control Authority, 22, 48, 54
Allied Economic Directorate, 46
Allied High Commission, 112
Alphand, Hervé, 4, 21–2, 39, 48–9, 51, 61, 73, 90, 99
Anglo-French Economic Co-operation Committee, 48, 125
   established, 5
   examination of Monnet Plan, 9, 11
   and long-term programmes, 129
Anglo-French Steel Agreement, 31
Attlee, Clement, 22
   and Anglo-French integration, 9
   becomes Prime Minister, xi
   chairman of the Economic Policy Committee, 130
   and coal imports, 40, 42
   and Monnet Plan, 10
Auriol, Vincent, 110

Baudet, Philippe, 105
Berlin Airlift, 135
Bevin, Ernest
   and Anglo-French customs union, 3, 19, 126
   and Anglo-French relations, 1–2
   becomes Foreign Secretary, xi, 45
   and Bizonal steel industry, 72, 90
   and British coal industry, 100
   and British steel industry, 31
   and coal imports, 41–2
   and Commonwealth, 106
   death, 107, 120
   disillusionment with Council of Foreign Ministers, 80
   and dismantling of German industry, 76–7, 108
   and European steel integration, 32–3, 96
   and Franco-German relations, 111
   and French Government of Léon Blum, 35
   and German economic recovery, 128
   and German steel production, 118

   'grand design', 1–2, 125, 127–8
   illness, 106
   and long-term programmes, 93
   and Marshall Aid, 89
   and Monnet Plan, 9–10
   and Ruhr, status of, 3
   and Saar, 52, 56, 58–60, 62
   and Schuman Plan, 105–7
   USA, attitude towards, 128, 135
Bidault, Georges
   and Anglo-French economic co-operation, 4
   and Anglo-French Union, 2
   and German coal supplies, 48–9
   and German level of industry, 71, 87
   and Marshall Aid, 89
   replaced by Schuman, 111
   and Saar, 55, 58, 62
Bipartite Board, 65
Bipartite Economic Panel, 74
Bizone, 104
   formation, 65
   fusion with French zone, 61
   long-term programme
Blum, Léon, 9, 19, 34, 110, 125
Board of Trade
   and Anglo-French Co-operation, 5–8, 30, 126
   and European customs union, 126
   and Monnet Plan, 15–16
   and steel forecast, 28–9
Bridges, Edward, 15, 36
Brussels, Treaty of, 128
Butt, David, 125
Byrnes, James, 56, 67

Cairncross, Alec, 28
Central Economic Planning Staff (CEPS), 18, 28, 132–3
Chauvel, Jean, 4
Churchill, Winston, 139
   Anglo-French Union, offer of, xi
   return to office, 120
   United States of Europe, proposal for, 110
Clay, Lucius, 39, 69, 92–3
Coal Control Group, 83
Combined Steel Group, 87, 115–16, 119

Index

Committee of European Economic
   Co-operation (CEEC)
  Bizonal delegation, 91
  established, 89
  see also Organisation for European
    Economic Co-operation
Control Office for Germany and Austria,
  21, 46, 50
Cooper, Duff, 1
  and Anglo-French integration, 4
  Board of Trade, attitude towards, 10
  and the Ruhr, status of, 3
  and the Saar, 56
Council of Europe, 137
Council of Foreign Ministers (CFM)
  established, xi
  London, 62, 80
  Moscow, 19, 29, 41, 50, 56–7, 70, 80
  New York, 34, 56
  Paris, 22, 47, 67
Couve de Murville, Maurice, 56–7
Cripps, Stafford
  and Anglo-French economic
    co-operation, 9
  Bevin, relations with, 130
  and European investment programmes,
    97
  and European steel integration, 97
  and French economy, 131
  and long-term programmes, 93
  and Monnet Plan, 17, 125
  Morrison, stands in for, 19
  President of the Board of Trade, 6, 9

Department of Overseas Trade
  Report on the Saar, 53
Douglas, Lewis, 42, 82, 102
Duncanson, John, 23, 28
Dunkirk, Treaty of, 19, 41, 59, 65, 69–70,
  126

Economic Commission for Europe, 6, 29
  Coal Committee, 63, 100, 103–4
Economic Co-operation Administration,
  103
Economic Intelligence Department, 26
Economic Policy Committee, 93, 107, 130
Economic Section of the Cabinet Office, 7
  and Anglo-French integration, 13–14, 132
  and Bevin's European policy, 127
  and European steel production, 29
Economic Survey, 28
Economic White Paper, 9, 15, 17–18
Economist, The, 11, 46

Edelman, Maurice, 97
Eden, Anthony
  and Anglo-French Union, xi
  at Potsdam, 45
Essen
  Anglo-French coal conference, 45
European Coal and Steel Community, 120,
  137
  see also Schuman Plan
European Coal Organisation, 37–44
  and British imports, 100
  and Ruhr, 46
  and Saar, 59, 62
European Economic Co-operation
  Committee of Ministers, 96
European Economic Co-operation (London)
  Committee
  see London Committee
European Recovery Programme, 89–104
  and American coal for France, 65
  and Anglo-French relations, 128–32
  and British coal, 100–4
  and British economic recovery, 128
  customs union, proposal for, 126
  and International Authority for the Ruhr,
    81

Fould, René, 29
François-Poncet, André, 96
Frankfurt
  Anglo-American discussions on German
    administration, 69–70
Franks, Oliver, 89–90, 107
Fraser, Ronald, 43
Fuel Committee, 41–2

Gasperi, Alcide de, 110
Gaitskell, Hugh, 102
Gaulle, Charles de, xi
German Industry Committee
  and Saar, 52
Germany
  British zone, cost of, 3
  Federal Republic, 84, 87, 94, 106
  Level of Industry Plan, 22, 55, 70, 78, 90,
    98
  Occupation Statute, 84
  steel production and consumption, 21, 52
  see also Ruhr and Saar
Gouin, Félix, 38

Hague, The
  Congress, 137
Hall, Robert, 132–3, 135, 138

Hall-Patch, Edmund, 4, 9, 72, 105, 130–1, 133, 136
Harriman, Avrell, 103
Harvey, Oliver, 2, 57, 70, 77, 96, 111
Hayter, William, 119
Hirsch, Étienne, 132
Hitchman, Alan, 132
Hoffman, Paul, 76, 136
Hoyer-Millar, Frederic, 4
Humphrey, George, 76
  Humphrey Committee, 76–9, 86, 109

Inter-Allied Reparations Agency (IARA), 56, 64, 74
Intergovernmental Study Group, 112–13, 117
International Authority for the Ruhr, 81–2
  abolition, 119
  and European integration, 82, 111, 118
  German membership, 85
Iron and Steel Development Plan, 31–2

Jenkins, Gilmour, 73
Joint Export–Import Agency (JEIA), 68, 81

Kirkpatrick, Ivone, 107, 117
Korean War, 113
Kurochkin, General, 48

Lee, Frank, 30
  and European economic integration, 30
  working party on German steel industry, 23–5, 28
Lintott, Harry, 9
  and British coal exports, 101
  and Monnet Plan, 12
London
  conference on Germany 81, 106, 111
  tripartite talks on German steel industry, 73
London Committee, 31, 59, 92–3, 95
  and British coal exports, 102–3
  and European integration, 128
Lord President's Office, 6–7

Makins, Roger, 43, 61, 107
  and Anglo-French integration, 130–1, 133
  attitude to Bevin's European policy, 127
Marjolin, Robert, 9, 99
Marshall, George
  and German level of industry, 72
  and Saar, 58–9, 62, 71
Marshall Plan
  see European Recovery Programme

Massigli, René
  and Anglo-American Control Groups, 83
  and coal supplies, 34, 37
  and German steel production, 74
  and Intergovernmental Study Group, 117
  and International Authority for the Ruhr, 82
  and Military Law no.75, 84
  and Saar, 59
Mayhew, Christopher, 130
McNeil, Hector, 9, 41, 103
Meade, James, 12, 16
Military Law no.75, 83–4
Military Security Board, 84, 86, 108, 109, 114
Ministry of Fuel and Power, 40, 41, 46
  and Anglo-French economic integration, 15
  and British coal exports, 38, 102–4
  and European steel integration, 96
  and Saar coal production, 60
  and Schuman Plan, 107
Ministry of Supply
  and Anglo-French Co-operation, 7, 15
  and European Coal Organisation, 37
  and European steel integration, 96, 98
  and OEEC, 99
Moch, Jules, 34
Molotov, Vyacheslav Mikailovich, 58, 62, 89
Monde, Le, 1
Monnet, Jean
  Adenauer, telegram to, 120
  and Anglo-French relations, 133, 138
  and Anglo-French Union, xi, 139
  and Franco-German relations, 122, 133
  Plowden, meeting with, 132–4
  and Schuman Plan, 105–6, 137
Monnet Plan, 8, 34, 106, 136
  Anglo-French discussion of, 11, 65
  Cabinet discussion of, 10
  and coal supplies, 34–5, 49–50
  and German steel production, 14, 21, 26
  and long-term programmes, 129, 131
Morrison, Herbert
  Foreign Secretary, 119
  illness, 19
  Monnet, conversation with, 34
Moscow Sliding Scale, 50, 61

National Coal Board, 101
New Statesman, The, 97
New York
  conference on Germany, 113, 115, 117

Index

Noiret, General, 69
North Atlantic Treaty Organisation (NATO), 113, 117, 135
North German Coal Control, 44

Observer, The, 16
Operation Severance, 83
Organisation for European Economic Co-operation (OEEC), 92–4, 97–9
  see also Committee of European Economic Co-operation
Overseas Negotiations Committee, 102
Overseas Reconstruction Committee, 22–3, 25, 47, 57, 71

Paris
  Anglo-French discussions on Monnet Plan, 11
  Anglo-French discussions on steel production, 25, 36
  Council of Foreign Ministers, 22, 47, 67
  Marshall Plan conference, 71–2, 89, 95, 100
  peace conference, 4
  tripartite talks leading to Petersberg Protocol, 85, 108
Permanent Under-Secretaries' Committee, 106
Pertinax, 56
Petersberg Protocol, 86, 109, 115, 135
Petsche, Maurice, 97
Plowden, Edwin, 18
  Monnet, meeting with, 132, 135, 138
Potsdam Conference, xi, 3, 44, 47, 51, 77
Production Committee, 103
Prohibited and Limited Industries, 113

Quai d'Orsay, 39
Queuille, Henri, 131

Ramadier, Paul
  conversation with Bevin on Anglo-French Union, 126
  expels Communists from government, 72
Robertson, Brian, 48, 69–70, 76, 93
Robinson, Austin, 28

Ruhr, 67–88
  coal supplies, 3, 41, 46
  status, xiii, 3
  steel production, 5

Saar, 51–66
  Agreement, 64, 120
  coal for France, 42, 43, 62, 120
  currency reform, 58–9, 62
  and European integration, 110
  and Schuman Plan, 120
  status, xiii
  steel exports, 21, 23, 79
Salzgitter, 85
Sargent, Orme, 127
Schuman, Robert, 77, 85
  Adenauer, talks with, 111
  Bevin, talks with, 134
  at New York Conference, 114, 117
  and Saar, 121
Schuman Plan, 87, 105–24
  see also European Coal and Steel Community
Shinwell, Emanuel, 42, 47
Steering Committee on Economic Development, 14–15, 17
Sterling Area, 129, 131
Stevens, Roger, 105, 111, 118
Strang, William, 75, 81–2

Tennessee Valley Authority, 110
Thyssen, 86–87, 108, 112, 115
Times, The, 19
Transitional Period Committee, 37
Treasury
  and Anglo-French co-operation, 1, 11, 129
  and European steel integration, 95
Turner, Mark, 21, 23

Uri, Pierre, 132

Washington Conference, 94
Western Department, 1–2, 4
Wilmot, John, 26
Wolf, George, 75, 76

DATE DUE

HIGHSMITH #45230   Printed in USA